Preaching in Belfast, 1747–72

Belfast in 1757 (Linen Hall Library)

PREACHING IN BELFAST, 1747–72

A selection of the sermons of James Saurin

EDITED BY

Raymond Gillespie and Roibeard Ó Gallachóir

FOUR COURTS PRESS • DUBLIN

in association with

THE REPRESENTATIVE CHURCH BODY LIBRARY

Set in 11 pt on 12.5 pt Ehrhardt for
FOUR COURTS PRESS LTD
7 Malpas Street, Dublin 8, Ireland
www.fourcourtspress.ie
and in North America for
FOUR COURTS PRESS
c/o ISBS, 920 N.E. 58th Avenue, Suite 300, Portland, OR 97213.

A catalogue record for this title is available from the British Library.

ISBN 978-1-84682-535-4

Printed in England
by Antony Rowe Ltd, Chippenham, Wilts.

CONTENTS

ILLUSTRATIONS

PREFACE

This is the seventh volume in the texts and calendars series published by Four Courts Press in association with the Representative Church Body Library. The series seeks to provide critical editions of significant Church of Ireland archives and manuscripts with substantial interpretative and explanatory apparatus.

However, this volume, which presents a selection of the sermons of James Saurin, breaks new ground. The previous volumes in the series have all dealt with aspects of parish administration and, in particular, have explored what can be learnt from an examination of vestry records. The sermons of James Saurin have less to do with the minutiae of parish life and rather more to do with the place of the Church of Ireland as a minority community in the rapidly developing town of Belfast expressed through the medium of theological and biblical reflection. This volume is different also in that it presents a selection, rather than a complete transcription, of the sermons in the Saurin collection. It is intended to give a sense, by selecting from what is one of the largest surviving collections of parochial sermons from eighteenth-century Ireland, of how the vicar of Belfast nurtured his flock week by week through the medium of preaching.

I am grateful to Professor Raymond Gillespie for suggesting this project and for bringing to bear upon it his unrivalled knowledge of the history of Belfast, and to Roibeard Ó Gallachóir for his diligent transcription of the often heavily revised sermon texts. I am grateful also to the dean of Belfast, the Very Revd John Mann, to Paul Gilmore and to the staff of the Representative Church Body Library for facilitating this project in different ways.

The publication of this volume has been greatly assisted by a generous grant from Malcolm Macourt, in memory of his father, the Ven. W.A. Macourt, and by the continued support of the Representative Church Body.

RAYMOND REFAUSSÉ
Series Editor

INTRODUCTION

This edition takes the form of a selection of twenty-four sermons from a collection of sixty-one preserved in seven volumes in St Anne's cathedral, Belfast. The sermons were originally preached by the vicar of Belfast in the middle of the eighteenth century, James Saurin. The survival of such a collection is rare since, despite the ubiquity of parochial sermons in the eighteenth century and their role in shaping the outlook of their hearers, few clergy took the pains to ensure the preservation of their sermon texts.[1] Some, it is true, resorted to print to ensure that their words might be preserved and circulated more widely. The establishment of a press at Belfast in the 1690s seemed to augur well for those who wished to use the latest technology to disseminate their thoughts. However, in the early eighteenth century the Belfast printers were firmly Presbyterian and while some, such as James Blow, were not adverse to profiting from the sale of psalters for use in the established church they drew the line at publishing other works associated with that church. The market for print in early eighteenth-century Ulster was thin and most Belfast printers contented themselves with reprinting well-tried devotional works on which the financial risk was limited. It was only on the back of the political excitement generated by the Volunteer movement that one Belfast printer, James Magee, saw the commercial potential of sermon publication.[2] Thus in the 1750s James Saurin had few local outlets for his work and it is not surprising that it should have remained in manuscript. That does not mean that his manuscript sermons were regarded as unimportant. They were preserved by Saurin and his clerical descendants both for their utility as a collection of ready-made discourses and for their content. The repeated use of these texts for preaching into the early nineteenth century, evidenced by that dates of use recorded at the beginning of each sermon, testifies to their significance as more than simply ephemeral events.

1 Jeffrey S. Chamberlain, 'Parish preaching in the long eighteenth century' in Keith Francis and William Gibson (eds), *Oxford handbook of the British sermon, 1689–1901* (Oxford, 2012), pp 47–8.
2 Michael O'Connor, '"Ears stunned with the din of arms": Belfast, Volunteer sermons and James Magee, 1779–1781', *Eighteenth-Century Ireland*, 26 (2011), pp 51–79.

THE PREACHER: JAMES SAURIN

When James Saurin became vicar of Belfast in June 1747 he was twenty-seven years old. He was born in London on 6 March 1720 and baptized Jacques Louis by his father, the minister of the conforming Huguenot Savoy church, on 17 March.[3] His father, Louis, had come to London about a decade earlier as minister of the church, following in the steps of his elder brother (and James's godfather) Jacques Saurin (fig. 1).[4] Jacques had ministered to the Threadneedle Street Huguenot congregation in London from 1701 to 1706 but later moved to The Hague where he became one of the most distinguished preachers of the eighteenth century.[5] Five volumes of his sermons were published in his lifetime and after his death his son edited seven additional volumes. From the middle of the eighteenth century, English translations were available. James probably had some contact with his uncle and godfather since Jacques' son, Anthony, entered Trinity College Dublin in 1738, the year before James graduated from Trinity.[6] In 1727 Louis Saurin moved to Ireland and quickly acquired two ecclesiastical positions that he would hold until his death in 1749: the precentorship of Christ Church, Dublin, and the deanery of Ardagh. These were joined by the archdeaconry of Derry in 1736. Why he decided to move to Ireland is unclear. Jacques, brother of Louis, clearly had Irish connections and in 1725 he was buying books for Archbishop William King of Dublin at auctions in Holland where he was living.[7] In January 1726 Louis was being considered in England in connection with the precentorship of Christ Church, Dublin, and his case seems to have been taken up by Archbishop Boulter of Armagh. Louis also had powerful English friends, including William Wake, the archbishop of Canterbury, who recommended him as 'one of the chief French ministers in London' to the bishop of Derry.[8]

The household that Louis Saurin established in Dublin, probably in the recently developed and fashionable parish of St Ann, was not divorced from

3 William Minet and Susan Minet (eds), *Registers of the church of the Savoy, Spring Garden and Les Grecs*. Publications of the Huguenot Society of London 26 (London, 1921), p. 47.

4 George Beeman, 'Notes on the sites and history of the French churches in London', *Proceedings of the Huguenot Society of London*, 8 (1905–8), pp 19–20.

5 W.M. Machée, 'Huguenot clergy lists, 1548–1916', *Proceedings of the Huguenot Society of London*, 11 (1915–7), p. 290.

6 G.D. Burtchaell and T.U. Sadlier, *Alumni Dublinenses* (Dublin, 1935), p. 735.

7 Trinity College, Dublin, MS 750/8/58.

8 *Letters written by his excellency Hugh Boulter, DD, lord primate of all Ireland* (2 vols, Oxford, 1769), i, pp 129, 135, 146, 155–6; Leonard Forster (ed.), *A calendar of the correspondence of J.H. Ott (1658–1671)*. Publications of the Huguenot Society of London 47 (London, 1960), p. 43.

1 Jacques Saurin, uncle of James Saurin, vicar of Belfast

his earlier life. He developed contacts with the conforming French Protestant congregation in Dublin and in the 1730s and 1740s officiated at baptisms and other occasions for the Dublin Huguenot congregation.[9] His will, written in 1746, was in French and he left £10 to the Huguenot church of St Patrick and St Mary in Dublin, suggesting the links with his origins. How much of this sense of a French heritage was communicated to his son James is not clear.[10]

James was brought up in a scholarly household. His father was at home in the world of books and he was regarded as something of a bookish man, being consulted by Archbishop Bolton of Cashel about what he should buy and how such books might be obtained.[11] Louis appears in the subscription list of some ten works printed in Dublin in the early eighteenth century. Some of these were what one might expect including theological works, such as Joseph Harrison's *Scriptural exposition* (1748) and Calliard's *Sermons* (1728), or works in French such as Anthony Desvoeux's *Trois sermons* (1745) or Charles Vilette's *Essai sur la felicite* (1748). Others related to Ireland and its history, including John Keogh's *Zoologia medicinalis Hibernica* (1739), the 1739 edition of Sir James Ware's works or William Knowler's *Strafford's letters and despatches* (1740). Yet others were more general works such as Gilbert Burnett's *History … of my own times* (1734) or the first volume of the third edition of Chamber's *Cyclopedia* (1740). James, too, bought books and appears on subscription lists of the 1750s after which he seems to have become a rather lackadaisical book purchaser. With his father he subscribed to Desvoeux's *Trois sermons* (1745) but his other purchases were in English. While he certainly purchased Maclaine's *Ecclesiastical history* when it was published in 1767 he bought little theology, only John Roche's *Moravian heresy* (1751). He seemed happier with James Simon's *Essay on Irish coins* (1749) or Chetwood's *Voyages* (1751), and Richard Barton's *Lectures on natural philosophy* (1751) may have attracted him because of Barton's descriptions of experiments with petrified wood at Lough Neagh, close to James's home in Belfast. It is difficult to know what others books James may have read since he rarely quoted any directly in his sermons, his only direct quotation being from the sermons of the distinguished Archbishop Tillotson, but there are also clear allusions to *The whole duty of man*, a very influential work that shaped the outlook

9 J. Diggs la Touche (ed.), *Register of the French conformed churches of St Patrick and St Mary, Dublin* (Dublin, 1893), pp 49, 51, 54, 57, 58, 60, 61, 62, 65, 66, 70, 130, 228.

10 Dorothy North (ed.), *Huguenot wills and administrations in England and Ireland, 1617–1848*. Publications of the Huguenot Society of London 60 (London, 2007), p. 389.

11 Public Record Office of Northern Ireland, D562/457, 499

of many in eighteenth-century England and Ireland. However, Saurin clearly had a considerable knowledge of the bible and was able to bring verses from very diverse parts of scripture together in long thematic passages. Those linkages are not the sort that might be made by a concordance or even a bible with cross references but rather are the result of wide reading and placing verses from diverse parts of the text together to explicate the meaning of particular texts. That he relied on his memory rather than a text is also suggested by the fact that the biblical quotations and allusions in his sermons are often slightly inaccurate indicating that he was not reading from a text. For Saurin the bible was a work that recorded a continuing revelation in which one part might illuminate another through careful juxtaposition of texts and his frequent reading of both Old and New Testaments and memorizing parts of the text allowed him to do this.

James was educated at Dr St Paul's school in Dublin and entered Trinity College, Dublin, in November 1734, aged fifteen, and graduated with a BA in the Spring of 1739.[12] He was presumably ordained shortly after when he reached the canonical age of twenty-three, and this would accord with the earliest date of preaching of 20 March 1743 given in the surviving sermons (3).[13] What James Saurin did from this date until his appointment as vicar of Shankill, of which Belfast was the largest element, in 1747 is unclear. The dates and places of preaching noted on the sermons themselves suggest that he was in Dublin and preached in a number of churches there.[14] The surviving parish records for those parishes do not mention him, which might indicate that his connection with those parishes was rather informal. However, after his appointment to Shankill he returned to a number of those churches over the years suggesting that the connection was more enduring but its exact nature is not known. How and why he acquired the living of Shankill is also unclear. The patronage of the living was in the hands of the Chichester family, earls of Donegall, but in 1747 it was in the hands of trustees since the absentee fourth earl was held to be weak-minded and it was presumably through contacts with the trustees in Dublin that Saurin was found suitable for the living of Shankill.

James Saurin was appointed to the living of Shankill on 2 June 1747 and moved to Belfast almost immediately.[15] On 28 June 1747 he preached his first recorded sermon in Belfast on the subject of prayer (no. 5 in appendix 1). The sermon was specially written for the occasion but it betrays little hint of the circumstances in which it was preached. Themes that would emerge in the later sermons – especially the need for a gen-

12 Burtchaell and Sadlier, *Alumni Dublinenses*, p. 735.
13 Sermon numbers in Arabic refer to items in appendix 1.
14 See appendix 2.
15 J.B. Leslie, *Clergy of Connor* (Belfast, 1993), p. 118.

uinely felt religion as opposed to an outward form – were certainly present in it but there is no hint that Saurin was setting out an agenda for his ministry. Perhaps only towards the end is there a passage that suggests that Saurin was setting out his expectations of his new congregation.

> Consider the behaviour of the generality of mankind in our churches & religious assemblies where every thing concurs to animate our devotion & where if it is not to be found, we vainly seek for it in the closet. Consider I say the behaviour of the generality of our people & what lukewarmness & coldness appears in their outward deportment? What roving, rambling eyes whilst their lips mutter praise? What readiness to absent themselves from the worship of God upon every idle pretence, to admit that for an excuse from it which they dare not pledge as much for the most trifling engagements. No sense of the great Being they adore seems to overawe their service, no warmth of affection seasons their words, all carries the face of tediousness & disgust & the most rational becoming duty terminates in meer form, shews unpleasing to God and useless to ourselves.[16]

Complaints about misbehaviour and coolness in churches were certainly frequent in eighteenth-century Ireland. Saurin's contemporary, John Wesley, discovered how Belfast audiences might react to preaching over his ten visits to the town between 1756 and 1785. In 1756 many left his sermon early 'in haste', in 1760 and 1762 while the hearers were 'serious and attentive' they were all poor since the rich did not care for religion. In 1769 they 'had no ears to hear' and in 1771 Wesley 'never saw so large a congregation there [in the market place at Belfast] before, nor one so remarkably stupid and ill mannered: yet a few should be excepted even gentlemen, who seemed to know sense from nonsense, I have found as sensible men at Dublin as Belfast, but men so self sufficient I have not found'. Things improved over time so that by 1773 'their behaviour was remarkably decent' but in 1778 Wesley noted of his Belfast hearers 'I doubt the bulk of them were nearly concerned in my text'.[17] However, at the end of Saurin's first sermon his Belfast congregation could have had no doubt about his expectations of them as a parish community.

James was joined in Belfast by his mother, Henriette Cornel de Bretonniere, after the death of his father, who was buried in St Ann's church in Dublin in September 1749. His mother was presumably sup-

16 St Anne's Cathedral, Belfast, Saurin sermons, vol. 1, pp 140–1; also pp 214–15 below.

17 *The journal of the Rev. John Wesley* (4 vols, 1840), ii, p. 362 (23.7.1756); ii, pp 508–9 (5. 5.1760), iii, pp 85–6 (21.4.1762); p. 360 (6.4.1769); p. 415 (3.7.1771), p. 472 (15.6.1773); iv, p. 120 (9.6.1778).

ported by the land in Meath left to her by her husband but all James inherited was a gold watch.[18] His mother died at Belfast in April 1753 and was buried in the parish churchyard there.[19] Two years later, in July 1755, James married Jane Johnston, the widow of James Duff of Belfast.[20] Her father, William Johnston, who was a minor customs official, had been instrumental in establishing the Belfast water supply with a lease from the trustees of the earl of Donegall in 1733 of all the water in the vicinity of Belfast but he seems to have made little profit on the venture and could hardly be seen as a major figure in the town.[21] However, the family of her first husband, James Duff, were prominent figures in the established church. Patrick Duff was the earl of Donegall's agent and constable of Belfast castle at the beginning of the eighteenth century and John Duff, probably her father-in-law, who died in 1753, was sovereign of the town in 1729–30, 1741–3 and 1746–7 and 1753.[22] Jane died in 1760, some twelve years before James.[23] They had three sons and at least one daughter: William (later attorney general of Ireland), Mark Anthony, James (later bishop of Dromore) (fig. 2) and Sarah.

The evidence for James Saurin's life in Belfast is relatively sparse, partly because of its routine nature. The three existing parish registers for his years in Belfast record his activities in baptising, marrying and burying his parishioners and the sermons record his preaching but little else has survived. He showed little interest in the formal politics of the town, unlike his successor as vicar, William Bristow, who was sovereign ten times between 1786 and his death in 1798. Saurin waited until 1753 to become a freeman of Belfast and until September 1768 before becoming a burgess suggesting that, although he would have been a natural nominee of the Chichester family for such a post, he was reluctant to become involved in the political life of the town.[24] His absence from the political scene does not mean that he was not involved in wider urban life. He was resident in Belfast for most of his working life. His movements can be reconstructed from the dates of preaching of his sermons (appendix 2). In the first eight years at Belfast he spent most of the year in the town but usually spent a

18 North (ed.), *Huguenot wills*, p. 389.

19 Raymond Gillespie and Alison O'Keeffe (eds), *Register of the parish of Shankill, Belfast, 1745–1761* (Dublin, 2006), p. 181.

20 Gillespie and O'Keeffe (eds), *Register of the parish of Shankill, Belfast*, p. 210.

21 George Benn, *A history of the town of Belfast* (Belfast, 1877), pp 487–8.

22 R.M. Young (ed.), *The town book of the corporation of Belfast* (Belfast, 1896), pp 194–7; Benn, *A history of the town of Belfast*, p. 728.

23 Arthur Vicars, *Index to the prerogative wills of Ireland, 1536–1810* (Dublin, 1897), p. 415; *Belfast News Letter*, 25 Mar. 1760. Curiously there is no entry for her burial in the Belfast register.

24 Young (ed.), *Town book of the corporation of Belfast*, pp 237, 296.

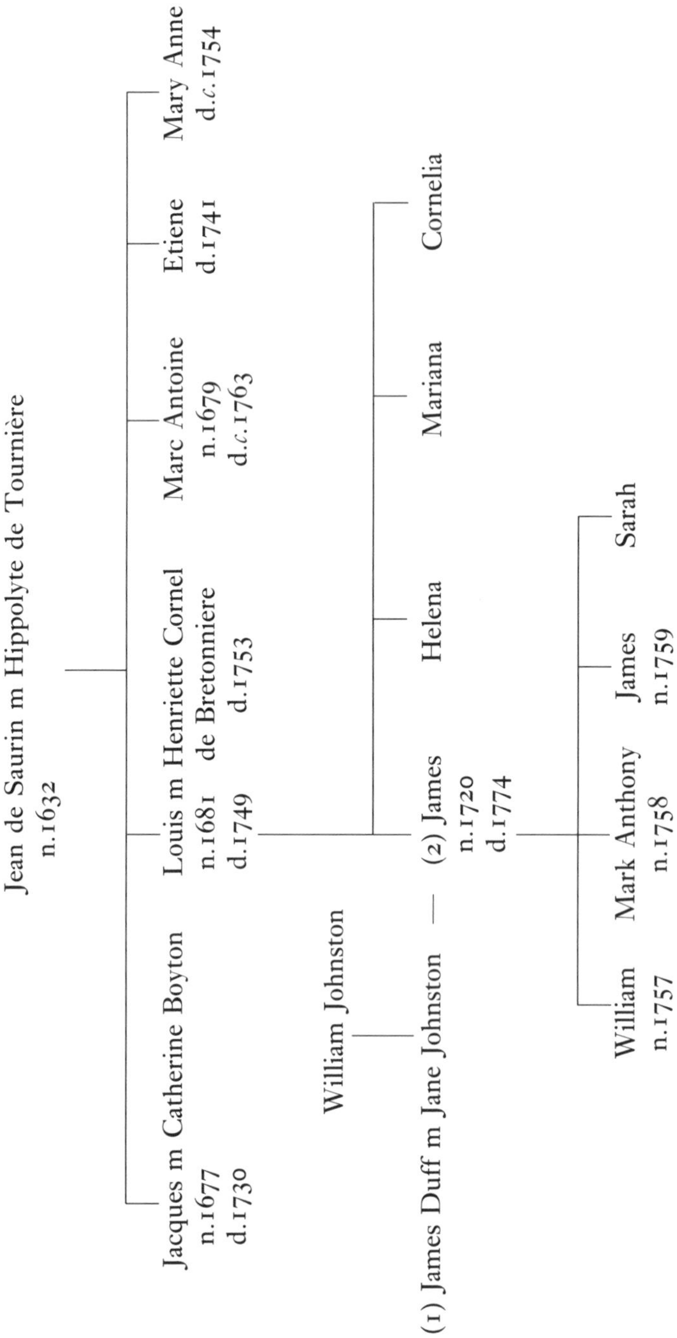

2 The Saurin family

short period each year in Dublin, although in 1754 and 1755 he spent almost three months each year in the capital. In 1755 he also went to Bath for the first time. While it is not clear why he was absent from Belfast for such extended periods it may be connected with his marriage in 1755, possibly some form of honeymoon, or possibly to take the medicinal waters at Bath for a medical complaint. After 1755 his visits to Dublin became more infrequent. However, in 1766 he spent almost six months in Bath and in 1768 almost three months in Dublin. Over these periods of absence the cure was served by his curates, especially William Tisdall in the 1760s, whose names appear in the parish registers as undertaking the normal business of baptizing, marrying and burying.

Perhaps Saurin's most important contribution to the life of Belfast came in the middle of the 1750s. In 1756–7 a combination of trade slump and food shortages created a crisis in the town. The parish registers kept by Saurin reveal a surge in burials in the autumn of 1756 and this rise in the death rate hit the poorest worst.[25] As the situation worsened over the summer of 1756 the town authorities feared the breakdown of order and in August their fears were realized in the shape of food riots in the town that persisted into November.[26] This was not the first such crisis and there had been an earlier crisis in 1750–1. That had resulted in the foundation of a charitable society in August 1752 with Saurin as the first name on the list of committee members. The role of the committee was to operate a lottery to raise money for the building of a poor house and the building of a new parish church since it was claimed that the old one was 'old and ruinous and not large enough to contain [the] parishioners', an aspect of the scheme that seems to have been Saurin's initiative.[27] However, the lottery scheme collapsed in confusion in 1753 with allegations of fraud being made against the managers, including Saurin. The scheme was eventually transformed into then Belfast Charitable Society which, from 1767, ran more successful lottery schemes and by 1771 it had already begun the building of a poor house on land granted by the earl of Donegall on Donegall Street. In all this Saurin was instrumental and acted as the intermediary between the earl of Donegall and the local committee, reflecting his 'gentry' status in the town between landlord and merchants.[28] Saurin's charitable activities were not confined to the poor house. In reaction to the

25 Gillespie and O'Keeffe (eds), *Register of the parish of Shankill, Belfast*, pp 32–6. For the wider context see L.M. Cullen, John Shovlin and Thomas Truxes (eds), *The Bordeaux – Dublin letters* (Oxford, 2013), pp 18–20.
26 Benn, *A history of the town of Belfast*, pp 593–7.
27 *Belfast News Letter*, Oct. 1752.
28 For the details see R.M. Strain, *Belfast and its charitable society* (Oxford, 1961), chs 4–5, and for Saurin as intermediary, pp 25, 38.

1756–7 crisis another society was established in Belfast for the relief of the poor, in which Saurin was again a prime mover. By May 1757 the new society was relieving 635 people. From its origins Saurin was one of the directors of the scheme, raising funds and disbursing them to the deserving poor. He was the first of those named as one of the overseers of the poor at the meeting to establish the poor law in the market house on 17 December 1756 and he continued to be named as one of the collectors and distributors of charity until August 1758.[29]

It may well be claimed that the relief of the poor was one of Saurin's professional responsibilities. His predecessor had certainly been involved in the collection and distribution of poor relief in 1740 and in sermon XXIII Saurin declared of the rich 'Let their wealth minister to the wants of others, supply their necessities, be spent in acts of Charity & beneficence'.[30] Saurin contributed to other charities such as the Society for the Relief of Protestant Strangers in Dublin.[31] However, Saurin's activities went further than this. Charity was not simply a religious duty but an important element in the organization of society. As the *Belfast News Letter* observed of the poor relief scheme of 1756, 'many subordinated advantages may be expected to arise from the method proposed such as a Reformation of Manners amongst the lower orders of our people and a general increase of sobriety and industry'.[32] While Saurin had no doubts that the world was shaped by the working out of God's providence (sermon XXIII) he also held that all people were equal before that God and that social inequalities were man-made, but necessary. According to sermon XI:

> For tho' the Distinctions of this World be indeed highly useful to answer the ends & purposes of Human Society, yet is it manifest that those are accidental & arbitrary differences, fitted to the present State of Mankind, & absolutely to cease with this, but still an equality is preserved in other respects, sufficient to shew the end & Destination of all Men to be the same.

However, such inequalities of wealth were necessary to make society work as sermon VII explained:

> To consider things as they are now modelled, & as the necessities of Society require, there is a plain & visible subordination between Men.

29 *Belfast News Letter*, 17 Dec. 1756, 14 Oct. 1757, 1 Aug. 1758; Benn, *A history of the town of Belfast*, pp 596–7.

30 *Belfast News Letter*, 5 Feb. 1739/40. Sermon numbers in Roman refer to the number in this edition.

31 *Belfast News Letter*, 26 Jan. 1753.

32 *Belfast News Letter*, 14 Dec. 1756.

> Some are placed upon an eminence, invested with authority & power commanding the service & obedience *of others people* tho' in a much less conspicuous station, yet thro' the easiness of their circumstances, & the plenty they are blessed with move on in a lower but still a pleasant sphere, whilst many thro' necessity, penury, & want, are obliged thro' constant drudgery & toil, to be instruments & agents in the hands of those above them & to depend upon their own industry & the good will of others for their maintenance & support.

What held this unequal society together was a system of trust or morality. As he put it in sermon XVIII:

> All Society is founded upon a mutual compact & agreement, a reciprocal trust & confidence in each other, which is the true & only cement that keeps us together, No entercourse can be carried on among Men but upon such a supposition. If we treat with others, we must understand that they carry on the same design with ourselves, & as we mean to act fairly with them in discharging our just obligations to them, that they in like manner intend to keep up exactly & rigorously to the terms in consideration of which we enter into such engagements. But Injustice & dishonesty at once dissolves this compact, It means the very reverse of what we do, It breaks thro' the sacredness of bonds & obligations, It is restrained by no terms or conditions, It offers a manifest violence to us, It encroaches upon our natural rights, it invades all property & dominion, It overturns the sense of law & equity; Hence must Society sink & be destroyed, Men are kept together by no link or bond, An end is put to trust, confidence, & faith in each other, Nothing but rapine & violence ensues, Every Man's hand is against his Brothers Suspicions take place of reliance & good opinion, & Communication and entercourse with others for ever cease & vanish.

The system of morality that promoted trust and contained the excesses of unrestrained human nature was provided by religion, or as Saurin put it in sermon IV:

> For Religion teaches us our Duty, what we owe to God, the submission & obedience that we are to pay to him, the particulars in & by which we can manifest it, what offices are due from one Man to another in the different Relations stands in to them, & what we owe to ourselves as Guardians & Stewards of sundry gifts, graces and abilities, since it informs us of the true grounds of these & such like Duties, & if properly dwelt upon, carries us to the performance of

> them by the most actuating & enlivening motives, we cannot without the Study of Religion know how to act, or which way to determine our choice amidst jarring & opposite interests & desires, Our Passions left to themselves without proper management grow wild & extravagant, Tumultuous & overbearing appetites take place of better regulated principles & produce those infinite mischeifs which we daily see in the World.

The system could be self regulating so that too much ambition or covetousness could lead to decline and fall under the control of God's providence or as sermon XIV expressed it:

> Providence has established general Laws, in consequence of which certain temporal evils unavoidably follow upon the committal of certain actions, unless prevented by the interposition of God *&* over-ruled by a particular act of his power. Thus according to general laws, prodigality Luxury & vice bring a Man to poverty, consume & eat up the fortune that was entrusted to him for the welfare of his Children, & reduce an innocent & harmless family to distress & poverty.

Morality provided a way in which the worst excess of human nature could be controlled and without it the civil power would be forced to act, as in sermon X:

> those, who are endued with a Civil & Legislative power, appointed to watch over the welfare & prosperity of that Community, to which they belong, Because without some authority, to inflict punishment upon those, who disturb it's peace & quiet, Society could not subsist, but must necessarily fan into confusion & disorder. Every-one in a low rank would become liable to the insult of those above him, & power & wealth might range lawless & uncontrolled thro' the World, whence in Scripture are Magistrates represented, as the Vice-Regents of God upon Earth.

In this context it is hardly surprising that so many of Saurin's sermons should be about 'social' sins such as pride (sermon III), anger (sermon V), fraud (sermon XVIII), ambition and time wasting (sermon XV). Charity, therefore, was not simply a religious duty; it was a social imperative intended to ensure that the temporary, but necessary, distinctions of social order were maintained. Both morality and prudence required that the poor were not oppressed by the greater and they in turn respected their place in the social order by behaving according to their station on life. Saurin did not simply preach these ideas, he put them into practice.

James Saurin died suddenly on Tuesday 4 August 1772, aged fifty-two. He may have been unwell for the previous two months as he disappears from the surviving evidence in May of that year. There are no indications of his preaching activities after May 1772 and in the same month, according to the parish register, he baptized a number of children, but does not appear in the register thereafter, although he did attend the bishop's visitation at Lisburn on 27 May.[33] He was buried in the churchyard of the parish church of Belfast on 6 August.[34] Over the next year his goods and some land that he had accumulated was sold by his executors.[35] In his last years Saurin may well have lost some of his enthusiasm for the social order that was laid out in his sermons. Instead of becoming an oasis of order and stability Belfast and its region became an increasingly disturbed place with the rise of agrarian violence, promoted by the activities of a local agrarian secret society, the Hearts of Steel.[36] In May 1772, a few weeks before his death, Saurin headed a subscription list to provide a reward for information leading to the capture of those members of the Hearts of Steel who attacked a soldier in Belfast and on 27 May he was one of those who signed a petition to the bishop of Down and Connor condemning the 'barbarous and illegal practices of those deluded people who style themselves Hearts of Steel'. The aim of the petition was 'to record the indispensable duty of obedience and submission to the laws, the respect due to the magistracy and the obligation that every member of society is under of preserving the peace'.[37] The language could almost have been drawn from one of Saurin's own sermons.

Whatever Saurin thought about his contemporaries they certainly respected him. The Church of Ireland Belfast merchant John Black wrote in 1765 that 'The Belfast community is happy … in having so worthy and reverend a clergy who preach by their good example of Christian charity as well as by sermon precept. Long, long may you enjoy and imitate so pious and good a ministry'.[38] Generations after James were similarly affectionate. The *Belfast News Letter* wrote on 7 August 1772 that he was

33 *Belfast News Letter*, 29 May 1772.
34 St Anne's Cathedral, Belfast, third Belfast register, p. 200.
35 *Belfast News Letter*, 23–27 July 1773, 15–18 June 1773.
36 W.A. Maguire, 'Lord Donegall and the Hearts of Steel', *Irish Historical Studies*, 21: 84 (Sept. 1979), pp 351–76. For John Wesley's comments on the Hearts of Steel impact on Belfast see *Journal of the Rev. John Wesley*, iii, p. 472 (15.6.1773).
37 *Belfast News Letter*, 19 May 1772, 29 May 1772.
38 Quoted in Isaac Ward, 'The Black family', *Ulster Journal of Archaeology*, 2nd ser, 8 (1902), p. 185.

> A good man who, by a regular and faithful discharge of the duties of his office, his constant attention to the wants and distress of the poor, to whom he was a liberal benefactor, his polite and affable behaviour, the sweetness and cheerfulness of his temper and conversation, and the uniform practices of all the relative and social virtues gained the love and esteem of all ranks and denominations in this place. In short it may justly be said that he was 'an Israelite indeed, in whom there is no guile'.[39]

This was a reputation that would endure. George Benn, writing almost a century later in 1877, noted that when St George's church was being built in 1811, on the site of the old parish church, 'the workmen engaged in making the foundations so respected Mr Saurin's grave that they arched it over and that … his remains now lie under the communion table in that church'.[40]

THE HEARERS: THE CHURCH OF IRELAND COMMUNITY IN BELFAST

The Church of Ireland community in mid-eighteenth-century Belfast was relatively small. A list drawn up by the Presbyterian minister of the second Belfast congregation, James Kirkpatrick, in 1713 as part of a dispute with the Church of Ireland minister, William Tisdall, named seventy-eight Church of Ireland individuals in Belfast and if most of these represented heads of families then this might provide an order of magnitude of about 400 for the small community. This estimate is broadly in line with that of Archdeacon Pococke in 1754 who guessed there were sixty Church of Ireland families, 'most of them of the lower rank', but to judge from the number of baptisms in the parish register this might be a slight underestimate.[41] According to Saurin's own reckoning some 209 attended the Belfast Christmas communion services in 1765, 201 at Easter 1766 and 204 at Easter 1768.[42] While family size may have been about five some of these would not have been confirmed, and therefore not able to communicate, and others may have been absent so that a communicating family of three may be reasonable, giving an estimate of about seventy Church of Ireland families in the parish or perhaps about 350 individuals.

39 *Belfast News Letter*, 7 Aug. 1772. The allusion is to Nathaniel in John 1.47.
40 Benn, *A history of the town of Belfast*, pp 384–5.
41 James Kirkpatrick, *An historical essay on the loyalty of Presbyterians in Great Britain and Ireland* ([Belfast], 1713), pp 434–5; Gillespie and O'Keeffe (eds), *Register of the parish of Shankill, Belfast,* pp 26–8.
42 St Anne's Cathedral, Belfast, third Belfast register, p. 419.

Whatever the exact size of the Church of Ireland community it was clearly a minority one given that the population of the town was about 8,500 in almost 2,000 houses in 1757.[43] It is even more difficult to make statements about the social make-up of the community since the parish registers rarely recorded occupations. However, by the middle of the eighteenth century there were few of the Church of Ireland congregation that belonged to the social elite of the town. As the Presbyterian minister James Kirkpatrick put it in 1713 'there are indeed very few in Belfast of the communion of the established church who are considerable dealers'. There were a few 'of the best station in town' but most 'follow the handicraft trades of tobacco spinners, tailors, shoemakers, smiths, saddler, glovers, butchers, carpenters, etc'. By the middle of the century the army garrison at Belfast had also become an important part of the Church of Ireland community and the presence of soldiers is frequently recorded in the parish register. Only a few on Kirkpatrick's list of members of the Church of Ireland in Belfast can be identified with certainty but those that can be support this generalization, being tradesmen rather than larger merchants. As Kirkpatrick realized, this was a relatively recent development and before the 1690s the Church of Ireland had been more powerful among the mercantile community but by 1713 some were dead, others had moved to estates outside the town and the children of others had entered the professions.[44]

It is somewhat easier to understand the theological outlook of the community to which Saurin preached. The patron of the living, the Chichester family, had always been at the godlier end of the theological spectrum, and hence the clergy who had served Belfast before Saurin had not been of a high church inclination. On only one occasion had Saurin's predecessors shown such tendencies. William Tisdall, who had been vicar of Belfast from 1704 until 1736, had caused considerable trouble in the town over the issue of tithes and the position of the clergy that most people were keen not to replicate. Given Saurin's Huguenot background it is likely that he shared the low church theological outlook of his parishioners. The clearest evidence is in his preaching on the sacrament of holy communion. In one of his most frequently preached sermons (VIII) on I Cor. 11.9 Saurin warned his congregation about the dangers of receiving the sacrament unworthily at a time when many churchmen were trying to promote more communion services and more frequent reception of the sacrament. That his congregation took his warnings seriously and shared his views is suggested by the numbers that Saurin recorded at his monthly communions in 1767. Over 1767, omitting

43 Raymond Gillespie and Stephen Royle, *Belfast: part 1, to 1840*. Irish Historic Towns Atlas 12 (Dublin, 2003), p. 10.

44 Kirkpatrick, *Historical essay*, pp 435, 436. For the merchant community see Jean Agnew, *Belfast merchant families in the seventeenth century* (Dublin, 1996).

Christmas and Easter, the average number of communicants was under fifty or about 13 per cent of the community.[45] All this points to a parish orientated to the godly end of the theological spectrum with preaching rather than the Eucharist as the centre of the community.

While the Church of Ireland population had its own characteristics it would be wrong to see it as separate from the wider Presbyterian-dominated population of the town. Many of the political sentiments and concerns with social order that characterize Saurin's sermons are also present in the sermons of some of the Presbyterian ministers of the town. The single example of a 'political' sermon preached by Saurin on the peace of Aix-La-Chapelle in 1749 (XIII), which ended the War of the Austrian Succession, can be matched by a sermon preached on the same day by Gilbert Kennedy, the minister of the Second Belfast Presbyterian church.[46] The themes of the two preachers were very similar reflecting the underlying Whig assumptions held by both men, with their fear of tyranny and absolutism linked to Catholicism and their desire for an ordered society underpinned by civil and religious rights. Saurin's sermon dwelt at least as much on the 1745 rising and the fear it had generated and it should also be read against Gilbert Kennedy's sermon preached on 18 December 1745 at the fast ordered by the government in response to the Jacobite rising in Scotland.[47] Again there are similarities in the ideas of the two preachers: both emphasizing the wickedness of absolute power and its link with Catholicism.

In part, the similarities of political and social convictions between the Belfast Church of Ireland community and its Presbyterian counterpart stemmed from their reactions to common problems associated with the town's development. Belfast during the period of Saurin's ministry was undergoing dramatic changes that affected all its inhabitants. Its population almost doubled between the 1750s and the 1770s and this was affected in a changed physical layout of the town. In 1752 the trustees of the Donegall estate obtained a private act of parliament to allow them to make new leases of the town despite the fact that Lord Donegall was a ward of Chancery. In 1757 the fourth earl of Donegall died and was succeeded by his nephew, the fifth earl, who began to take a more active interest in Belfast, producing a map of the town in that year (see *frontispiece*). These two developments led to a transformation of the topography of the town with the laying out of new streets, such as Donegall Street (originally called Linenhall Street), and the

45 St Anne's Cathedral, Belfast, third Belfast register, p. 419.

46 Gilbert Kennedy, *The great blessing of peace and truth in our days: a sermon preached at Belfast on Tuesday, April 25th 1749* (Belfast, 1749).

47 Gilbert Kennedy, *The wicked ruler or the mischiefs of arbitrary power* (Belfast, 1745).

rebuilding of older parts of the town, such as High Street, that had fallen into decay. At the top of the new Donegall Street the earl granted a site for the new poor house and on the street itself, opposite the new church, he constructed a linen hall. All this changed the social topography of Belfast, shifting the social gravity of the town away from High Street and Waring Street towards Donegall Street. These developments were funded by an upsurge in the trade of the town after the problems of the early eighteenth century and, increasingly, it was to make its name as an industrial and commercial centre rather than simply as a port. The appearance of an early provincial bank in Belfast between 1751 and 1757, for instance, points to this shift in activities.[48] Again the emergence of new industrial activities in the late eighteenth century, such as linen (and later cotton), transformed the economic structure of the town. All this gave opportunities for new families to establish themselves in Belfast. A few merchant magnates such as the Gregg and Cunningham families, who developed the trans-Atlantic trade as an important source of wealth, certainly appeared but there were more who made money in industry and retailing, thus creating unprecedented social mobility so that most of the families who had dominated Belfast in the early eighteenth century had vanished by 1800.[49] Associated with this transformation in its economic structures and rapid social mobility Belfast came to be a centre of polite sociability in which radical political ideas could later flourish on the back of Enlightenment sensibilities.[50] Even John Wesley recognized Belfast in 1785 as an oasis of civility commenting, 'I often wondered that among so civil a people we can do but little good'.[51]

This was the modern, fashionable world that Saurin had begun to see emerge in his lifetime. In Sermon XVI he urged his parishioners to 'betake themselves to some profitable entertainments to fill up these empty spaces of their life, such as reading [and] useful conversation'. Improving knowledge and polite conversation were part of this new world of assembly rooms and balls. According to sermon XXI 'the sole end of all conversation is to unite us together in closer bonds of friendship & love, to relax the mind by an innocent & inoffensive mirth & joy, to minister to the pleasure of others, at the same time that we minister to our own'. Indeed so important was language and conversation in this world that Saurin dedicated two sermons

48 Benn, *A history of the town of Belfast*, pp 465–7.

49 For an overview of these developments see Raymond Gillespie, *Early Belfast: the origins and growth of an Ulster town to 1750* (Belfast, 2007), pp 167–71; Norman Gamble, 'The business community and trade of Belfast, 1676–1800' (PhD, Trinity College, Dublin, 1978), esp. pp 25–40.

50 S.J. Connolly, 'Improving town, 1750–1820' in S.J. Connolly (ed.), *Belfast 400* (Liverpool, 2013), pp 161–78.

51 *Journal of the Rev. John Wesley*, iv, p. 300 (9.6.1785).

3a Belfast parish church *c.*1685, redrawn from Thomas Phillips' perspective map of the town (British Library, Maps K Top 51 37).

(XXI and XXIV) to explaining how to achieve conversation 'improving to ourselves, & inoffensive to others on appropriate conversations'. The arrival of ideas of sociability, with assembly rooms and polite conversation, in a trading town demonstrated that, as one man put it in a description of Belfast in 1738, 'trade don't always spoil politeness'.[52] For all that, Saurin's Belfast was rapidly changing. Emblematic of this was the fate of Saurin's old church, on the site of the present St George's church, which was described in 1753 as 'old and ruinous' (figs 3a–b).[53] It was closed and demolished in 1774 and a new church, which rather optimistically had seating for 990, was built on the newly created and fashionable Donegall Street on the site of the present St Anne's cathedral. Given this pace of change in Belfast's social world it is perhaps not strange that so many of Saurin's sermons should be about how to achieve social stability and order.

52 T.G.F. Paterson (ed.), 'Belfast in 1738', *Ulster Journal of Archaeology*, 3rd ser., 2 (1939), p. 122. Swift's satirical work on the art of conversation was reprinted in Belfast in 1738.
53 *Belfast News Letter*, 6 July 1753

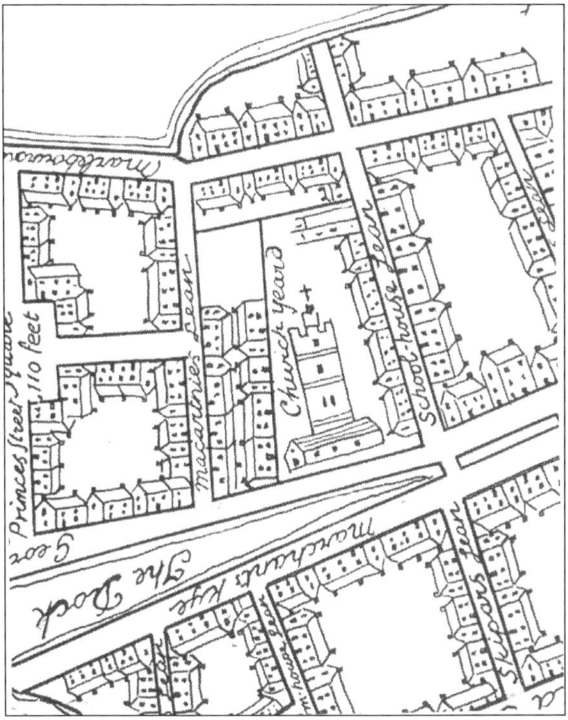

3b Belfast parish church *c.*1715, from John Maclanachan's map of Belfast (Public Record Office of Northern Ireland, T733/1).

THE SERMONS

Given Saurin's family background it is hardly surprising that he was regarded by his contemporaries as a good preacher. In 1758 the Belfast merchant John Black recorded that he had heard an 'excellent sermon' by Saurin on one Sunday morning.[54] Saurin was also a diligent preacher. We know nothing about how he composed his sermons but it is unlikely that he sat down and wrote a single complete draft for each sermon. There were presumably sermon outlines or other notes that have not survived. Saurin wrote his sermons in full, as was normal in the eighteenth century, in small booklets (15 x 21 cms) that could be easily carried into the pulpit. In contrast, extempore preaching was more characteristic of dissenting clergy. The handwriting was usually large for legibility in poorly-lit churches. He left

54 Public Record Office of Northern Ireland, D719/51. The letter is dated 1 Sept. which was a Friday. The previous Sunday would have been 27 Aug. and from Saurin's notes the sermon in question was no. 60 in the list in Appendix 1 on Matt 22.37.

the back of each page blank for additions.[55] The surviving text is usually heavily revised and some of this may have been done even before the sermon was preached for the first time, unlike many preachers who regarded the written text as final. Even in case of the sermon 'on the peace', preached only once in 1749 (XIII), Saurin made a number of alterations after writing it out and, presumably, before delivery. While we know little about Saurin's delivery it does seem that he was aware of the importance of the act of preaching. For example, he was careful about his choice of words, often revising his text with no apparent change of meaning but for rhetorical effect, and he underlined words and phrases (usually biblical quotations) that he wished to emphasize, and gaps in the continuous prose text may indicate pauses, all of which conveys some sense of the style of delivery.

The format of each sermon was fairly standard, being logically developed using heads or 'considerations'. The sermon began with the announcement of the text and then sometimes a short justification of the subject. The text was then broken down into four or, rarely, five heads on which the preacher would discourse before concluding with an 'application' and finally a short prayer. Such a practice certainly helped listeners to follow the arguments and it also provided a structure for any who might be taking notes of the sermon to refresh their memories later. The text is heavily infused with the language of and allusions to the bible and, to a lesser extent, the Book of Common Prayer and rarely does Saurin introduce local or personal illustrations or other material derived from his wider reading. In all, Saurin's sermons were models of their time – logical and biblical but not abstruse; devotional and practical rather than theological; and not too long. Most of the sermons edited here are about 3,500 words that, given a usual reading speed of 130 words a minute, would have lasted about twenty-five minutes; dissenting sermons were usually much longer. A case in point is the 1749 Presbyterian sermon on the Peace of Aix-La-Chapelle preached by Gilbert Kennedy that, in its printed form, is nearly twice the length of that preached on the same subject on same day by Saurin.

Two notes in the existing volumes provide evidence for the history of the sermon collection. The first is a note dated January 1882, probably by Lewis Richards, at the front of volume 4, that identifies these sermons as Saurin's and records that they were passed to his son, James, who was curate of St Doulough's and later bishop of Dromore, and then to Saurin's grandson, also James, who was archdeacon of Dromore. The lists giving the details of when and where each sermon was preached at the start of each text suggests that Saurin's son made good use of his father's sermons although his grandson also preached some, with one sermon (V) being still in use in 1845, though such longevity was atypical. On James Saurin's death

55 Chamberlain, 'Parish preaching in the long eighteenth century', p. 48.

in 1879 the sermons passed into the hands of the great-grandson of the original preacher, Lewis Richards, rector of Drumglass in Tyrone.[56] Since they were bound into volumes by Richardson of Dungannon before 1882 (the note in vol. 4 was dated in that year) it seems that it was Richards who arranged the sermon booklets into their present form and had them bound. Richards died on 6 November 1910 and the sermons passed to his son-in-law, Revd Kivas Brunskill, rector of Donaghendry.[57] A letter pasted into vol. 6 from Brunskill to the bishop of Down, dated 1 Jan. 1911, recorded that 'some time ago the Dean of Belfast told me that you were forming an episcopal library at Culloden [the bishop's residence in north Down] & I thought that perhaps you might be glad to have these old papers so intimately connected with your United Diocese. Should you be able to find room for them on your shelves I'll gladly forward them as in the Episcopal library they will find a safe resting place'. The volumes were duly forwarded in February 1911. They remained in the bishop's library until that was amalgamated with the Down Connor & Dromore diocesan library in Belfast, which had been founded in 1854, and located in the diocesan offices. When that library was broken up the sermons were moved to the library in St Anne's cathedral in Belfast where they now remain.

This outline history goes some way to explaining the nature of the collection. The sermons are of a kind that was the mainstay of parochial preaching. There are, for example, no sermons written for the high points of annual Protestant celebration such as 23 October, 5 November or King William's birthday on 4 November. Again, during the period of Saurin's incumbency of Belfast the government proclaimed two days of thanksgiving and eight fast days, all of which would have required special sermons, yet only one (XIII) has survived in the collection. The surviving sermons show little interest in confessional disputation. There are certainly a few in which there are the usual attacks on aspects of Catholicism. Sermon XXII, for instance, is a direct challenge to papal power while specific Catholic traits, such as monasticism, relics, pilgrimage and superstitious ceremonies, all came under attack in sermons II, XIX and XXII. Saurin thought that Catholicism's power was spent and he claimed in sermon IV that it was 'losing ground'. Much more dangerous, according to Saurin, were deists, the incredulous, free thinkers and those who would have morality without religion, all people that he attacked in sermons IV, XVI and XX. For Saurin religion was revealed religion. That revelation came through scripture and that revelation was to be inwardly felt rather than being a matter of set forms or rituals. Perhaps curiously in a town dominated by

56 For whom see W.E.C. Fleming, *Armagh clergy, 1800–2000* (Armagh, 2001), pp 440–1.

57 For whom see Fleming, *Armagh clergy*, p. 197

Presbyterian dissenters there is little in the sermons that could be seen as defence of the principles of an established church. It may be that such sermons have simply not been preserved. The passage of the sermons from generation to generation ensured that the local and the particular were winnowed out of the collection as of limited utility in other circumstances.

The ways in which the sermons that have survived relate to Saurin's wider preaching is not known although appendix 2 suggests that they formed the main bulk of his oratory. There is no evidence to indicate how he chose the subjects on which he opted to preach but the frequency of preaching of any sermon may be an indication of the popularity of its subject with hearers. The liturgical year seems to have played a relatively small part in deciding on a sermon topic. There are certainly sermons in the collection for Christmas and Easter, reflecting on the nativity and the resurrection (IX, XII, XVII), and there are a few pastoral sermons such as that for confirmation (I).[58] However, apart from these particular occasions, the fact that the same corpus was regularly preached in Belfast suggests that these contained general truths that Saurin felt were important to the inhabitants of the parish. Saurin probably also chose topics that he thought appropriate or relevant to his congregation and then matched a biblical text to the theme. Hence sermons on social order form a large part of Saurin's corpus. It was probably common for Saurin to chastise his hearers and some sermons may have been inspired by specific events that are not now recoverable, although detailed analysis of the *Belfast News letter* for the period when sermons were preached might yield some clues. A case in point may be sermon no. 32 in appendix 1, preached in Belfast on 22 August 1756. A few weeks earlier, in early August, there had been food shortages and grain riots in Belfast in which grain had been looted.[59] The sermon was clearly not composed for the occasion since it had already been preached eight times before, yet it was remarkably apposite for the circumstances. Taking as his text Philippians 4.11 ('I have learned in whatsoever state I am therewith to be content'), Saurin urged his hearers to accept 'a resigned, cheerful & willing submission to our present state when it is out of our power to alter and amend it' and that people should behave as was 'proper for their station' since the world was 'ordered & disposed by a just & a gracious God' and, citing Job, urged that we 'submit ourselves to his dispensations'. The poor should labour for their goods and shake off idleness and sloth. Poverty, he suggested, was more than com-

58 How important confirmation was in Belfast is unclear but one list, between 1765 and 1783, names 21 to be confirmed, 15 males and six females, all between the ages of 12 and 36, though most were in the 12–16 age range; St Anne's Cathedral, Belfast, third Belfast register, p. 419.

59 Benn, *A history of the town of Belfast*, pp 594–5.

pensated for by the gifts of God such as health and friends so that 'we all enjoy more than we deserve'. This was undoubtedly an appropriate message for times of difficulty and Saurin may have used it as such, preaching it in Belfast in January 1750/1 during a previous demographic crisis. The power of the sermon comes not from its words but rather the context in which those words were spoken, where general thrusts took on a particular significance because of the context in which they were spoken. To accept one's lot was a much more powerful message in the wake of grain riots than on other occasions but it was suitable for a wide range of general uses also. This application of general texts to specific situations may have been a characteristic of Saurin's preaching. Sermon 49 in appendix 1 was preached in Belfast on 31 October 1756 in the run up to the November grain riots in the town. Again this sermon was not addressed to any specific problem and had been preached five times before but contained elements particularly relevant to the immediate situation. Preaching on the story of Ananias's gift of land to the early church and his retention of part of the sale price Saurin speculated that this money was to be used for the relief of the poor, although scripture does not say this, since for Christians 'assisting their indigent brethren was their indispensable duty' and the early church 'judged it proper that a public fund should be made for the relief of the poor & indigent brethren that by these means those in more easy circumstances might assist the want of others and by an excellent distribution set them upon a sort of equality'. A month later a poor relief scheme on exactly these lines was established in Belfast. One final example, again from the food crisis of late 1756, demonstrates the same principle. Sermon 37 in appendix 1 was preached in Belfast on 14 November, its sixth delivery, on the story of the rich man and Lazarus in Luke 16.31. While much of the focus of the sermon is on miracles, Saurin did tell his hearers that Lazarus had the 'reward of his patience & submission to the severe dispensations of providence', the same message as sermon 32 with particular relevance in the strained social tensions created by a harvest crisis. Again it may be significant that both of these sermons were also preached in late 1750 and early 1751 when another demographic crisis was gripping Belfast. It seems clear that in reading Saurin's sermons context is central to understanding their reception and the absence of topical or specific local references may not be as significant a problem as first appears in using these sermons. A good deal more work needs to be done in providing the context for each delivery of a sermon and, for instance, an examination of Saurin's pattern of preaching during the credit crisis in Belfast between 1770 and 1773, following the collapse of the London market for Irish linen, may yield interesting results.

CONCLUSIONS

The survival of James Saurin's sermons is remarkable and certainly constitutes one of the largest collections of parochial sermons surviving from eighteenth-century Ireland. They do not reflect the full range of sermons for parochial occasions, lacking, as they do, the corpus of sermons preached on political and special occasions, but they do represent the majority of the sermons delivered by Saurin over his lifetime as appendix 2 suggests. While the texts of the sermons lack anything by way of local or specific references to contemporary affairs that does not mean that they are any the less expressions of public life, since it is possible to locate the sermons within a spatial and temporal context because they have dates and places of preaching attached to them. As such they provide a way into the mind of their preacher but also a perspective on what listeners heard. In this way they reveal something of the mentality of at least one section of the Protestant community in an Irish provincial town in the middle of the eighteenth century. Used carefully, they may contain much more evidence of the outlook of the under-documented minority Church of Ireland in Belfast than might be apparent at first glance.

EDITORIAL CONVENTIONS

The text is a selection of twenty-four sermons from a collection of sixty-one preserved in seven volumes in St Anne's cathedral, Belfast. The selection has been made in an attempt to present a representative sample of the existing sermons. Thus some of the sermons for special occasions, such as Easter, Christmas and Confirmation, are included. Most of the sermons were for normal Sunday preaching and here popularity, measured by the number of times preached, and a concern to reflect Saurin's social and theological ideas have been the criteria in making the selection. A full list of the collection is included in appendix 1 and a guide to Saurin's preaching in appendix 2. The sermons selected for editing here are allocated sequential Roman numerals at the beginning of each sermon while the number in the collection list in appendix 1 is included in Arabic numbers together with the manuscript volume from which the sermon is drawn.

The text comprises a transcription of the selected sermons, now in St Anne's cathedral, Belfast. The spelling has not been modernized. Saurin usually wrote on one side of the page and on the opposite blank page he sometimes added material to be included and in the edition this has been inserted at the appropriate point and indicated by a note. Where an alternative version of parts of the sermon exist these have been printed as an appendix to the original text. Saurin's punctuation is erratic, usually using a comma where a full point may be more appropriate, but this has not been modernized. Sources of biblical references and allusions are given in the notes. Abbreviations for biblical books are given in the index. All biblical citations are from the Authorised Version.

Dates have been given old style and in the preaching lists the year had been taken as starting on 25 March, as in the manuscript, but in appendix 2 it has been taken as starting on 1 January.

The following editorial conventions have been used:

[ ]	editorial matter
Opportunities tendered	deletion
<in heaven>	interlineation
...	text illegible or missing

Text underlined is underlined in MS.

TEXT

Sermon I

Volume 1(6)

[p. 145] Belfast at a Confirmation July ye 22d 1747
Ditto at Ditto July 19th 1752
Ditto at Ditto Aug ye 4th 1767

[p. 146] In the Twenty Eight Chapter of the Gospel by St. Matthew & at the nineteenth verse.

Go ye therefore & teach all Nations baptising them in the Name of the Father & of the Son & of the Holy Ghost

Our Blessed Saviour having now Fulfilled the Great work, for which he came into the World, exhibited to Men the most perfect & compleat pattern of the sublimest virtues, wrought the most astonishing Miracles, offered up his life to God for the sins of Mankind [p. 147] & gloriously triumphed over all the powers of Death & the Grave, sets himself to compleat his important task, by commissioning his Apostles to publish *& preach the Doctrine to remote and distant Nations* <the glad tidings of his Gospel to the most remote & distant parts of the Earth>. Go ye therefore, & teach all Nations, baptising them in the name of the Father, & of the Son & of the Holy Ghost.

My design at present is not to enquire into every particular deductible from these words, I shall confine myself to such General Reflections, upon the nature of Christian Baptism, as may best lead us to understand the end [p. 148] for which Confirmation was appointed, & the Design of our Church, in requiring the observance of <this> decent & solemn ordinance.

And these I shall reduce to the four following. 1st. The Institution of Baptism, or the <general> Command here given, to <go &> baptise all Nations, 2nd. The stress, which is laid upon teaching & instructing the Nations, before they are admitted to Baptism. Go ye therefore & teach all Nations, baptising them in the name of the Father, & of the Son, & of the Holy Ghost. 3rd. If the Command be such, I shall consider, it comes [p. 149] to pass, that Baptism is administered to infants, who are incapable of Instruction, & Lastly from the practice of Infant Baptism, I shall *deduce* <infer> in the fourth place, the wisdom & use of Confirmation, & the proper Duty of those, who come to partake of this Rite.

1st Consid[eration]:

The first & most obvious Remark upon these words, is the Institution of Baptism or the Command <here given> to go & baptise all Nations.

It was customary with the Jewish Doctors, upon the admission of any new Disciple, into their sect or school, to make use of some external [p. 150] Baptism, or outward Rites, as a sign of their authority & power; we find this practised by John the Baptist, who regularly baptised *these that* <all such as> came to him & accepted the terms of that Repentance which he preached, & a Greater than John the Baptist, O[ur] B[lessed] S[aviour] himself, upon entering on his <S[acred]> Ministry, submitted to the like Baptism, both to show his approbation at this pious Custom & to lessen the prejudices of the Jews against him, for thus it became him to fulfill all righteousness,[1] whence it may not perhaps be unreasonable to suppose that the Baptism which he was now instituting, was appointed in conformity to this ancient usage.

[p. 151] But however this was *not* as the Gospel was intended to succeed the Law, it is much more probable, that Baptism was ordained to take place of Circumcision, established *by* <among> the Jews by God himself to be an outward sign of the Covenant, which he had made with them, & an earnest of the blessings which were to be the consequence of their diligent Observance of it.

And a very proper Emblem of the Gospel Covenant, is our Christian Baptism, which being of a simple Nature in itself, is admirably well suited, to the Genius of a Religion, divested of all that load of Ceremonious practices, rigorously, tho' wisely required by the [p. 152] Laws of Moses, which can be performed at all times, & in all places, which by it's outward sign, pure & clear water, is particularly expressive of that inward purity & holiness of life, <so essentially required & insisted upon under this oeconomy>...[2] & which as it was celebrated in the Eastern & hot countries, by immersion & plunging into water, & which we endeavour to imitate as far as the Nature of our Climate will allow, by covering with water, the face of the Person baptised, was a just representation of our Death unto sin & our Resurrection unto life, according to the allusion of the Apostle in the 6th Chapter to the Romans, that as many [p. 153] as were baptised into Jesus Christ, were baptised into his Death, that like as we have been planted in the likeness of his Death, we should be also in the likeness of his Resurrection.[3]

And it is with respect to this, that the form of Baptism was instituted, in the name of the father, & of the son, & of the Holy Ghost, that the whole Scheme of Christianity, & the whole plan of our Redemption, might *be set forth* <be laid before us> in one view, as contrived, executed & completed by the father, son & Holy Ghost, into whose service we are then initiated, & to [p. 154] whose honour we are hence-forward to *dedicate* <devote> our hearts & affections, in *sure and certain* hopes of being included within the Covenant of Grace & made partaken of its invaluable priviledges to wit, the answer of a good Conscience, towards God, by the Resurrection of Jesus Christ, who is gone into Heaven, & is on the right hand of God, Angels, & authorities, & powers, being made subject unto him.[4]

2nd Cons[ideration]:

Nor were the Apostles commissioned to baptise only, they were in a particular manner commanded to instruct the [p. 155] Nations, before they admitted them to Baptism, which is the 2nd thing observable in the words of the Text. For both Jews & Gentiles were called to this Baptism, Christianity was intended for them both, the Blessing of Christ's coming were *gathered to them equally* <indiscriminately tendered out to both>, & therefore the nature *of his religion was to be opened to them & its precepts were to be explained* <& principles of the Religion which he taught were equally to be explained to both, before they could judge whether they were to receive it or not>. The idolatry of the one, & the better grounded prejudices of the other, were to be sapped & undermined, the <former> were to be shown the folly & absurdity of multiplying the objects of their worship, that they might be brought to acknowledge the Unity of a God, & the [p. 156][5] spirituality of his Nature whilst the Jews with whom the Unity of a God was a primary & fundamental principle, were to be made sensible, even from their own Scriptures, that the Laws on which they so much valued themselves, was but a type & shadow of good things to come,[6] that in Christ Jesus, they met with the accomplishment of ancient Prophecies, & the full completion of former Predictions, & that every Circumstance relating to him, his birth & parentage, his virtues & powers shewed him to be the true Messiah, whom they had so long expected, for whose coming they had so ardently wished, & to whom God had bore witness by such great & signal wonders wrought in their presence, as placed the reality of [p. 157] them beyond every possibility of doubt or suspicion and these necessary evils were etc.[7] [p. 158] to be attained, by the gentle means of argument & persuasion, by proposing this Religion to their understanding, submitting it to their judgment, appealing *to their reason and common sense for the truth & certainty of what they offered* <for the truth of it, to their own reason & common sense>. For neither Christ nor his apostles were acquainted with the barbarous and unchristian methods, of forcing the Consciences of Men, of encreasing the number of their followers, by employing fire & sword, & delivering up obstinate unbelievers to Secular Powers, of enlightening the mind by torturing the body, or of convincing the heart by destroying the Man; Christ gloried in the number [p. 159] of his Disciples, but he gloried in the sincerity of their profession, & <in> the cheerfulness of their service, He knew, that *Religion* <Christianity> could stand the test of the most nice & unprejudiced enquiry, & therefore before *he would allow any to be baptised into it* <any were allowed *to* admission into it by baptism>, he would have their notions rectified, their doubts renewed & their faith settled, that the Baptism they received might be their own choice & a voluntary act of their own understanding.

But if teaching & instructing, was <thus> to precede Baptism, how comes it to pass that <in contradiction to so positive a command> Infants are baptised, altho' [p. 160] from their tender age, they are altogether incapable of Instruction; *the solution of which difficulty which* <this> is the third reflection naturally resulting from the *command* <words> of the Text.

3rd Consid[eration]:

It is true indeed that <in> the first Institution of Baptism, this sacred ordinance was chiefly intended for Persons *grown up to years of discretion & who* <of a mature age, & such as> were capable of entering into contract, & of chusing for themselves, but it is as true, that whatever advantages attend this Institution, the Children of Christian Parents seem to have a [p. 161] natural right to them, for they are born Heirs to these promises & hopes, of which Baptism is the earnest & the seal, since to us & <to> our Children, were the promises made,[8] their own incapacity & want of understanding cannot deprive them of these benefits, nor is there any absurdity in admitting then by an outward Rite, as parties in that Covenant, of which they actually reap the fruits, & are hereafter to obey the terms and conditions. This was the case with the Jews, their Circumcision was as much a Contract with God as our Baptism, God made them promises [p. 162] on his part, & they engaged themselves to perform certain Duties on theirs, & yet it was appointed *by God* to be solemnized on the eigth day *after* <from> the birth of the Child, whence it *follows* <is> that if Infant Baptism has nothing more than this, to justifie the use of it, far from being absurd & irrational, it is plainly conformable to what God himself had enjoined to his own favourite & chosen People.

But indeed the matter is far from resting here, it were easier to show, from the *earliest & most primitive* <whole practices of antiquity, in> the earliest & most primitive times, that every Christian Parent regularly [p. 163] brought his Child to be admitted to Baptism, in the presence of the Congregation, & tho' it cannot be directly proved that there were Children in the two housholds of Lydia or Stephana, *baptised* <which we are told were baptised> by St. Paul, yet the probability seems to be on that side.[9] Nor is this practice of Infant Baptism less *detestable* <to be vindicated> if exclusive of any warrant from scripture, or from the practice of the Ancient Church, we consider the propriety of it upon the grounds of Natural Reason *alone* <only>.

For is it not highly proper & becoming, that Parents perswaded of the truth of the Religion they profess, [p. 164] convinced of the high advantages, with which a ready adherence to it, is attended, & touched with a sincere & affectionate regard for it, should endeavour to putt their Children in the same happy circumstances with themselves, should at their births present & dedicate them up to God, acknowledge that they consider them as an heritage & gift that cometh of the Lord,[10] & that therefore they are desirous to enter them into Covenant with him, by obliging themselves in the most solemn manner, to give them all the instructions in their power, & to lay before them *the Nature* as strongly as they can, the Nature of the Obligation they have found themselves under for their sakes, [p. 165][11] even to go so far as to promise in their names by the Intervention of Persons who are judged properly qualified to discharge this trust, that they ... shall take this engagement upon themselves, when-ever they are capable of understanding or their Parents & Sponsors have taught them what that Engagement was.

And was this Holy Institution of Baptism, as religiously observed, as it was at first piously meant, all Objections to it would vanish, & the Wisdom & propriety of it be universally acknowledged.

But when as is too often the case, we conform to it to comply with an established custom without any sense of Religion or of the importance of what we are doing, when Days [p. 166][12] of this sort are considered as Days set apart for Intemperance, rioting & except when sponsors are chosen, who from their age, or situation are incapable of making good their promises, it is not much to be wondered at if the Institution itself suffers, & the abuses we make of it, bring it into contempt & disrepute.

4th Cons[ideration]:

And Hence from the Practice of Infant Baptism, follows as the last Reflection the Wisdom & use of Confirmation.

For as the Contract was made by the Parent or Sponsor, for the Child, before he could understand [p. 167] it's sense & meaning, it becomes very proper to have the Child himself, when he is sufficiently instructed to do so, to have him, I say renew his vows & promises with his own mouth, make an open Declaration, that he looks upon himself, as bound to be true to those engagements, which have been entered into for him, that he takes upon himself the terms of this Covenant, expects from the mercy & goodness of God, such helps & assistances, as may enable him to *follow* <comply with> the conditions of it, <& to entitle himself to the rewards promised to those who sedulously & diligently fulfil them>.

This is the End & Design of Confirmation, as every Circumstance [p. 168] attending it plainly shews; For it is intended for those only, who are grown up to such year's of Discretion, as make them capable of knowing the Grounds, upon which their faith stands, They are examined before hand, whether they have had sufficient instruction given them by their Parents, & are acquainted with the Nature of the promise, which they are going to make. They are brought into the Church, that every Member of the same may be a witness of their solemn promises, & as it were, bear testimony to their admission into the flock of Christ. There they solemnly asked, in the presence [p. 169] of God, whether they renew the promise & vow, that was made in their name at their baptism, whether they publickly ratify & confirm the same in their own persons, & acknowledge themselves bound to believe, & to do all those things, which their God fathers and God mothers then undertook for them, the form & manner of admitting them, being reserved for those, who holding the first & chiefest rank in the Government of our Church, are the likeliest by their authority & weight, to make the stronger & more lasting Impression upon them, and the better to enable them to *be true to their engagement* <do this>, they have the joint [p. 170] prayers of *those who are present* <all present>, who by the Interest they naturally take in the welfare of these Persons, to many of whom, they are particularly attached, by the close ties of friendship & blood, may be supposed, powerfully to intercede for them, & *to plead their case at the throne of Grace* <earnestly to recommend them to the fav[our] & acceptance of God>, to all which affecting circumstances, is added the Imposition of hands, as an outward sign to denote the love & great Blessings <which> they may reasonably expect, from <*this ordinance, this pious act,* this ordinance>, for if every private act of Devotion, accompanied with zeal & attention, with fervency ardor, procures unto us new & additional mercies, can we in the least [p. 171] doubt, but that God will favourably accept of a Religious Rite performed with this view, & sanctify the use & Intention of it to the lasting benefit of those, who partake of it with proper & becoming dispositions.

Applic[ation]:

Such a Solemnity thus requires from you, who are the more immediate subjects of it, the utmost seriousness & attention, You are now happily come to a fuller use of your Reason & understanding, You are voluntarily of your own accord taking upon yourselves the Obligations, which Christianity [p. 172] lays you under, You are renewing with you own mouths, the vows & promises which were made for you at your Baptism & therefore now become accountable for your actions, & answerable for them to the Great Judge of Heaven & Earth, those faults which the weakness of your Reason might once have excused, stand now openly condemned by the consent of your own wills, & the rebukes of an enlightened & better instructed conscience.

You are now *going* to launch out into a World, where you are to meet with numberless temptations, where you shall find yourselves perpetually beset with people whose [p. 173] boast it is, to corrupt innocence, & to make pure & unsullied hearts as tainted & vitious as their own, in continual danger of being led away by the torrent of evil examples, or what is still more fatal, of being ridiculed & laughed out of Religion by Libertines & Infidels, & in such perplexing circumstances, what is more proper, to preserve your inexperienced Youth from ruin, that continued sense of Religion, & a const[ant] rememberance of the sacredness of our Baptismal vows.

You are actualy engaging in the different Callings & occupations of life, & expecting from your success in these, <the> your future [p. 174] temporal welfare & happiness, but can you hope for the Blessing of God, to prosper your Worldly undertakings, if at your first setting out, you should break the most solemn promises, violate the most sacred engagements, & live totally regardless of God, & of *the* <your> Duty *you owe* <to> Him.

Let therefore each of you, seriously ask & examine yourselves, whether you can resolve to live in conformity to that Religion, of which you this day make so publick a profession, whether you are determined to forsake the pomps & vanities of this wicked World, & to let the rule of God's commands, <be> the [p. 175] chief & governing principles of your actions.

By acting thus in the dawn of life, before prejudices & vitious habits have taken root, you will find the paths of Religion become easie & pleasant, your progress thro' the World smooth & unencumbered, & your whole lives be attended with that peace & satisfaction of mind, which are the Inseparable Companions of him, whose early foundation was laid upon the unshaded principles of Religion, & the fear of God.

As for those among us, who are of a more advanced <age> not directly concerned in the occasion of our present [p. 176] meeting, still should this engage then a call to their minds the promises & vows, which they themselves formerly made at their Baptism, & which they have since, often, & solemnly renewed at the Sacrament of the Lord's Supper, <to consider>, how far their past & present conduct corresponds with these. They have promised to renounce the Devil & all his works, the pomps & vanities of this wicked World, & do their <actions> agree with this profession? Do they savour of mortyfication & self denyal? Do not the pleasures of this World; the idle pursuits of vanity & folly, the greedy desire of wealth & power, too often [p. 177] ingress their thoughts & affections? They have been graciously admitted into Covenant with God, entitled to the priviledges of God's chosen & elect Peoples, Do they not upon this very account, too often grow remiss, carless, & indifferent, presume too much, upon the mercy & goodness of God, & make no other use of his great & signal benefits, *but* <than> to encourage themselves in sin, & because to sentence denounced against. the<ir> glib words, is *hid* <not speedily> executed, to set their hearts more fully to do evil.[13]

To Conclude. Whatever may be the conduct of others, Let our's at least [p. 178] [be] such, as manifests the heartiness & readiness of our principles, let the promises, which we have already made to God, & those which many of us are now called upon to make, be so many Inducements to virtue, & so many motives to the practice of piety & *virtue* <holiness> God is in the midst of us, in a particular manner giving the most secret intentions of our hearts, judging of the sincerity of our professions, & laying us in remembrance before him the promises we bind ourselves to. If any presume to come to him, irreligiously & inconsiderately, wantonly & idly, his all seeing eye, notes their hypocrisie, & pierces through their [p. 179] artful disguise, but if any draw nigh to him in sincerity, & with an upright heart, resolved to make good <their> promises, to act up to their profession, God will favourably receive them, he will embrace them with the arms of his mercy, & in no time <he will> make them feel the whole feat & value of that kind & Gracious visitation of O[ur] B[lessed] S[aviour] very applicable to the present circumstances, Suffer the little Children to come unto me, & forbid them not, for such is the Kingdom of God.[14]

Sermon II

Volume 1 (10)

[p. 299] Belfast April ye 17th 1748

Do. July ye 23rd 1749

St. Ann's Dub[lin] March ye 25th 1750

Belfast April ye 5th 1752. Sunday after Easter

Do. September ye 1st 1754

Do. March ye 13th 1757

Do. September ye 30th 1759

Do. December ye 27th 1761

Do. April ye 21st 1765

Do. April ye 10th 1768. Sunday after Easter

St. Dulough[15] Sep: 12th 1790[16]

Do. May 26 1793

Do. April 1795

Do. April 10 1796

Do. Oct: 29 1790

Do. Nov 2. 1800

Rosenallis Nov: 14. 1802[17]

M[oun]t. Melich[18] Oct: 14. 1804

Rosenallis Dec: 15. 1805

Do. Nov 23. 1806

M[oun]t. Melich Jan: 12. 1807

Rosenallis Jan: 1. 1809

[p. 300] M[oun]t. Melich Dec: 9. 1810

Rosenallis Jan: 13. 1810

[p. 301] In the Third Chapter of St. Paul's Second Epistle to Timothy at the Fifth Verse

Having a Form of Godliness, but denying the power there-of.

In the Beginning of this Chapter, the Apostle fore-tells the Great *depravity* Corruption, into which Men <were to> fall, not-withstanding the Holiness & *transcendant* purity of the Religion, they professed; This know also *saith he* that in the last days perilous times shall come, for Men shall be Lovers of their own selves, covetous, [p. 302] proud, blasphemers, dis-obedient to Parents, unthankful, unholy, Without natural affection, truce breakers, false accusers, incontinent, fierce, despisers of those that are good, Traitors, heady, high minded, Lovers of pleasures more than Lovers of God, Having a Form of Godliness, but denying the power thereof.[19]

And this Prediction has accordingly been exactly fulfilled, Not to mention the many Crimes & vices *that*,<which> prevail in the World to the utter disgrace of Christianity, the particular Charge in the Text is literally & exactly true; Many are sollicitous & preserve the form, *the image* the outward [p. 303] *and empty* representation of Godliness or Religion, whilst they deny the power there of, *are careless and indifferent about the natural & immediate consequences of their profession and show no regard or concern for the essence, the stance and end of all religion* <and give themselves no trouble to maintain the essence of it in its genuine purity & perfection>.

And <Now> as a mistake of this Nature is most fatal in itself, & of <the most> dangerous consequence to the World in General *and most deceitful to those who are under the delusion of it*, I shall endeav[ou]r in the following Discourse to Lay before you <some of> the most striking & palpable <lines in the> Character*s* of those, who *can* <may> truly be said to have the Form of Godliness only, & to deny the power thereof <that from seeing ye folly & insufficiency of these we may be led to ye chief & only end of all religion, as strict obedience to ye will of our Father which is in heaven>.
And these I shall reduce to the ... [p. 304][20] *and less danger & Lastly They who* <*that*> *have real & substantial virtues but who by their principle they act upon & intention they have in view*. ...[21]

1st Part:

[p. 304] The First. *They* <I shall mention who> have a Form of Godliness without the power of if <are they> whose Religion consists in Orthodoxy in opinion & a sound faith *at the very time that they* <the very time that they> neglect the practical Duties <naturally> resulting from *it* this Profession.

Orthodoxy in opinion, & a sound faith *is* <are> doubtless the true & chief foundation of a Religious Life, & the possession of *it* <them> a high & invaluable advantage; Every [p. 305] Good Man must be careful to acquire & preserve *it* <them>, & Happy are they, who by their own endeavours & the assistances of God's Grace, have been able to see thro' the errors & mistakes of others, & to embrace a pure & unmixed faith, genuine & incorrupt.

But the Higher this advantage, the Greater sure the influence which it ought to have upon our Lives, the weightier & more clear the motives by which we are acted, & the more *glaring and conspicious* <shining & exalted> the virtues, which these intended to produce.

And yet is not the *contrary and* reverse of this often to be seen? Are there not Men every day to be met with, whose Religion if it be narrowly enquired into, consists only in the bare belief of certain [p. 306] *points & articles* truths, & a tenacious adherence to certain points & Articles of faith? Are there not daily instances of Persons in the World, who whilst they are miserably *divided* <torn> into parties & factions, about matters of mere Speculation in Religion, agree to *debase &* dishonour the faith, they profess by their own bad lives & dissolute manners, who as strenuous as they seem to be, for the defence & preservation of *certain* <particular> opinions in Religion, are remarkably cold & Languid in the maintenance of the Precepts & Moral Commands of it, little desirous to secure them in their original perfection, & by the faithfull observance of them to recommend the Doctrines & principles they appear so fond of.

[p. 307] And of what use is <such> a jejune & empty faith without a conduct corresponding thereto, of what advantage to fill our minds with a multitude of sound & true ideas, if these are in some sense cloistered up there, & never suffered to influence or affect the heart, of what advantage to spend much time upon Religious truths, many of them of the utmost importance to the practice of Morality, & all of some use & improvement, if the Letter of the Law only be attended to, & the Spirit, the end of the Law totally neglected.

St James is very express upon this point, What doth it profit a Man, my Brethren, tho' a man say, that he hath faith, & hath not works, Can [p. 308] Faith save him? Thou believest there is one God, thou dost well, the

Devils also believe this,[22] they have a right faith & just apprehensions of God's power & truth, & the Great aggravation of their guilt *was* <is>, that with such a persuasion they continue*d* Slaves to sin, & the bitterest enemies of all Virtues & righteousness, & St Paul makes it possible for a Man to have the Gift of prophecy, to understand all mysteries, to have a faith capable of removing Mountains, & yet for want of the virtues necessarily resulting from this faith & knowledge to be really nothing to resemble sounding brass or a tinkling Cymbal, void of any true sense or meaning.[23]

[p. 309] 2nd Part.

But 2nd: They also have a form of Godliness without the power of it, who are very studious to comply with the Ceremonial parts of Religion, of whatever nature they be, but who <neither> consider *neither* the end nor ye tendency of them.

This was in a singular manner the practice of the Pharisees among the Jews, we see them tything mint, anise and cumin, & *yet* omitting <at ye same time> the weightier matters of the Law, superstitiously cleansing the outside of the Cup & platter, & leaving the inward part full of ravening & corruption,[24] observing days & months & years, & passing by the end for which [p. 310] these days & months & years were appointed.

And in this they have been exactly *copied* <followed> by the Professors of the Popish Religion, who by introducing an infinite variety of vain & useless modes & Ceremonies, have so far overshadowed the power of Godliness, as to retain almost nothing but the form of it, a faint & mere representation of what Religion ought to be.

For what can be called the form of Religion without the power *of it*, if their superstitious fastings be not so, when it is made a meritorious & well pleasing act before God, to abstain from *certain* <some kinds of> meats upon *certain* <stated> days, whilst *men are left at liberty* <full liberty is allowed them> to gratyfy their sensuality & gluttony upon the most [p. 311] costly wines & the most delicious foods?

What is the form of Religion without the power *of it*, if their Penances & temporal atonement for their sins be not so, when *men* <they> think, they do God & their own souls service by cruelly torturing & distracting their bodies, as if G[od] A[lone] took pleasure in the shedding of Human Blood, or a recompence could be made him for the transgression of his Laws, by inflicting upon one's self Corporal & Bodyly punishments.

What is the form of Religion without the power *of it* if their Pilgrimages be not so, when they expect to secure salvation to themselves by visiting the Tombs and Monuments of ancient Saints, & departed [p. 313] Venerable Men, by taking long & tedious Journies to Distant Countries, & offering a costly & expensive Worship to Shrines and Relicks.

And Blessed be God *who has* <we are> freed from such *errors and mistakes* <dangerous delusions>, & by a wise & reasonable Reformation <have> rescued *us* <ourselves> from <this heavy load of> superstition & Idolatry, but as certain as this is, & as true that no Ceremonies are retained amongst us, but *those* <what> *as* are truly useful & proper for the Improvement of Morality & Virtue[25] and setting these upon their true and only bastion serve God & religion. Is it not to be feared that too many among us take the form for the power of religion & imagine that they have kept up to the spirit of it when they have only been complying [p. 315] with some external duty highly important in itself but only to be properly *exercised* <estimated> by its consequences and effects.

I might produce many & striking instances of this, but I shall confine myself to one only as having a particular reference to our present circumstances, namely Laying a full & entire stress upon the bare observance of Great and solemn festivals, without considering the end for which they were principally appointed.

Called upon to commemorate the most important blessings, we generally comply with the ordinance of the Church, we are constant in our attendance in the House of God, we follow with seeming fervency & zeal the daily service of the Church, to do this more effectually we interrupt our usual entertainments & Callings, we finish & compleat the [p. 317] whole by partaking devoutly in the Sacrament of the Lord's Supper & in all appearance by forming strong and hearty purposes of amendment.

And so far indeed *has* <is> the Form of Religion strictly preserved <& maintained> first whether the power of it *was* <is> as much attended to, can only be determined by our subsequent behaviour; If all this outward shew is only out of Custom & Decency, If like those mentioned by the Prophet Ezekiel we speak one to another, every one to his Brother saying, Come I pray you, & hear what is the word, that cometh forth from the Lord, & we come unto him as the people cometh, & sit before him as his People, & hear his words,[26] but [p. 319] become by these better men & better Christians we have joined the power to the form of religion & by uniting them into one formed a compleate and perfect system, the only true and satisfactory one.

3rd Part:

Part 3rd. They who affect great warmth & zeal about matters of Religion, & *shew* <express> it by a sour ill-natured & uncharitable demeanour towards others, may well be said to have the Form of Godliness without the power of it.

These hear much said in favour of zeal in Religion, they know (& in this they are right) that it is *that* <zeal>, which gives a Spirit to Devotion, *that* <which> animates [p. 320] & enlivens every Virtuous or Religious act, *that* <which> makes that service acceptable to God, which otherwise would be lukewarm, neither hot nor cold, as St. John expresses it, to be spewed out of God's mouth.[27]

But at the same time mistaking the nature of *it* <this zeal>, & having neither understanding nor knowledge sufficient to direct or set bounds to it, they unavoidably run into all those extremes, which a blind zeal, unguided & undirected is apt to lead Men in, Being without knowledge, having no foundation to go upon, not knowing what Spirit they are of,[28] they necessarily err both in the application & measure of it, Hence do they take that for Religion, which not only is [p. 321] opposite to but totally destructive of it<'s very nature & essence> & for want of due moderation & temper, & a compassionate sense of the infirmities of others, too often defeat the wise and good ends, they have in view, their zeal degenerates into sourness & ill-nature, they become censorious, cruel & austere, & are themselves strong prejudices against taking up a Religion, which their ignorance <& mistaken notions, concerning it> place in so disadvantageous a light.

And now if there be no power of Godliness, no true & vital Christianity without Charity, sure these Men are as far from it, as they possibly can <be>, If they would have a true & genuine zeal, the real effect of Religion, Let it be [p. 323] *employed in correcting and amending their own evil & corrupt ways, in recommending virtue by their own powerful example in repressing <and discountenancing> vice in those under their immediate influence.*[29] Let their admonitions & reproofs be accompanied with moderation, with temper, with Charity, & tho' it be always good to be zealously affected in every good thing,[30] Let their care be to invite Men to the practice of Virtue & Religion by a truly Christian & benevolent Carriage, a meek and affectionate Demeanour, *which must inevitably gain in the end upon all those who have still either a humane or generous sentiment remaining in them.*[31]

[p. 324] 4th Part.

The 4th. & most remarkable instance of the Form of Godliness without the power *of it*, is to put on Religion as a mask, & make *a shew* <use of ye appearances> of it in our transactions & dealings the better to impose upon the World, & carry on our unjust designs with more *security* <secrecy> & less danger.

There is something so truly amiable & engaging in a *virtuous & Religious* Character, that the most dissolute & abandoned are themselves struck with its <beauty>, Men readyly & greedily trust to such an appearance, they know Religion & piety to be the only sure bond of all honesty & integrity, they place a full trust [p. 325] & confidence in a Person, of whom they entertain such an opinion & *make his words and person their security and protection* <willingly give themselves up to his care & management>.

The Consequence of which is, that Some to gain this credit, to acquire this esteem, to be trusted & confided in, pretend to virtues, which they have not, make a glittering & deluding shew of outward sanctity & Religion, & carry engraved upon their fore heads this Device, Holiness to the Lord,[32] whilst their real Character is the very reverse of this, whilst they *cozen* <defraud> & deceive those who rely upon them, whilst their Sanctity is Publick & external, & their virtue mere falsehood & hypocrisie. [p. 326] And how heinous, how detestable a Character is this! Considered with respect to others it is the basest & most iniquitous *that can be conceived.* It is concealing a bait under the most deceitful & ensnaring appearances, to allure others, as it were irresistibly, to their own destruction, It's principle is Dissimulation, falsehood insincerity, & lying.

Considered with respect to God, It is the most daring Insult, *that* <which> can be offered to his Divine Majesty. It rots & divests him at once of his Attributes, It supposes, that he neither knows, views nor observes our actions, It braves his severest threatnings & menaces, & resolves them all into the idle threats, or the [p. 328] weak & vain efforts of a feeble & impotent Being.

And Considered with respect to ourselves, it is the vainest & emptiest of all delusions, *The* <That> God whose wisdom & knowledge we thus defy, *is ever present & at hand to* mark<s> our transgressions, peirces thro' the greatest secrecy, *to* view<s> our artfulness & cunning, *& when all false colours at once removed by Death, to manifest our shame to the eyes of the whole World, & to render our confusion conspicuous & astonishing,*[33] For what is the hope of the Hypocrite when God comes to take away his [p. 330] Soul?[34] No better than a Spider's web,[35] which how artfully linked together is liable to be quashed & broke by every accident.

5th Part:

But Lastly the Form of Godliness without the power, *of it* is not confined to the Hypocrite & Dissembler, the false & deceitful only, there is another Sett, liable to the same charge, who tho' they have many real & excellent virtues, which they regularly practise, & which they are careful to maintain, yet *they* marr & defeat the good effect of them by the principles they act upon, & the intention they have [p. 331] in view.

For it is An upright intention, aching out of principle & for Conscience sake, *is the only thing* that <which> *can* <alone>which alone determines the Morality of our actions, & denominates them good or bad, virtuous or vitious, according to O[ur] B[lessed] S[aviour]'s observation, If thine eye be single, thy whole body shall be full of light,[36] & of this integrity none <surely> can judge but ourselves, The World consistently with justice, & to avoid the imputation of censoriousness and ill nature, must deem that Man charitable & beneficent, who performs Charitable & beneficent action, and call him pious & Religious, who [p. 332] practices the outward Duties of Religion & piety.

But a Man's own heart & Conscience may it consulted & advised with possibly shew <him> these very actions in <a more> true tho' a less satisfactory light, for may not many of them be founded upon a wrong motive, & *acted* <influenced> by Worldly not Religious considerations. Has not Pride & vain glory often times a share in our Charity & other good actions? Is not our Piety & Devotion less fervent than it is in the Publick worship of the Church, & Do we not sometime reap less comfort & satisfaction from [p. 333] those <silent> acts of Religion, which have no other witness, *than* <but> God & our own hearts, than we do from those, which are performed in the presence of the World, & attract the attention and admiration of Men, & consequently *whether* <May we not> by some such means as these *we do not* flatter ourselves with having the power of Religion, when in reality we only possess the form, the empty appearance of it.

And Let those who labour under delusions of this *nature*, or of any other kind *that* <which> I have mentioned but reflect what pains they are at, to appear what they really are not, to put on [p. 334] the outward garb of what they should be, & at the expence of their own ease & pleasure, to preserve & keep up their pretended Character, & then consider what little *profit & advantage, what trifling* benefit they draw from this, compared with the high & inestimable *ones* <advantage>, they should deduce from a sincere & unfeigned obedience to Religion, & the commands of God, & such a consideration will naturally induce them to *study &* seek after the power of Religion, & to desire the appearance & form of it, no further than as it is necessary, (& indeed it is absolutely so) *for* <to> the attainment of *the* <its real> Essence & substance *of it.*

[p. 335] The Pleasures of Religion those I mean of sincere & unaffected Religion are so solid, so real, so durable and lasting, that they make full & abundant amends for all the hardships & difficulties they may bring us under, They are ever present to support us in all the vicissitudes of Life, to soften & sweeten the greatest Calamities, & to raise comfort & joy in the most desponding & wretched circumstances we can find ourselves in.

Pursue then & make these the sole & only end of all your endeavours with Holy David seek the ground [p. 336] of your heart, prove & examine your thoughts, Look well if there be any way of wickedness in you,[37] if any undue motive, any Worldly consideration be the sole principle of your present actions.

Above all, Consider yourselves as continually acting in the presence of God himself, & before that Supreme Being, with whom no artifice or disguise, no delusion or deceit can avail, who searcheth the reins,[38] & knoweth the most secret thoughts of men, who can expose & punish our vices, tho' ever so prudently managed [p. 337] or artfully practised, & who can at once distinguish the false & Dissembler from the sincere & upright.

This *consideration* <awful thought> frequently indulged & brought to our minds, would effectually prevent such dangerous mistakes, it would guard us against resting too much upon the form of Religion, & neglecting it so entirely as some have lately done, who by reducing all to mere Speculative & empty notions, & preaching up as weak & unsupported Morality, have made the power inconsistent with the form, & by setting the one in opposition to the other, have really [p. 338] proved themselves Enemies to both.

When instead of this we should join them into one, use the form to promote the power, & make the power enhance the value of the form, that so by offering up both our souls and bodies, a reasonable, living, Holy & acceptable sacrifice[39] to God we may reap the fruits of so entire an oblation here on earth, & at our departure out of the World into the next, see the foundation we have been raising, remain firm & unmoveable to all Eternity.

Which God of his Infinite Mercy Grant etc. etc.

Appendix

[Note: Saurin significantly redrafted the second part of this sermon, writing on the back of the usual text of the sermon, so as to create an alternative section. The text of this revision is printed below].

[p. 312] I think myself warrented to say that the Form of Religion is more attended to come among us, than the Power; & the empty Shadow more than the real Substance of Religion. For is there not more form than Power, in that scrupulous exactness with which under pretence of serving God & of better discharging the duties of Religion, we interrupt upon certain days [p. 314] and seasons our vitious recreations & amuse men with no other view than to return to them again as soon as opportunity offers, & the time affixed as such periodical Devotions will allow. Is there not more form than power in our cold & languid attendance upon the worship of God, when we are present indeed in the body, but absent in the Spirit, bow our knee to God, & rove away from him in idle & rambling thoughts & wishes; Is there not more form than power in that contradictory mixture of Religion & uncharitableness, of Devotion & censoriousness, of Piety & intermperance which the lives of so many daily present us with, & in which they persevere not only without reluctance, but with the greatest security & satisfaction.

[p. 316] Is there not more form than power in that sollicitude which dying Persons so often shew of receiving in their last hours the benefit of the external ordinances of Religion, totally neglected the use of, either disrespectfully passing them by, or superstitiously reserving them for their last moments, as a sure & safe passport to carry them to happiness & Heaven without any further concern or endeavours of their own, finally Is there not more form than power in that loud and Religious cry of the Enthusiast, The temple of the Lord, the Temple of the Lord, the Temple of the Lord are these, whilst he is at no trouble [p. 318] to amend his ways & his doings, to execute judgment thoroughly between a Man & his neighbour, to free the stranger, the fatherless & widow from oppression,[40] & by such like acts of Moral goodness and virtue to do the will of his Great Creator.

Sermon III

Volume 2 (11)

[p. 1] Belfast May ye 15th 1748
Ditto September ye 3d 1749
Ditto November ye 3rd 1751
Ditto October ye 7th 1753
St. Luke Dub[lin] November ye 25th 1753
Belfast Aug: ye 8th 1756
Ditto March ye 12th 1758
Ditto September ye 21st 1760
Ditto April ye 24th 1763
Ditto July ye 7th 1765
Ditto June ye 4th 1769
Ditto December ye 1st 1771
St. Dourlogh's June ye 29th 1783[41]
Ditto may ye 22nd 1785, a very small congregation
Ditto August ye 25th 1785
Ditto June ye 24th 1787
Ditto August ye 16th 1789
Ditto June 19 1791
St. Michaels December 4th 1791
St. Dol[ough's] July 14th 1793
[p. 2] St. Dol[ough's] June 28 1795
Ditto June 16 1799
Rosenallis June 20 1802
Mt. Melich August 8 1802
Ditto October 27 1805
Rosenallis May 31 1807
Mt. Melich January 17 1808
Rosenallis July 22 1810
Mt. Melich May 26 1811
St. Peter's November 21 1813[42]
Ditto April 9 1815
Ditto June 15 1817
Dunonghmore[43] August 24 1817

[p. 3] In the Sixteenth Chapter of the Proverbs of Solomon at the fifth Verse.

Every one that is proud in heart is an Abomination to the Lord, tho' hand join in hand, he shall not be unpunished.

There is hardly <any> one Vice to which Men are more generally addicted than of Pride, against which the words of the Text are principally pointed. It is confined to no age, no condition, no rank or station in life, The High & the low, The Rich & the [p. 4] poor are more or less tainted with it, & often those the most, who have the least right & pretension to be so, if indeed any thing can give a right & pretension to what is deservedly condemned by the wisest of Men, as the just object of God's hatred & displeasure. Every one that is proud in heart, is an abomination to the Lord, tho' hand join in hand, he shall not be unpunished. In further Discoursing upon these words, I shall 1st Enquire into the Nature of Pride, 2dly Endeavour to shew it's bad & pernicious effects, & 3^{d} the *odiousness* <folly> & sinfulness of *such a depiction of heart and mind* <it>, in the sight both of God & Man.

[p. 5] 1st Part.

And here we must be careful to distinguish Pride from a just & laudable Emulation, which prompts us to equal, or even to excel by lawful & allowable means, those who have rendered themselves eminent in the World, & whose example we may therefore very properly, set before us, as a powerful Incentive to the performance of the same great & good actions. Neither is that affection of the Human mind, to be deemed Pride, which makes us desirous in all we do, to secure to ourselves the favourable opinion & approbation of others, provided this approbation be subordinate to that of God, & of our own hearts. [p. 6] There is *also* <like-wise> something exclusive of Pride, in the natural disposition we all have, to chuse & single out our Company, & to form friendships & connections with those, whose circumstances & characters are most conformable to our own. There is in one word, a Decency due to our Rank & Station in life, which sometimes requires a pompous outside, certain <Distinctions> to be observed for the sake of order & regularity, & a certain outward splendor, that can & often does subsist with any mixture of Pride & vanity.

But what constitutes the nature of this Passion is, 1st To imagine ourselves <free> from those faults & vices, which we really have, or to lessen & diminish [p. 7] those, which we cannot avoid seeing, 2^{d} To ascribe to ourselves virtues, which we have not, & to charge & amplify those, which we have, or 3d To reckon that virtue, excellence or merit, which is only an accidental & occasional advantage, often derived to us from others, than acquired by ourselves, or issuing from the wisdom of our own counsils.

1st. It is one property of Pride to make us imagine ourselves free from those faults & vices, which we really have, for the whole foundation of Pride is an excessive & immoderate self love, which shuts our eyes against the most glaring truths, & prevents our seeing objects thro' a right [p. 8] medium, We set out with a fixed & over-weening fondness for ourselves, & this easyly perswades us, that nothing odious or disagreeable can enter into our beloved Composition, hence if some Lines are too striking not to be perceived, Pride generally lessens the deformity of them, so as to convert them into Qualifications & accomplishments, & from the narrow boundaries between each virtue & it's opposite vice, finds means enough to convince us, that our very imperfections & defects are in reality ornamental & praise worthy. It changes Anger & Passion into a just & proper resentment, Covetousness & Avarice into a prudent & reasonable [p. 9] concern for futurity, & an unbounded thirst of Glory into a natural & laudable desire of fame, So very apt is self-love to lull us into a delusive security, to blind our judgment, & as the Prophet Isaiah expresses it, to call evil, good, & good evil to put darkness for light, & light for darkness.[44]

And the same method does Pride observe with respect to our Virtues, ascribing to us many, which we have not, & much over-valuing those which we really have. It raises it's structure upon some one perfection, which we are perhaps in possession of, but which it carries beyond it's proper [p. 10] bounds, for if we have deserved commendation & applause upon some particular account, it adjudges & arrogates the same to itself upon every other, It conceives, that eminence in one instance gives one a right to eminence & superiority in all-others, that because we understand one branch of learning, we are entitled to judge peremptorily of every other part of Science, that because we have done some conspicuous & remarkable action in our lives, we are therefore at liberty to command the respect & admiration of the whole World, or because we have some one Grace or virtue, that we possess them all in the highest degree Like the Men of Laodicea, fondly [p. 11] saying to ourselves, We are rich & encreased with goods, & have need of nothing, when in fact, we are wretched, miserable, poor, blind, & naked.[45]
And the better to compleat it's views, Pride in the last place substitutes accidental & occasional advantages in the room of solid & real excellencies.

It *makes a merit of* <derives merit to itself from> the very circumstances *we are born, the ranks in* <of birth & fortune, esteeming our> wealth, rank, honours & power, as part of our own intrinsic worth, appropriating these to ourselves, fancying they add a powerful & irresistible weight to every thing we say or do, & make abundant amends for what [p. 12] ever other Qualifications we want, claiming upon so pifling a distinction, respect & superiority, representing us to ourselves, as highly exalted above the rest of Mankind, entitled to their homage veneration & servile attendance, & engaging us, to think more highly of ourselves, than we ought to think, & not soberly, according as God hath dealt unto every man the measure of his gifts.[46]

And from so unjust & unfair a value we put upon ourselves, follow as a natural consequence many fatal evils, the bad effects of which [p. 15][47] I come now in the second place to lay before you.

2nd Part.

And 1st. The mischiefs arising to ourselves from such an excessive Pride are many & obvious; it sets us upon desiring & actually undertaking, what we are neither capable of performing *it* <nor> of attaining to, upon grasping at Dignities & Stations, too high & elevated for us, & which, if <our extravagant wishes were listened to>, would only serve to expose our *own* weakness, & to place our defects & incapacity in a more conspicuous light. But as it more generally [p. 16] happens, that such ill-grounded expectations are not attended with the desired success, Pride *makes* <causes> disappointments of this kind <to> fall on us with tenfold weight, because it ever represents them to us, as a real injury offered to *our merit* & and injurious slight & contempt, if those superior talents, which we vainly boast to possess. And this in the end produces total discontent & dissatisfaction, taking us off from whatever is easie & pleasant in our condition, to dwell upon the imaginary cravings of an *extravagent* <inordinate> self conceit, whence it is observed that the Proud Man is generally <the> most [p. 17] fretful & uneasie, founding his happiness upon such enjoyments, as are the furthest out of his reach, & carrying incessantly about him the torturing & excruciating passions of envy & jealousie. Nor are the evil & fatal effects of Pride confined to ourselves only, they affect all those, with whom we have to do, For as it lessens our own defects, or increases our own perfection, so for the same reason does it diminish the real virtues of others, & either swells their imperfections, or ascribes to them faults & vices, which they have not, without attending to the many good qualities, which perhaps fully compensate for those they have. [p. 18] Hence that contempt, which the Proud Man Manifests for others, which he shews in his looks, in his words, in his gesture & whole deportment, Hence that eagerness to seek for applause & commendation, where with to feed & nourish up his vanity, Hence that offensive haughtiness, with which he treats his Inferiors, that affectation of rising above his equals, & coveting to put himself upon a level with his Superiors, Hence that sourness & moroseness of temper, that positiveness & obstinacy, those bitter & injurious expressions, which interrupt the sweets of friendship & social converse, & hence the folly of distinguishing himself by [p. 19] his Pomp, <his> luxury, & <his> grandeur, by unnecessary & ruinous expences, which often lay him under a necessity of contracting debts which he is never able to pay, & of pursuing such measures, as inevitably end in the ruin of *both* himself, & of those, who are *very dependant upon him* <deceived by his appearance>.

And A Vice of so evil a tendency to us & others, can not fail of having a most fatal Influence over the Duties, which immediately relate to God; This Pride for instance, which diverts our eyes from the God, who dispenses <to us> the advantages we enjoy, to fix them upon our own merits & sufficiency, which takes us oft from all dependence upon him, to trust to our own [p. 20] strength & ability, presumptuously asking with King Nebuchadnezzar, Is not this Great Babylon, that I have built for the House of the Kingdom, by the might of my power, & for the hour of my Majesty?[48] T'is Pride which induces us to murmur under *hard dispensations & trials* <affliction & trouble> to consider as unmerited & unjust; what meekness & humility of Spirit would represent, as highly useful & beneficial to us, T'is Pride, which obstructs the Great work of our conversion, by falsely perswading us, that we have no vices to correct, no faults to amend, nor no defects to set right, in one word, T'is [p. 21] Pride, which prevents our leading to greater perfection, acquiring the Graces, which we want, improving those we have & making proper & suitable advances in virtue & goodness. And now from the bare exposition of this Vice, we may casuly furnish ourselves with argu[me]nts to evinice the <folly> & sinfulness of it, which is the third & last thing to be spoken to.

3rd Part

First. It is of all passions the less suited to the condition of Man in this World.

There is something so humbling & mortifying in the very [p. 22] frame & complexion of our Being, That it might be expected, we would rather need arguments to support us under the sense of our meanness & insufficiency, than of words to convince us of the truth & reality of it. That Creatures such as we are, who dwell in Houses of clay, whose foundation is in the dust, which are crushed before the moth,[49] driven to & fro as a leaf, & as the dry stubble,[50] That Beings, whose breath is in their nostrils, whose goodliness is as the flower of the field, withering as the grass, & fading away, as the green herb,[51] That [p. 23] Men subject to numberless infirmities, liable to infinite Diseases, exposed to a variety of unthought of accidents, That they whose knowledge the least difficulties perplex, whose curiosity every pebble & insignificant Insect set bounds to, *That men* whose Virtue is endangered by every temptation, whom Passions & violent Appetites continually wrack & distract, That Beings who live as we do here, whose beginning is listlessness & indigence, whose Growth is only feebleness, insufficiency & whose end is corruption & death. That Creatures of this sort should be proud, vain, & arrogant, is one of the most astonishing & striking [p. 24] instances of the corruption of the human heart, which will appear in a still more shocking light, if we consider 2d. The little foundation there is for pride & conceit in the several pretences, upon which we generally build it. Is it the abundance of our riches & wealth, that render us thus assuming? What gave we that we have not received? Are not these more commonly the consequence of other People's merit & industry, than of our own? Can they secure us from danger, ensure our health, or prolong our days for one single moment? Can we take them along with us, when we dye, or extend the enjoyment of them [p. 25] beyond this World, nay rather Can we promise to ourselves the possession of them for any time, May they not make themselves wings & fly away;[52] or may not the Great master & Supreme Proprietor of all things, deprive us of them, to bestow them upon whom he pleaseth? So it [is] the strength of Genius & understanding that exalts the Pride of Man? What is our knowledge, when compared to the number of things <which> we are totally ignorant of? Does it *extend to* <penetrate into> the substance & nature of things? Can we contemplate the works of God without being lost in perplexity & amazement? Can we even comprehend our own [p. 26] nature & the secret springs of our own Being, & Are not the smallest motions of our bodies, with the simplest operations of our souls, far beyond the conception of the Wisest Men? Is it the Glitter of Titles, or the superiority of Rank & station that *we pride ourselves upon* <swell our vain hearts>? What are all these, but accidental advantages, the result of circumstances & situations? Do they make any *real* <very> considerable difference, in the real state & condition of Men? Did not the same God *make* <form> us all? Did he not create us for one & the same purpose? Are not the poor & the Mighty, the Noble & the Ignoble, perfectly upon [p. 27] all equality with respect to all the lasting advantages, or the real miseries of life? Finally. Do any exalt upon the sense of beauty or the advantage of outward Comeliness of Grace? What is this, but the fleeting superiority of one'*s* moment's Continence, which it is in the power of every succeeding Distemper to interrupt or efface which every suceeding year *must* <necessarily> impairs above all, which Death that certain dweller, will sooner or later destroy, & perhaps in the full of it's bloom, reduce to *the* <a> most hideous & loathsome Spectacle.

3rd. Pride generally fails if success seldom attains the end it has in [p. 29] view.[53] It seeks for esteem, & in return it meets with contempt, It aims at regard & admiration, & it only excites laughter or pity, according to the just observation of Solomon, A Man's pride shall bring him low, but honour shall uphold the humble in Spirit.[54] And indeed nothing less is to be expected from it, for as the proud Man despises every one but himself, so is he deservedly entitled to the contempt of all Men, as he builds his own greatness upon the depression of others, so is it natural for every one to pull down his pompous & injurious Structure, as he attacks every one's self-love & self-conceit, so does he well deserve to [p. 30] have them all combining (into one) to frustrate his designs, & by all possible means to humble & mortify him, for such is the Inconsistency of Pride, that tho' it induces us to contemn the whole world, it *makes it at that very time* founds our hopes of happiness <at the same time> upon the good opinion & aplause of those for whom we manifest the highest contempt, & the single thought, that we are not sufficiently admired, even by the Persons we treat with most disdain, is alone capable of poysoning & embittring all the pleasure & satisfaction of our lives.

Lastly. Pride is directly opposite to the Spirit of Religion & inconsistent [p. 31] with the practice of it. (We have already seen it's pernicious affects with respect to the Duties, which more immediately relate to God, & the same are extended to all other duties recommended & enjoined by Religion.) If religion requires us to be Compassionate, tender-hearted, ready to communicate, & to relieve the wants of others, Pride hardens our hearts, engages us to look down with disdain upon the miseries of our fellow Creatures, abolishes in our imaginations the very Relations, which subsists between them & us, & reduces us to stand single, & by ourselves, apart from the rest of Mankind [p. 32] & Religion would have us follow the Example of O[ur] B[lessed] S[aviour] in the practice of the same meekness, humility, condescension, charity & love, which added such distinguished lustre to his whole life & conversation. Pride carries us on in direct contradiction to this, & the Course of Action it traces out for us, is in very instance, the reverse of our divine Model. If again Religion demands from us upon certain occasions the Sacrifice of our ease, our pleasure & our wealth, Pride prevents the oblation. It stands in need of all these to support it's extravagant pretensions, It renders us careless [p. 33] & indifferent about every serious concern, too often tempts us to pursue our own ends at the expence of Conscience & Duty. And accordingly has God, not only denounced the severest judgments 1st every one, who is proud in heart,[55] that has frequently *brought* < inflicted> them *down* upon him even in this life, tumbling him down from his height, blasting & confounding all his hopes of Grandeur, exposing him to the just slight & contempt of others, thus did he act with Haman, whose haughtiness would admit of no equal or Competitor,[56] thus with Herod, smiting him with a sore & dreadful Disease, as he was [p. 34] feeding upon the impious praises of a multitude of vile Sycophants,[57] & thus with Nebachadnezzar, whom by an hitherto unheard of Judgment, he reduced to the State of a Brute, driving in from Men, appointing his dwelling with the beasts of the field, making him to eat grass as an ox,[58] & to be wet with the Dew of Heaven, till his Reason returned unto him, & he honoured the King of Heaven, & acknowledged, that all those that walk in pride, he was able to abase.[59] And tho' there may be some, who as the Prophet tells us, hold the height of the Hills, [p. 35] make their nests as high as the Eagle's,[60] & that any seeming Interruption, not have <we> an <undoubted> Assurance from the mouth of God himself, that he will one day bring them down from thence, tho' hand join in hand, they shall not go unpunished,[61] their lofty looks shall in the end be humbled & their haughtiness brought low, for the Day of the Lord of Hosts shall be upon every one that is proud & lofty, & upon every one, that is lifted up, & he shall be brought low, And the loftiness of Man shall be bowed down & [p. 36] the haughtiness of Man shall be made low, & the Lord alone shall be exalted on that day.[62]

Applic[ation]:

(Since then Pride is a Vice of dangerous a Nature,) Let us with all diligence secure our hearts against the eluding blandishments of so seducing Passion; The most effectual way to do this, is frequently to reflect upon that Period, which is not far from *every one* <any> of us, in which all the vain Distinctions of this World, all our Pomp & luxury, every thing [p. 37] which now flatters or cherishes our self-love, shall vanish away, in which ...[63] <turned again into that Dust, out of which we were originally taken, one common Grave is to receive us all>, when summoned before an Impartial Tribunal, we shall *all* be weighed in an even ballance, without regard to rank, ability, or wealth, when our vain & Chimerical Greatness <with which we are so unaccountably infatuated>, shall appear [less] than Vanity itself, & be laid open [to] the notice & observation of men & of Angels. Indulge such a thought, no Arrogance can be great enough to withstand it's power, no Pride so [p. 38] vetted but what it must compound, one so proud in heart, but what it must crash & bring down. May that God, who resisteth the proud, but giveth grace to the Humble,[64] pour into our hearts those excellent virtues of meekness & humility, that we in Imitation of O[ur] B[lessed] S[aviour]'s example, making ourselves humble & of no Reputation,[65] may with him …[66] in Glory, & instead of the short & transitory honours of this World, secure ourselves the permanent & solid series of the next. For thus saith the High & lofty one, that inhabiteth eternity, whose name is Holy, I dwell [p. 39] in the high & *lofty* Holy place with him also, that is of a contrite & humble Spirit, revive the Spirit of the humble, & to revive the Spirit of the contrite ones,[67] and Blessed, for ever Blessed are the poor in Spirit, for their's is the Kingdom of Heaven.[68]

Appendix

[Note: pages 13 and 14 are a later insert written in a hand that is not Saurin's, but possibly that of his son, and represents a reworking of the sermon.]
In the sixteenth Chapter of the Proverbs of Solomon at the fifth Verse.
Every one that is proud in Heart is an abomination to the Lord, tho' Hand join in Hand he shall not be unpunished.

[p. 13] If we view the whole Catalogue of human vices, we shall find no one, to which men are more generally addicted than to that of pride, it's confined to no age, no condition, no rank, or Station in Life, the high, & the low, the Rich & the poor are more or less tainted with it; God has therefore been graciously pleased, by the mouth of the wise man, to declare his aversion to it, saying no in this manner under an additional obligation to guard against it, for it is an abomination unto him, it shall not be unpunished; attend therefore M[y] B[rethren], whilst Endeavour to shew it's pernicious Effects, it's folly & sinfulness in the sight both of God & man.

[p. 14] If we view the whole Catalogue of human vices, we shall find none to which men are more generally addicted, than to Pride, tis confined to no age, no condition, no rank or station in Life, the high & the low, the rich & the poor, are more or less tainted with it; therefore did it deserve, the observation of the wise man that God has been therefore graciously pleased, by the oath of the wise man, to declare his aversion to it, saying no in the manner under an additional obligation to guard against it, for it is an abomination unto him, it shall not go unpunished, attend follow me then my B[rethren] whilst Endeavour to shew it's pernicious effects, it's folly & sinfulness, in the sight of both God & Man.

Sermon IV

Volume 2 (12)

[p. 40]

Belfast June ye 19th 1748
Ditto December ye 17th 1749
Ditto December ye 15th 1751
Ditto January ye 13th 1754
Ditto April ye 20th 1755
Dublin St. Ann's June ye 27th 1756
Ditto St. Michael's July ye 4th 1756
Belfast October ye 30th 1757
Ditto November ye 26th 1758
Ditto November ye 2nd 1760
Ditto January ye 16th 1763
Ditto February ye 3rd 1765
Ditto March ye 22nd 1767
Ditto August ye 21st 1768
Ditto January ye 13th 1771
Ditto March ye 22nd 1772
Rosenallis September 7 1806[69]
Mt. Melich September 1806
Ditto August 14 1808
Rosenallis April 5 1810
Mt. Melich March 24 1811

[p. 41] In the Fourth Chapter of the Prophecy of the Prophet Hosea & at the Sixth Verse

My People are destroyed for lack of knowledge.

The Knowledge which God by the mouth of the Prophet Hosea complains his People were destroyed for lack of, is the Knowledge of Religion, as it comprehends our Duty to God, our neighbour & ourselves, and their ignorance here-in [p. 42] *it* proceeded not so much from any incapacity

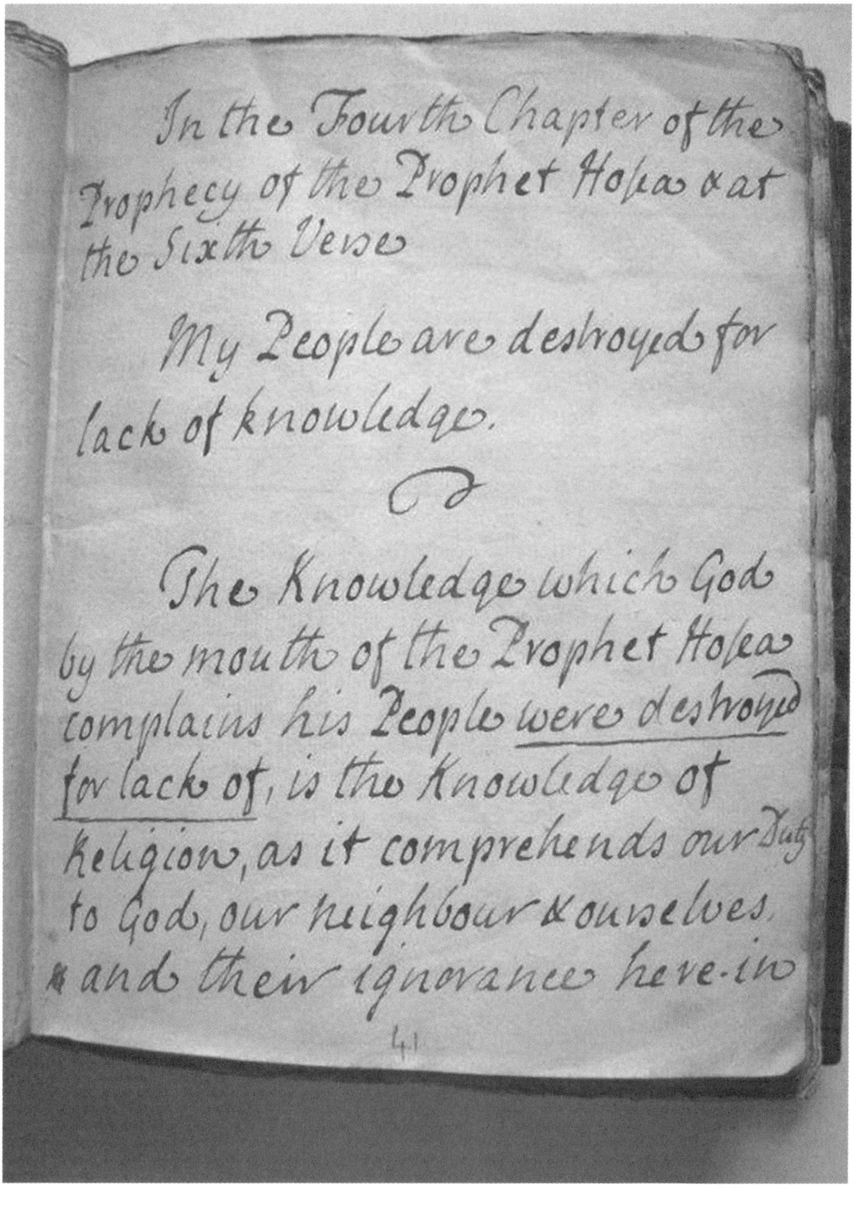
In the Fourth Chapter of the
Prophecy of the Prophet Hosea & at
the Sixth Verse

My People are destroyed for
lack of knowledge.

The Knowledge which God
by the mouth of the Prophet Hosea
complains his People were destroyed
for lack of, is the Knowledge of
Religion, as it comprehends our Duty
to God, our neighbour & ourselves,
and their ignorance here-in

41

4 Opening page of Sermon IV (12) in Saurin's hand, written in large letters for pulpit legibility.

they were under of coming to the *true* <right> knowledge of it, as from a willing indifference *& disregard for it*, a stupid carelessness *& inconsideration* about matters of this important Nature, & a total neglect of the means naturally conducing there-to.

It were easie to draw a Parallel between the conduct of God's People & our's in this respect, & it is with a view of applying the Complaint now before us to ourselves, & thereby of exciting us to the Study of Religion, a Study of all others the most *noble, the most* useful, *the most* <and> becoming, that I [p. 43] have chosen the words of the Prophet Hosea from whence I propose 1st to shew *his observations as applicable to us & demonstrate that the people are in lack of knowledge* < how truly the prophets observation *is applicable to us*>& 2d *to shew the* <the evil &> mischeivious consequences that attend *the lack of Divine knowledge they are destroyed for by it 3d to offer some Directions whereby we may the better and easier come to the attainment of it* <their being so. They are destroyed for lack of it>.[70]

1st Part:

And *to verify* <in order to show how truly> the Prophet's observation <is applicable to ourselves> it is not necessary that we [p. 45] should include all the People in General under this charge, or apply to every Individual what only belongs to the Greater number among them; As low as the State of Religion is now reduced & as little as the Study of *religion* it is at present attended to, there are Many upon whom the Contagion has not yet gained, whose chief & principal *aim* <care> is to acquire the saving knowledge of the truths, who apply their time, their parts, their leisure *in improving themselves in it or in aiding & assisting others in their researches* <the Religious improvement of themselves, or others>, who like David love the law of God, & make it [p. 46] their meditation *night &*< all the> day,[71] & by whose unwearied pains & diligence the truths of Religion are preserved, & hitherto maintained in some repute.

But the misfortune is, that there are but few who think in this manner, & if some among us study Religion, the Generality <certainly> do not; if we look abroad into the World, & examine what little Care is taken for the most part to train up Youth in the knowledge of Religion, how much pains & time are spent upon teaching them everything else but this. If we observe how superficial the little knowledge is which they do acquire, consisting [p. 48] chiefly of words & sounds to which they fix no sense or meaning *we shall find that the result of such a beginning. must be total ignorance of religion in the end that not* < If moreover we consider, how few are capable of teaching others, from the want of proper Knowledge in themselves, we shall find little reason to wonder, that so many continue ignorant of the truth & certainly of Religion, that not being> sufficiently grounded, in the <necessity &> importance of it,[72] the Cares and sollicitudes of the World, with which they are taken up in the next Period of their lives, choke what little principles were instilled in them & efface the early impressions that were made upon their minds.

And in <The> consequences of *this* <which> is *do* <that> we very rarely see Persons educated in this careless manner, enquiring at all after Religion when they [p. 50] grow up to years of discretion, or applying themselves to the study of it with any degree of diligence & attention. They look upon it as the business of their early *younger years & would*, <years with which they have at present no concern & would> think it an injury *done them were they* <done them>, even to suspect <that they were> pursuing such a knowledge or meant to for the attainment of it, their own *endeavours* <labours>[73] or the counsil <& advice> of others, whence it is that men *presumably* <implicitly> continue in the Religion of their Fathers, adhere stedfastly to their principles, *swallow down their errors & absurdities* & transmit them *down* to their Posterity without further choice or discernment.

[p. 51] This then being the Case of the Generality of our People as well as of that of the Jews, the *consequence* <inference> which the Prophet draws from it, is strictly applicable to *them* <us as well as them> that they are destroyed for lack of this Divine knowledge, an Emphatical & strong expression to denote the Great & mighty evils that inevitably arise from such a neglect, the particular consideration of which is the 2nd thing intended to be spoken to.

2nd Part

And the 1st Evil I shall mention arising [p. 52] from the want of Religious knowledge is the *being exposed* Danger of falling into many errors & mistakes concerning the truths of Religion.

Hardly had the good seed been sown, but tares sprang up, nourished and cherished by an evil Spirit.[74] A number of pernicious destructive Tenets were propagated, by the suitableness *and agreeableness* of which to men's corrupt & depraved appetites, a ready admission was made for them & favourable & encouraging reception.

These were many & of various [p. 53] kinds, there is a mode of fashion for them as there is for every thing else in the World. They make use of Novelty to introduce them<selves> & taking advantage of the <natural> fickleness & understanding of Men *who are generally inconstant in all their ways* they vary & transform themselves into a multitude of shapes.

It would far exceed the limits of this Discourse to enumerate the many errors, that have crept into Religion & the monstrous corruptions they have given rise to; The most prevailing in our time & age is to [p. 54] lessen as far as possible the Sacredness, usefulness & expediency of a Divine Revelation, to set up in opposition to it the sufficiency of our own Reason, to weaken the great Sanctions of God's Laws, the rewards & punishments of another Life by expatiating upon the eternal & original fitness of Virtue & the praise & glory there is in <practising> it for it's own sake, without any respect to the consequences of it *to true relegion of all its outward form*, to undervalue the *necessity* <use> of the <outward> acts & ordinances of *it* <Religion>, & to preach up Morality bare & unsupported.

Now <if this be & ever was the case>, if we be exposed to errors [p. 55] of *this* <a> dangerous tendency, if there be Men whose pleasure & boast consists in withdrawing others from the truth by deceitful arguments, glossed over with the highest professions of regard & veneration for Religion, if errors of this kind be common & obvious pressed upon us in conversation & more openly inculcated in print, Is not a large share of Religious knowledge required to prevent our being ensnared by such delusions, not only to convince ourselves of the weakness & *fallacy* <absurdity> of them, but to *prevent* <hinder> the deception of others, & stop the Growth & progress of *such* <false and> sophistical principles.

[p. 56] Ye do err says our Divine Lord not knowing the Scriptures,[75] It is neglecting this fountain of real knowledge that leads us into these *deceits* <mistakes>, Did we lay the foundation of our whole System in due & serious study of the truths which these Sacred Oracles contain, we should not *this easyly* be tossed to & fro < in this manner> & carried about with every wind of doctrine by the sleight of men, & cunning craftiness, whereby they lye in wait to deceive but should grow up into him in all things, which is the head, even Christ, making increase of the body unto the [p. 57] edifying of ourselves in love.[76]

2nd: As the want of Religious knowledge introduces *& propagates* errors & mistakes in opinion, so is it one of the chief causes of that Corruption & degeneracy of manners, which obtains thro' the World.

For *as* <since> Religion teaches us our Duty, what we owe to God, the submission & obedience that we are to pay to him, the particulars in & by which we can manifest it, what offices are due from one Man to another in the different Relations *he* stands in to *t*hem, & what we owe to ourselves as Guardians & [p. 58] Stewards of sundry gifts, graces and abilities, *as* <since> it informs us of the true grounds of these & such like Duties,[77] & if properly dwelt upon, carries us to the performance of them by the most actuating & enlivening motives, we cannot without the Study of Religion know how to act, or which way to determine our choice amidst *that most ...ited of* jarring & opposite interests & desires, Our Passions left to themselves without proper management grow wild & extravagant, Tumultuous & overbearing appetites take place of better regulated principles & produce those infinite mischiefs which we daily see in the World.

[p. 59] For can it be deemed probable, that if Men were *early* instructed in the principles of Christianity & *applied* <made> them*selves to* the *study of it with any care or attention* <object of their care and study> *that* they could willingly run into all the excesses which they now so ... *give in*, that the early sense they had imbibed would produce it's effect, & tho' appetites & Passions *should* <might> for some time *gain an ascendancy* <bear rule>, that the first Impression would not again revive & prevent their continuing long in such a State of perverseness & depravity.

And this is strongly confirmed [p. 60] by experience, Those upon whose Religious education some pains have been taken, who *by the piety of their parents and the wisdom of their mothers* have been duly instructed in Religion, if they do go out of the path they were trained in, *do* generally return into it again, the principles they have at bottom recover their lost power, & produce a happy tho' a later effect, & hence appears the truth of Solomon's observation that when wisdom (& by wisdom he always means Religion) when wisdom entreth into the heart, & knowledge is pleasant unto the [p. 61] Soul, Discretion shall preserve a Man, & understanding shall keep him, to deliver him from the way of the evil Man from the Man that speaketh toward things,[78] & David's method not to sin against the Lord was to hide his word within his heart.[79]

3rd: Another disadvantage visibly *arising* <accruing> from the lack of Religious knowledge is, that hereby we are deprived of the benefits that attend the performance of the different acts of Religion.

Because without some sort [p. 63] of previous knowledge & some little acquaintance with the principles of Christianity, it is to little purpose to attend the House of God, to partake of his Sacraments or to read his word.

If we do attend the House of God, & joyn in the Publick Service of the Church unacquainted with the Qualifications requisite to make such a worship acceptable to him, nor made sensible of the awfulness, purity & Holiness of the Being adore, *our whole devotion is faint, cold & languid, whatever we there hear is in some sense lost for the* <we content ourselves with a formal lifeless attendance, we neither enter into the spirit, nor know the nature of the Duty & Service we come to offer, & whatever we may there hear, we lose the fruits & advantage of, for the>[80] Instructions we receive are always upon a supposition, that we understand Religion to a certain degree, & the chief end of Publick Discourses is [p. 64] more to press & recommend what we do know, than to teach us what we do not.

If we come to the Sacrament of the Lord's Supper, the same evil consequence accompanies us even there, we *lose the benefit* <forego the advantage> of an institution, no further useful than as it inspires us with *the highest and most peircing sense of God's mercy & compassion and of our own demerits & indignity & no other wise capable of doing this than as its free Nature and that design are apprehended and understood by us* us with <a high sense of God's mercy and of our own demerits, and no further capable of doing this than as the Scheme of Man's Redemption & the Terms of our reconciliation with God by the death & suffering of Jesus Christ are apprehended & understood by us.>

And if we read the Scriptures & seek for knowledge in them, we [p. 66] <find our labour fruitless & ineffectual>, the words of them are unto us as the Book mentioned by the Prophet Isaiah, which is delivered to him that is not learned,[81] with this charge, Read this I pray thee, but immediately returned to the Prophet with this Humbling confession, I am not learned.

4th. The Last bad Consequence I shall mention from the lack of Divine knowledge,[82] is the want of proper strength & support to enable us to go thro' the different changes & vicissitudes of life with any [p. 67] comfort or satisfaction.

In the World says O[ur] S[aviour] ye shall have tribulation,[83] but let not your hearts be troubled, ye believe in God, believe also in me,[84] Faith in God & faith in Christ, the pleasing & comfortable hopes of a Glorious Immortality, the joys of Religion & the reviving prospect of a happy eternity here-after, are the great the only true & solid foundation against that infinite variety of evils to which we are daily subject. Without such a perswasion as this *are attended with*, man in his [p. 68] present State is the most miserable of God's Creatures. The noble faculties of Reason & understanding with which he is endued, only serve to make him the more wretched, to foresee every possible misfortune, to recall every past one & to prolong the Duration of it to a distant Period. But when <once> Religion is fixed in the heart, & suffered to <have it's natural & proper influence> it immediately enlarges our notions, raises our nature, fills our mind with unspeakable comfort & hope, & by placing objects in their true & proper light, it Draws joy & satisfaction even from the most gloomy & ill-boding appearances; [p. 70] God is then in the midst of us *continually in our thoughts & the subject of our constant meditation & therefore should we not be revived <his providence, direction and minsitration of things below are continually in our thoughts to strengthen & revive us.>* The thoughts of his Providence are continually present to our minds, to strengthen & revive us, to disarm affliction of it's sting, to give a relish to prosperity, to spread calmness & composure all around us & to make even the approach of Death easie & supportable, In Solomon's words,[85] When we go, they shall lead us, when we sleep they shall keep us, & when we awake they shall talk with us, for his commandment is a lamp, & his law is light, & reproofs of instruction are the way of life.[86]

The many & Great Inconveniences thus arising from the want of Religious knowledge, can only be remedied by our early & diligent [p. 75][87] endeavours after the attainment of it, & to make this the easier, certain Directions are to be observed, which I *am now to … & … place to set before you* <come now by way of conclusion to set before now>.

3rd Part.

And as useful as they may be, they are not equally so to all, Some thro' want of leisure or Capacity cannot follow them exactly, Others who have long continued in a State of ignorance & *stupid insesnibility* <stupidity> are too much accustomed to inconsideration *& thoughtlessness*, to be taken out of their usual tract of thoughtlessness [p. 76] & inadvertence.

But they chiefly concern & are principally intended for the Young & those, who are still Novices in Religion, whose tender minds are susceptible of any Impression, who are laying the foundation of their faith, & upon whose first setting out *generally* depends <in great measure> their future *good or evil* conduct & it's tendency to good or evil, And Blessed be God who has raised up a Spirit of Religious Improvement through-out this Nation, & by putting it in the hearts of Men to establish a [p. 77] number of Schools properly calculated to answer this end, gives us a prospect of seeing true Religion gain ground & spread itself to the ruin *of* and subversion of Popish Idolatry and Romish Superstition.

Would we then Study Religion *& apply ourselves to the knowledge of it* <& meet with success in this important work>, the first Direction we are to observe is to *begin* Learn before all things the principles of Religion in general, & especially to become thoroughly acquainted with those arguments upon which consists the Certainty authority & veracity of them.

And this is one mistake [p. 78] often attending our Instruction in Religion that we begin where we *should* <ought to> end, we are first taught the Doctrines of Religion before our hearts are prepared for the due reception of them by convincing us of the excellency and perfection of *their origins* < him that delivers them.>

This is the Reason that men judge so hastily of them, that they renounce some as absurd, treat others as inconsistent, & expose the whole System to ridicule & contempt, whilst there is in reality such a Gradual progress in Religion, that to an impartial mind it carries conviction with it & manifests the wisdom & propriety [p. 79] of the whole, & the argum[en]ts *on* <upon> which it is founded are so plain *simple* & easie to be understood, that they must be felt by every <sincere & diligent enquirer>, So gracious was God in adapting *it* <them> to the meanest capacity, & thus putting the greatest & most valuable concern of all in every one's power.

2nd: We are not to confine ourselves to the meer truths & Doctrines of Religion only, but to take in the Precepts & Moral deduction from them, which are chiefly intended for the Rule & Guidance of our [p. 80] lives.

For this purpose were all the Doctrines designed, & to this do they constantly refer, for this did the Son of God appear in the World, for this did God make *such* <those> clear & repeated Revelations of himself *& by our faithful and diligent observance of his laws and precepts*, <and by this> can we only make a proper & suitable return to him for *his* <such Great> & Spiritual blessings.

Without Indeed unless this be the end of our endeavours, the truths of Religion shall not appear to us to have any weight or to carry any evidence with them, our Passions [p. 81] will exclude & shut out the most glaring light, & raise scruples & difficulties in our minds *in* <upon> the simplest matters, & therefore O[ur] S[aviour] lays it down as a mixed maxim, that if any Man will do God's will, he shall know of the doctrine whether it be of God, or whether he spoke of himself,[88] Study Religion with a hearty resolution of living conformably to it, Make the precepts & commands of it the standing rule of your Conduct, Consider all the Doctrines with respect to the practical improvement you can draw from them, & this is the true, the only method of attaining to that perfect, [p. 82] that saving & edyfiying knowledge, without which all other is empty & defective.

3rd: When we study Religion, Let us be careful to distinguish what is essential to it, from what is not so that we may proportion & direct our activity accordingly.

In Religion as in every other Science there are certain truths of greater importance that others, certain things taught & recommended by it, which are not of themselves absolutely necessary & intrinsically good, but are fit & becoming instrum[en]ts to attain the end it has in view; & these are often the very parts in [p. 84] Religion we are the fondest of, & the *most* <only> solicitous about, because we conceive them consistent with the gratyfying of our Passions or the Indulging or our appetites, *but of this & the Danger of mistaking the form for the Power of Religion I have lately had occasion to speak more at large, & shall therefore omit the further consideration of it at present to*[89] <I shall> add but one Direction more, & that is in our study of Religion & perusal of the Holy Scriptures to strengthen our faith against the pernicious Doctrine of Popery, & the ensnaring & deluding arguments of Infidelity & Deism.

[p. 85] We live in an Age where both these mistakes are to be dreaded, Popery on the one hand & Incredulity on the other hang over us, & threaten Religion, the former indeed thro' the present circumstances of things seems to be losing ground, & probably will continue to decrease, not-withstanding the prodigious & indefatigable zeal of it's Votaries, but the latter it is every Good Man's duty strenuously to oppose. Like a violent & impetuous Stream it daily makes it's way, & battles the opposition that is made to it by Religious & well-disposed Men, Youth at it's first setting out [p. 86] *is in clearest danger from it & Parents & Masters should endeavour as far as their abilites allow, to fortify and secure them against it* <in great danger of falling a sacrifice to it, unless care & caution be used to arm them against such delusions>; the way to do this effectually is by shewing to them the use and expediency of the Sacred Scriptures, by filling their mind with a sacred regard & reverential awe for them, by putting into their hands some of those excellent Treatises, to which the present Controversies have given life, & as much as is consistent with their circumstances, to improve & impress upon them what they read in a friendly & familiar Conversation.

[p. 87] Applic[ation]:

And Let no one think these Rules as strict to be observed, or these Directions too severe to be followed, When we *reflect* <consider> all that G[od] Almighty had done to bring us to the knowledge of his will, when we reflect, that the Religion we are to study, was revealed unto us <from

Heaven> by the Son of God himself, attested by his own blood, confirmed in an extraordinary manner, accompanied with signs & wonders, when we observe that nothing more is req[uire]d from us in it than the pursuance of our own happiness by the best & likeliest means to effect <it>, Can it be [p. 88] thought too much on our part, to add our heartiest endeavours to God's undeserved mercies, *can any thing be deemed baser than by our own neglect & indolence to frustrate the gracious mercies of God & defeat his merciful. purposes & might we not justly fear that as we do not chuse to retain God in our thoughts or to serve him as he directs he should deliver us up to our own reprobate hearts & persuade us to fall a sacrifice to idolatry, Superstition & Infidelity* <& to proportions our activity & diligence to the measure & importance of them?>

The Study of Religion is more extraordinary [incu]mbent who <Especially if we add this very weighty consideration, we are> happily obscured from that darkness into which other <Nations> are involved, *have* <that we> enjoy the [p. 89] valuable benefit of reading the word of God *&*, <of> keeping it in our Houses, *who* <that we> are members of a Church, where his worship is performed in a Language that we all understand, where the means of knowledge are in our power, & not cloistered up in selfish & interested hands, where the fountain of truth is always open for us to partake of the happy Streams of it continually flowing for our advantage.

Let us then improve this blessed opportunity, which Many earnestly covet after, but cannot obtain. Let us study religion with eagerness & solicitude, <in sure & steadfast assurance that> the Comforts we shall reap from it, <with> the inw[ar]d *satisfaction.* [p. 90] Complacency of mind, inseparable from such an enquiry, shall make abundant amends for whatever pains we may now be at; And God whose will & Revelation we thus make the end of our endeav[ou]rs, he whose word we exercise ourselves day & night, to whose perfect knowledge we are ambitious of attaining, shall here-after delight himself in encreasinig our knowledge, in furnishing us with new objects for improvement & admiration, in displaying & opening to our view the immense treasures of his wisdom & goodness, in giving to us the fruition of himself in his eternal & glorious Kingdom, where without toil or labour, without study or [p. 91] application, we shall be enabled [to] see him as he is, to adore his power & admire his works, & with Angels & Archangels to ascribe to him all honour Dominion & praise for ever & ever.

Appendix

[Note: This represents an alternative version of the application section and was written later than the application of the original text] [p. 71] Applic[ation]:

Such are the great Inconveniencies that attend a want of sufficient knowledge, in Religion, & therefore Such the reasons that should induce us to study it with the *nicest* greatest application & care, They recommend themselves & carry conviction to every serious & considerate mind, but in a more particular manner ought they to have the stronger influence upon us, who thro' the tender mercy of our God,[90] are happily rescued out of that ignorance & darkness into which other Nations are involved who enjoy the valuable benefit of reading the word of God & of keeping it in our houses, who are Members of a Church where his worship is performed in a language that we all understand, [p. 72] where the means of knowledge are always in our power & not cloistered up in selfish & presumptuous hands, where the fountain of truth is ever open, & the happy streams of it are continually flowing for our good & advantage, a priviledge this, which the gay part of the World may make a jest of, & the luxury & degeneracy of the present times may contemn & despise but which is so closely & intimately connected with every Civil blessing we possess that the loss of the one must totally destroy the other, & the removing of God's candle-stick from <among us>,[91] prove in truth the removing of every thing, that is justly held valuable & sacred.

Let us then dread to neglect & disregard it, Let us consecrate to our improvement under it a proper portion of our time, Let us with [p. 73] humble reverence observe the days & seasons more particulary dedicated to religious offices & instruction.

Let us study Religion with earnestness & sollicitude in sure & never failing hope that the Comfort which we shall reap from it with the inward complacency of mind inseparable from such an enquiry, shall make abundant amends for all the pains we may now be at.

And God whose will & Revelation we thus make the end of our endeav[ou]rs in whose words we exercise ourselves day & night, to whose perfect knowledge we are thus ambitious of attaining, shall in a future Oeconomy of light & perspicaity, encrease our knowledge, furnish us with new objects for improvement & admiration, [p. 74] more fully open to our view the immense treasures of his wisdom & goodness, & so lead us to the full & entire fruition of himself in his eternal & Glorious Kingdom where without toil or labour, without study or application we shall be enabled to see him as he is, to adore his power, to admire his works, & with Angels & Archangels to ascribe unto him all honour Dominion & praise for ever & ever.

Sermon V

Volume 2(13)

Belfast June ye 4th 1749
Ditto September ye 9th 1750
Ditto January ye 7th 1753
Ditto December ye 12th 1756
Ditto September ye 6th 1761
Ditto May ye 29th 1763
Ditto March ye 3rd 1765
Ditto October ye 18th 1767
Ditto July ye 16th 1769
Ditto May ye 17th 1772
Rosenallis November 17 1810[92]
Anaclone January 6 1822[93]
Annamore 13 April 1822[94]
Leagal July 1827
Ditto June 1828 E[vening] L[ecture]
Ditto June 1831
Hacknahay 17 August 1845 S:C[95]

[p. 93] In the Fourteenth Chapter of the Proverbs of Solomon at the Twenty ninth Verse.

He that is slow to wrath is of great understanding, but he that is hasty of Spirit exalteth folly.

The wisdom of Solomon here cautions us against the sin of anger, a sin which it's frequent & daily committal, may represent as trivial & insignificant, but which the wise King considered as the height of folly, & the true mark of a weak & narrow understanding, He that is slow to wrath is of great understanding, but he that is hasty of Spirit exalteth folly.

[p. 94] In discoursing upon these words, I shall consider 1st. The Nature of Anger, & endeavour to shew in what cases, & under what circumstances it becomes sinful & prohibited, 2nd. *I shall set forth* The extreme & fatal mischiefs *that* <which> attend this unruly Passion *& which may serve as proper disuasives from it*, & Lastly *I shall offer some Direction by way of prevention against it* <The best means to free us from ye power & Tyranny of it.>

1st Part.

Anger like all other Passions was intended to answer several wise ends. To view it indeed in it's present state, & *consider the effects which it generally produces* <consequences>, one might suspect that such a principle never came from God <but rather> took it's rise in the corruption and depravity of our Nature, But to trace it [p. 95] up to it's origin, & reduce it to it's pristine use to see it placed as a Guard to secure us *against* <from> danger, awakening our caution at the prospect of an injury offered, or intended to be offered to us, alarming our fears at the invasion of our property, the blasting of our fame, the lessening of our influence, exciting our just indignation, when the cause of Virtue & Religion is openly betrayed, the name of God profaned, & the most Sacred Characters treated with scorn & derision *it cannot be deemed but* <to see if I say under such circumstances we must allow> that a tendency to warmth & resentment is *then truly* <often> laudable & becoming, that a languid indifference in *such* <some> cases is both absurd & improper & *a facet … from far below the Dignity of our nature* <what neither Reason nor Religion requires from us>; Accordingly <we> have the example of the best & wisest Men to justifie anger upon *certain* <these & the like> occasions, Moses of whom it is recorded, that he was the meekest Man upon Earth up to it's origin, waxed [p. 96] hot when he saw the molten Calf, & the defection of God's People,[96] and a far greater than Moses Jesus Christ himself is particularly said to have looked with anger upon the Pharisees, because of the hardness of their hearts,[97] whence St Paul *exhorts* <directs> us to be angry & sin not,[98] intimating that Anger was some-times not only void of blame, but even our Duty, & absolutely necessary to our own preservation & well being.

But then we too often pervert the use of this principle, and transfer it from proper to improper objects, It is needless to define anger, we all feel it more sensibly & clearly than words can describe it. What concerns us more is to determine, in what cases it become sinful & prohibited, and this it does when it is causless, when it [p. 97] excessive, & when it is permanent and of long continuance.

Anger I say is sinful *& prohibited*, when it is causeless without sufficient grounds to warrant resentment & virulence; And this is frequently & for the most part the case with the angry & furious Person, His passions are so accustomed to bear rule, & to launch out into the most violent & outrageous starts of fury & madness, that they make no distinction between one provocation & another. Every little disappointment, every trifling accident *to a considerate Man the subject of contempt & laughter*, unhinge the Passionate Man's reason, open the flood-gates of violence & fury, & cause the same commotions within him, that the most plausible reason for the keenest resentment could [p. 98] possibly justifie.

And was this the end & design, for which so laudable a passion was at first given unto us? Was it to excite and raise a Storm within us upon every trivial occasion? *Was it* To kindle a fire ever ready to break out with new fury? *Was it* To make every insignificant accident an Engine to force out wrath & violence?

But tho' there may be sufficient grounds of anger & resentment, yet is it *sinful &* prohibited if in the 2nd place it be exclusive, & immoderate in it's degree.

There is a species of anger which nothing can excuse, whose guilt no provocation can palliate, whose stain no injury can wash off, & of this sort is that furious madness *that* <which> manifests itself in opprobrious [p. 99] injurious, reproachful language, *that* <which> carries us such great lengths as to make us forget all sense of decency & good manners, all regard for truth & sincerity, & what is worse, *that* <which> directly strikes at the very foundations of Religion, breaking out in oaths & imprecations, in profane swearing & inconsiderate cursing, *that* <which> are now become the *almost* inseparable attendants of anger, & the sole indications of the greatness & reality of it.

This kind of anger it is, which our Blessed Saviour so sharply reproves in his Divine Sermon on the Mount, Whosoever is angry with his Brother without cause, shall be in danger of the judgment, & whoso-ever shall say to his Brother Raca, shall be in danger of [p. 100] the Council, but whoso-ever shall say thou fool shall be in danger of hell fire,[99] And sure he must be in extreme danger, who not content with risking & branding his neighbour, makes the tremendous name of God instrumental to his passion, and adds to the guilt of anger the weighty & crushing load of blasphemy and profaneness.

Lastly. That anger is sinful, which is of long continuance, permanent and lasting.

It must be confessed that the first impressions *that* <which> an injury or the prospect of an injury make upon the mind, are often mechanical &

involuntary, they rise & start of themselves before we [p. 102] have time and power to prevent & stifle them, & the best meaning & best natured Persons are some-times betrayed into this without design or without any evil intention.

But then the difference lyes here, that such a Man's passion is of short duration, that no sooner has he time to come to himself but he sees his folly and exerts his utmost power to repress the impetuous sallies of his <temper>, that he checks the growth and progress of them <that he endeavours to> reduce them within due & proper bounds, *& never suffers them to gain so far upon him as to turn into a fixed & settled habit of rancour& resentment which must be the inevitable & unavoidable consequence of wrath when encouraged, cherished and dwelt upon for which reason it is* that he never suffers them to take such deep root, as to turn into as fixed & settled principle of rancour & resentment, as to engage him to wish desire or contrive the misery & unhappiness of those who have occasioned his anger, as to rejoice when his Enemy falleth, or be glad when he stumbleth,[100] as to harbour any malicious implacable revengeful thoughts, all which are the unavoidable consequences of wrath if encouraged, cherished & dwelt upon, for which reason it is &[101] that St. Paul in his precept upon the lawfulness of anger in certain cases, makes the short continuance of it [p. 103] an inseparable circumstance Be ye angry & sin not, & to do *it* <so> effectually let not the Sun go down upon your wrath,[102] close not the day with an angry & wrathful disposition, but before the time draws near for rest & composure, let every unruly passion be calmed, & both body & mind prepared to enjoy the destined peace & quiet.

These few *short* & imperfect reflections may <suffice to> give us a notion of anger & of the circumstances *that* <which> render it sinful, I now come in the 2nd. Place to consider the great & fatal mischiefs which rise from this passion of anger, which I offer as proper disswasives from it, & <of> which Solomon gives us his opinion in the words <of the Text>, he that is slow to wrath is of great understanding, but he that is hasty of Spirit, exalteth [p. 105] folly.

2nd Part.

And the 1st evil consequence of a Passionate & violent temper that I shall mention which demonstrates it's folly is the uneasiness & anxiety it *causes to the unhappy possessor* <occasions> whenever it is encouraged.[103]

The Storms of anger are of all other passions the most boisterous & tumultuous, they tear & distract the mind, they deprive it of all pleasing

& agreeable sensation, they raise the most wracking & tormenting ideas. Every black & uneasie passion reside in the angry Man's breast, & conspire together to encrease & effect his misery. Pride, jealousie, envy, suspicions, by turn move & torment him, an unnatural fermentation disorders his whole frame, his blood & spirits continually boil within him, his distorted looks, his furious [p. 106] eyes, his babbling without cause, his faultring speech, his rancorous bitter & envenomed tongue, full bespeak the inward agitation of his mind, Reason & reflection have no power & empire over him, Passion & resentment take their place & work their own dire & cruel effects; Unacquainted with the suggestions of that wisdom which is pure peaceable & gentle, Left a prey to the inward gnawings of his impetuous & uneasie mind, Abandoned to the frantick & extravagant motions of his own unruly breast, He is tossed & driven to & fro, whither so ever these lead him, like the troubled sea when it cannot rest, whose waters *throw* <cast> up mire & dirt.[104] And Can any situation be conceived more restless and uneasie than this? Can there be any prospect of happiness, where so many concurring accidents meet to interrupt [p. 107] and disturb it, where the foundation of misery is so deeply laid & so many tormenters at hand to waste & consume our strength & spirits in anxious & unease pursuits.

But as fatal as these effects are, it were happy for the World if the evil consequences of anger were confined to the angry Man alone, the misfortune is, the same principle *that* <which> renders the passionate & cholerick person unhappy, effects the misery and unhappiness of all those with whom he has to deal.

It banishes that easy mild & peaceable carriage which is the very bond & cement of all private & domestic union, It introduces in a family strife, contention variance & jarring discord, It occasions a variety of intestine broils to the utter ruin & destruction of these little Common-wealths. The Husband the Father the Friend those [p. 108] tender & endearing Relations are sunk *to wreck* & lost in the fiery & violent Man. He pays no regard to those to whom by the ties of blood he owes, & for whom by the affections of his Nature he truly professes the highest value & regard, He indiscriminately and without distinction treats every one alike, His wrath distinguishes no objects nor makes any difference, Those whom he loves and cherishes most, frequently feel the greatest weight of his resentment, & often the meekest & mildest tempers become the greatest sufferers.

Hence a diffidence & distance which are destructive of all comfort & quiet, Hence an awe & dread upon the mind which are incompatible with an openness & frankness of behaviour, that season the pleasures of friendship & conversation, Hence those violent altercations, where [p. 109] warm and fiery tempers meet together each striving for the Mastery, obstinately persisting in their opinion, more bent upon conquest than upon procuring & promoting the peace of those with whom they converse, a Scene of horror too often to be met with, occasioned by a warmth & vehemence of temper, the gusts of which blind & obscure our judgment, cast a mist upon our understanding, & weakening the powers of our reason & conscience leave us under the Dominion of unbridled *& unruly* passions & appetites, which leads me to a third dreadful consequence of anger, the great & pressing dangers & temptations to which it lays us open.

Solomon has illustrated this by a strong & very proper figure, He that hath no rule over his own Spirit, is like a [p. 110] lily that is broken down & without walls,[105] As a City whose walls & forts are ruined & destroyed, is exposed to every attack of an enemy, lyes open & defenceless, can resist no insult, is liable to every danger, So the angry & wrathful Man who is without the guard of reason *& temper*, in whom passion & violence have quite excluded the aid of higher & more noble principles, is unarmed & unprovided against danger & temptation, gives these superior advantages over him, & runs himself into evils, which he never intended, nor never fore-saw.

And how truly does experience confirm this observation? Into what a multitude of different sins does this single passion lead us? What abuse of the glorious priviledge of speech [p. 111] does it occasion, opening those lips to dishonour God & Man which were intended to *bespeak* <proclaim> his praise & advance the happiness of our fellow Creatures? What tragical scenes of blood shed & murder, *that* arise from the impetuous sallies of an extravagant & outrageous temper? What feuds & animosities have their source in the suggestions of anger, heated by passion & <often> enflamed by wine? What friendships have the unguarded expressions of wrath & the unthinking & inconsiderate motions of violence & passion for ever dissolved? In a word what havock & destruction does it make ruining the fortune *endangering the virtue of others endangering the very being of Society* <of some opening a Door to the vices, of others endangering the Virtue of all.>

For when once passion & wrath are let loose, & suffered to range uncurbed, [p. 112] t'is hard to know where *it* <they> will stop, the Beginning of strife, <says Solomon> is as when one letteth out water, as a River *that* <which> overflows it's bank, ravages & destroys whatever comes into it's way, so the Inundations of passion & wrath over-turn all they meet with, & *leave* offer to the view nothing but waste and destruction, therefore are we very wisely cautioned to leave off contention before it be meddled with to abstain entirely from it, lest by handling, it become familiar to us, & carry us further than we ever intended or desired to go.[106]

The last thing I shall endeavour to do to disuade us from Last<ly, We may consider> anger *is to consider it*, with respect to Religion, & <we shall find it> as opposite to this, as it is to our own happiness, to the quiet of our [p. 113] families, to the peace & comfort of the World.

And this it is no hard matter to prove, who-ever is at all acquainted with the nature & genius of the Christian Religion, *that* <who> considers the tendency & design of it's precepts, the Charity, meekness & mildness that breathes thro' the whole, *that* <who> dwells upon the great examples of forbearance, patience & equanimity which are illustrated in the life & actions of O[ur] B[lessed] S[aviour] must acknowledge that nothing can be more contrary *& opposite* to this than an angry, violent wrathful disposition, for as universal love & good-will are the badge & characteristic of Christianity, so malice hatred rancour revenge & resentment, the necessary consequents of violent & lasting wrath, are the very [p. 114] reverse the very contrary of all these, They disable us from discharging those offices of Religion, which require the whole powers & faculties of a quiet calm and sedate mind. These prevent our addressing ourselves to God with any degree of composure & attention, the impetuous gusts of passion disturb & interrupt our service, the objects of our resentment present themselves to us, & stop at once the exercise of our Devotion and piety, These exclude the performance of those huridly compassionate charitable duties which Religion enjoins to be discharged with[ou]t any distinction & extends even to those, who have <first> offended *& greviously trespassed against us* <us>, These banish for ever from the midst of us, the assistance of God's Holy Spirit, whose fruits are love, [p. 115] meekness, gentleness *These engage God to withdraw his Divine grace from us & to leave us to the misery and restless cure of our own malice & rancour, whence are we expected the next … and the … terms* <upon all which dreadful acts it is that we are so often & so strongly exhorted>, to put away from us all bitterness & wrath, & anger & clamor & evil speaking with all malice, to be kind one to another, tender-hearted, forgiving one another, even as God for Christ's sake hath forgiven us.[107]

Since then an angry & wrathful disproportion is of so dangerous a tendency *so prejudicial to our present & to our future happiness*, Let us in the third place consider the best & likeliest means to free us from the power & tyranny of it.

[p. 116] 3^{d}. Part

If we would avoid anger, Let us beware of Pride & an over-grown opinion of ourselves, our qualifications & abilities.

This general & universal defect it is that takes us off from the consideration of our faults & imperfections, that represents us to ourselves as entitled to the particular regard & esteem of men *that challenges their highest veneration & respect* & thence carries at every disappointment either real or imaginary, a warmth & impatience in us, which breaks out in this violent & outrageous manner, Self-love heating the fire & vain presumption exciting the flame.

To counter-act the workings & devices of this Passion, we should oppose to it [p. 117] our frequent faults slips & miscarriages, the many great impropriety in our own behaviour, the just cause we give for the wrath & anger of others. Where we are offended, we should <before we give a loose to our passion> take time to reflect both upon the nature & occasion of the offence, satisfy ourselves whether we are of the first transgressors, & the original framer of the *injury* <offence> we complain of whether the injury be not undesigned & involuntary, the consequence of our own pride, no real being of itself, or whether there may not be some accidental circumstances to soften & lessen the guilt of the injury we have received.

Reflections like these calmly and deliberately made, will help to lay the heat of passion <at least> to *moderate to our violence impetuosity & quiet* <moderate>the squalls of [p. 118] wrath, before they have time to manifest themselves in open acts, of violence & rage.

2d. *If* To avoid anger, beware of those evils which are the strongest incentives to anger, Intemperance, Drunkenness, & the Company of warm & passionate Men.

The two former enflame our blood, the latter supplies it with immediate fuel, Intemperance encreases our natural warmth, slackens the guard of Reason, & consequently raises the force of Passion. The Company of violent & fiery Men, administers matter for this to work upon, & soon furnishes the wrath of others *appear* with proper <subjects on which to feed.> The already distempered mind is made worse by the poison it has imbibed, & the contradiction & perverseness, the obstinacy & stubbornness it meets with from it's [p. 119] fatuated Companions burn up the coals, set the whole on fire make no friendship says Solomon with an angry man & with a furious man thou shalt not go lest thou learn his way & get a snare to thy soul,[108] and if the company of an angry man may teach a weak one anger & wrath, how productive of this Passion must it be when we have a tendency to it in ourselves & the principles of wrath are kept alive & encouraged by it

3d Would you avoid anger, avoid those subjects, thoughts or employments which generally excite your anger.

Sometimes the sight of a person from whom an injury has been received kindles the flame, Shun the sight of this [p. 120] Person till time & reflection have done their work, & enabled you to think of him with less rancour & resentment.

Some-times the sly insinuations, the crafty reports, the malicious slander of an infamous whisperer put in motion the choler of the violent, turn your ears from such unworthy friends, listen not to their suggestions, & never encourage in entercourse, which must end in your own misery, Where no wood is, there the fire goeth out, so where there is no tale-bearer, strife ceaseth.[109]

Some-times the excess of party & the heat of a particular faction, carry us away from ourselves, fly from such engagements as pernicious & dangerous, allow them not to gain upon you, [p. 121] much less to present themselves to you under the mask of Religion, & to set off as agreeable to God & consonant to Reasons practices which lend to the disgrace of mankind & the dishonour of Human nature.

4th Would you avoid anger, reflect often upon the beauty happiness & comfort of a meek & mild temper, whom no discord ruffles, no violence distresses, no intention distracts, where every thing hides smooth & easy flowing in an even, quiet channel, whose motions are influenced by benevolence & directed by charity, which attracts the love, the esteem, the applause of Men, which brings it's own reward with it, & makes the ease & pleasure it now enjoys a [p. 122] fore-taste & pledge of that which is reserved for it here after. Blessed are the meek, for they shall inherit the Earth.[110]

Lastly. If we would have our labours successful & our endeavours to get the better of our natural warmth & passion, Let us have earnest frequent & hearty recourse to God, *the God of peace of love of concord* <the Great fountain of love & peace>, that he would be mercifully please to assist our wear endeavours with his Divine peace, to *forward* <bless> the *measures* <means> we *take* <use> to lessen the violence of passion *with choicest helpings*, to *put down* <temper> the natural savageness & wildness of our constitution, to shed the benign influence of his Holy Spirit into our hearts, and thus [p. 123] fit us to inherit his blessed Kingdom of Love, Joy & peace to which may we all attain this the Merits of J[esus] C[hrist] O[ur] L[ord].[111]

Sermon VI

Volume 2 (15)

[p. 157]

Belfast July ye 16th 1749
St. Luke's February ye 28th 1749/50
St. Warburg's December ye 16th 1750
St. Ann's March ye 10th 1750/51
Belfast April ye 21st 1751
New Church[112] June ye 23rd 1751
Belfast July the 14th 1754
Ditto May the 8th 1757
Ditto March ye 4th 1759
Ditto January ye 11th 1761
Dublin Castle Jan: ye 31st 1762
Belfast Feb: ye 26th 1764
Abbey Church Bath Aug. 24th 1766
St. Peter's Dublin Oct: ye 26th 1766
St. Andrew's ditto Nov. ye 2nd 1766

[p. 158] In the Seventeenth Chapter of the Acts of the Holy Apostles at the Twenty third Verse.

For as I passed by & beheld your Devotions, I found an Altar with this Inscription, to the unknown God, Whom therefore ye ignorantly worship, him declare I unto you.

These words are the beginning of St. Paul's famous Discourse at Athens before one of the most polite & learned Assemblies then in the World, The Doctrines he preached, had by their novelty excited the Curiosity of the*se People* <Athenians>, naturally fond of every thing <new> & uncommon, They were desirous to hear him themselves concerning these matters, & introduced him into their Council, that [p. 159] he might answer the charge brought against him of his being a Setter forth of Strange Gods, because he preached unto them Jesus and the Resurection.[113]

But neither the solemnity of the Place, the fame of those before whom he spoke, the importance of the accusation, nor the dangerous consequences of it, could awe him into silence or prevail on him to betray the cause that was committed to him, He resolutely and undauntedly attacked the Pagan Superstitions, stood up single to batle the arguments & reasonings of the greatest Heathen Philosophers, & began his Discourse with that confidence & noble freedom which the justice of a cause generally inspires, & the consciousness of acting up to one's duty *seldom* <seldom> fails of producing, Ye men of Athens I perceive [p. 160] that in all things ye are too superstitious, For as I passed by & beheld your Devotions, I found an Altar with this inscription To the unknown God, Whom therefore ye ignorantly worship, him declare I unto you.[114]

I shall not *up* take up *your* time in enquiring particularly into the <intent> & design of the Altar, which St Paul tells us was erected to the unknown God, *Many & various have been the conjectures of Men upon this subject but among the rest the following observations seem most plausible* <Amidst that variety of conjectures to which it has just rite, the following seems to be the best proposed that> As the Athenians were most remarkably superstitious, they had erected Altars to a multitude of Deities, & lest any one of them should *escape their notice & knowledge& by losing the honour due to them might subject them to severe judgem[en]ts* <thro' their ignorance be deprived of the proper homage that was due to him & so be induced to revenge the affront by inciting them with some sore & signal punishment> they had set up an Altar [p. 161] in honour of this or <of> any such unknown God to Express*ing* hereby the honour & veneration they would have been ready to offer to him had his nature & Essence been disclosed to them, So flagrant a piece of Superstition could well warrant the Apostle's taxing them with gross folly & Idolatry, & justifie the subject matter of his Discourse, which was to shew them the absurdity of the objects of their worship, & *to* engage them to transfer it from these to the one only god, the Creator & Maker of the Universe.

From this whole account we may deduce the three following observations, which I intend for the subject of the following Discourse, 1st. That every age & nation has felt the necessity there was of owning & acknowledging a Supreme Being, [p. 162] There is an altar set up to God, 2nd. That notwithstanding this universal sense of a Deity unassisted Reason thro' the abuse that had been made of it, was *insufficient* <unable> to discover clearly & fully to us both his Value & essence, This altar was erected to an unknown God, & 3rd. That Revelation, <& especially the preaching of the Gospel> has supplied what was wanting & represented God *to us* as he is in himself <& as he is with relation to us> for whom the World ignorantly worshippeth, him does it declare unto us.[115]

1st Part.

1st. Every age & nation has felt the necessity there was of owning & acknowledging a Supreme Being, There is an Altar set up to God.

However savage & unpolished these were, how little conversant so ever with other [p. 163] Men & the histories of the World, however remote from the means of improvement & knowledge they universally agree in the *sense they have of a deity* <acknowledgement of a God, however they may differ in the opinions concerning his attributes & the manner of his worship> or if there be some that have not yet thought upon this Subject which is very far from being proved, propose this truth to them, there must be some Supreme Being, & there will hardly be found any stupid & senseless enough not to perceive the force of the arguments upon which the truth of this proposition is founded.

As something now exists, it follows that there must be some original Creator and framer of things, that existed before what we now see & was the Cause of their existence, since it is impossible for what now is, to have given itself as Being, or to act before it was itself produced.

[p. 164] *I am* <We are> conscious of *my*<our> own existence, *I*<We >find *myself* <ourselves> endued with a power of judging, understanding & chusing for *myself* <ourselves> *& am*, <We are> satisfied *I* <We> have not been the cause of *my* <our> own existence, nor adorned *my* <our> Being with the powers with which it is furnished. This leads *me* <us> to *refer my* <ascribe our> existence to some other cause & to refer this from one to another, till *I am* <we are> forced to have recourse to some Supreme Cause existing of itself, & indebted to none but to the necessity of *his* <it's> nature for *his* <it's> present being, which as it was never made, so is it never to be destroyed.

The same truth is more clearly & sensibly deduced from the works of the Creation. We see every thing fitted & adapted in the wisest & most intelligent manner, all formed with some view, & all answering the end for which they were formed. *No man can deny but* <every one must own that> [p. 165] the Sun was intended to give us light & heat, the Clouds to supply us with genial showers to refresh the Earth & render it fruitful, The Winds to cleanse & fan the Air in which all Animals live, & prevent it's growing noxious hurtful & poysonous; *No man can deny but* <Every eye must see that> each plant & herb is fitted with delicate fibres & tubes to receive proper juices, & transmit them to the different parts necessary to encrease & preserve their being, *No man can deny* <& all acknowledge that the various> parts of the Human body are contrived with the greatest art, and disposed with such exactness, such delicacy, such symmetry and with all such consistency, as *to* attract the wonder and amazement of all unprejudiced persons, & powerfully publish the infinite wisdom of him that made them.

And Can these & such like things arise from blind Chance? Chance is a form without any sense or meaning, an [p. 166] expression only intended to conceal our ignorance, & which by being often used has at length imposed upon Men & been substituted for a cause.

Can they be produced by the meer laws of motion? But not to mention that many things appear in the World to be framed contrary to the known laws of motion, Can the subtilest motion we know of, produce any one thought or sign of intelligence, Modify matter, encrease it's motion, enlarge it at pleasure, and it will still remain what it was before, the same unintelligent undiscerning undesigning motion.

Can things have existed in this manner from all eternity & rolled on in the way we see them with[ou]t any change or interruption, But are there any remains of the antiquity of these endless & never ceasing ages, Are [p. 167] we not able to account for the rise & origin of Arts & Sciences, see the gradual discoveries of men, count their successive improvements, date their birth, almost fix their period? and is it to be imagined that Millions of ages have passed in which Men were quite idle & unactive, in which they made not time in a State of insensibility, till within four <or five> thousand Years an inconsiderable time in an eternity of ages, they suddenly shot out into new & extraordinary marks of discernment & knowledge.

Whence it is, that we find these arguments so strongly working upon the minds of Men, as to induce them to agree in owning, that these things had a beginning, *at first* and that there is some supreme Cause, which gave them being at first, & upon whom they [p. 168] depend evermore for support & preservation & that in consequence of such and opinion <we see>, Altars *have been ever* erected, Places of worship built, a form of Religion instituted in every part of the World, Nature forcing their assent to this truth, & the Creation strongly bespeaking a Creator, for as the Religious Psalmist expresses it, The Heavens declare the Glory of God, & the Firmament sheweth his handy works, Day unto day uttereth speech, & night unto night sheweth knowledge, There is no Speech nor language where their voice is not heard, Their line is gone out through all the Earth, & their words to the ends of the World.[116]

I am aware that this argument of the universal consent of Men in the acknowledgement of the being of a God *will be* <is generally> [p. 169] answered by alledging <on the other hand> the number of Persons there are *even in our time*, who proclaim aloud that they do not feel the force of such reasonings, nor own the existence of a Supreme cause. But the weakness of this objection may appear by observing, That a few such like examples of monstrous & astonishing insensibly are not sufficient to destroy or counterpoise the weight of the above proofs, & the joint & concurrent assent which they draw from the generality of wise *& undertsanding* <thinking> People. Nay it may further be said, that there is perhaps no one instance, nor ever has been of a Man who during the whole course of his life has never once felt within him a sense of the Divine Being, & who can say with a safe conscience that he never believed, nor never was able to convince himself that there was a God. There have been [p. 170] *many* <some> loud talkers & bablers against a God, *many* <some> that have boldly given themselves out for atheists, & professed they utterly disbelieved that there was any such Being, But how many of them have renounced this Doctrine before they died? how many have endeavoured with their expiring breath to attone for their impiety & folly by owning themselves convinced? What dread & terror has remained upon their mind, & how much have their guilty fears betrayed the inward anxiety & anguish of their heart.

But if the Being & existence of a God be thus universally agreed to, it's Nature & essence is not as generally *allowed* known, which brings me to the 2nd proposition I laid down that notwithstanding this universal sense of a Deity, unassisted Reason thro' the abuse Men [p. 171] had made of it, was unable to discover clearly both it's Nature & Essence.

2nd. Part.

I say, *unassisted* Reason perverted and abused, for it is highly probable that in it's first State & in it's original perfection it might have led us to the knowledge of the Divine Essence, the invisible things of him from the Creation of the World, being understood by the things that are made even his eternal power & God head,[117] but Men soon perverted the right use of it, & thro' prejudice partiality & passion sullied it's lustre, & rendered it both weak & deficient.

If it enabled them to discover the Being of a God, it failed them when ever they attempted to explain his Nature & operations, They were lost in a maze of error & mistake, They [p. 172] wandered about in search of the

Lord, if haply they might feel after him & find him,[118] They ascribed the Deity to every object about them, They placed it in the Sun Moon & stars, They deified their Deceased Kings and Heroes, They multiplied the objects of their worship without number & without measure, assigning to each their respective Provinces, making Gods of the hills & Gods of the vallies,[119] They fell down before Animals, plants & stones, They ascribed to the Godhead the most monstrous & shocking attributes, They gave them their own vile & detestable passions & affections, They considered revenge, cruelty, drunkenness, licentiousness as the particular characteristic of the Deities they worshipped and the actions they were chiefly intended to patronize, They changed the Glory of the uncorruptible God into an image [p. 173] made like to corruptible Man & to birds, and underfooted beasts & creeping things.[120]

Like unto the nature of the object they worshipped, was the service they performed in honour of it, for when once such absurd & impious notions were formed of the Deity, it was natural to frame a worship in conformity to these, Hence did Drunkenness licentiousness the most unbounded & unnatural corruption cruelty & barbarity, no less than the *sacrifice* <shedding> of human blood & the offering of their sons & daughters to Moloch,[121] become a chief principal and established part of their Religious service, It would be transgressing all the rules of Decency & discretion to mention particularly the different and monstrous excesses, that were *usual upon such occassions* <practised in their publick worship>, I shall only observe that these <hideous> Rites & Ceremonies naturally opened [p. 174] the way for the *practice* <admission> of all sin & vice, not only lessened the hatred that Men *should* <ought to> have for them but even made the committal of them in many cases meritorious & praise worthy, for whilst they abandoned themselves to all wickedness & impiety they were only imitating the example of & following the pattern set them by the Gods they adored.

And these things were acted not in some remote corner of the World, unenlightened & unimproved, not among savage Nations, or in illiterate Countries, but at Rome, at Ephesus, at Athens where Paul preached, in the different parts of Egypt, the Seats then of learning Philosophy & knowledge, here it was that Idolatry with all it's impious train was carried to it's height, and tho' it may be thought that the wisest among them <were sensible of> the folly of these things & maintained [p. 175] one Supreme Being to whom the other Deities were subordinate & inferior, not whilst these things were continued practiced & countenanced by them, we may conclude that either they had nothing very positive to say against them & only entertained some distant doubt and suspicion, or else that they were conscious, they had not abilities & powers of themselves to withstand the Current of popular prejudices, or to stop the Growth of Superstition thus enforced & established.

What astonishment must it then raise in us, to see men desirous to reduce us to this State again, labouring to persuade us that Reason of itself is able to teach us our duty, striving to represent Revelation as useless & unnecessary? No doubt we imagine that had we lived in these ages, we would have been able to see thro' the corruption [p. 176] of the time <& to guard against such palpable & manifest errors>, we feel our reason & conscience recoil back so strongly at the bare mention of these things, that we fondly flatter ourselves, we should never have run into the like excesses, nor been carried away by the like examples.

My Brethren We <indeed> detest these principles, we truly perceive the absurdity & unreasonableness of them, but whence does it proceed? Is it from the natural strength of our Reason left to itself? By no means, we have no greater inate powers than they, & had we no supernatural assistances we had still continued in the same deplorable way. But the Revelation we have been bred in from our Infancy, has refined our notions, enlarged our conceptions & enabled us to reason upon such matters with a Degree of confidence perspicuity & strength, beyond what all the boasted Philosophy of the Gentile World could [p. 177] ever *do* <attain to>, And this makes room for the last *thing* <consideration> I am to *speak of*<offer namely>, that Revelation <& especially ye preaching of ye Gospel> has supplied what was wanting & represented God *to us* as he is in himself <as he is in with relation to us> or whom the World ignorantly worshippeth, him does it declare unto us.

3rd. Part

And this it *does* <has most effectually done> by removing all false notions of God, & giving us proper & becoming ideas of him & <of> his Divine Attributes.

Instead of that prodigious multiplicity & variety of Deities that confounded the minds of the worshippers, it reduces the whole God-head to one simple undivided Essence, Spiritual & Incorporeal. It teaches us that this pure Immaterial Being pervades every part of this wide Universe, upholds all things by the word of his mouth, directs, [p. 178] governs & rules over all, It represents him to us as endued with infinite power and might, subject to none, uncontrolable in his actions, limited by nothing but the original rectitude of his Nature. It shews us that in him no undue biass, no partial affections, no improper passions take place or prevail, but that infinite perfection <regulates> all his actions, & universal integrity is the basis of his Dominion, It makes us consider his Justice & love of order & harmony, as essential to his Nature, viewing things as they are, treating them as such, proportioning his punishments, & rewards to their deserts, It ascribes unto him the most unblemished purity, the highest hatred for sin, the greatest love for virtue & uprightness. Above all It engages our regard & esteem for this Supreme Divine Excellent Being by setting him before us, [p. 179] not as an Austere & inflexible Master *not* void of bowels & pity but as a kind & merciful Creator compassionating the weakness of his Creatures, desirous of their happiness, ever ready to promote and advance it.

The Idols of the Heathens are silver & Gold, the work of Men's hands, They have mouths but they speak not, they have eyes, but they see not, They have ears but they hear not, they have noses but they smell not.[122] Who among the<m> *Gods* is like unto thee O Lord, who <among them> like unto thee O Lord, glorious in holiness fearful in praises doing wonders,[123] Glory & honour are in thy presence, strength & gladness are in they place,[124] Thine O Lord is the greatness & the [p. 180] power, for all that is in the Heaven & in the Earth are thine, thine is the Kingdom O Lord, & thou art exalted as head above all,[125] Before the Mountains were brought forth, or ever thou hadst formed the Earth & the World, even from everlasting to everlasting thou art God[126] *O Lord our God how excellent is thy name in all the earth.*[127]

These are the notions which Revelation gives us of God, notions highly consonant to our reason, notions which our Conscience greatly applauds, *notions* to which the worship it teaches us to offer to God is best suited & adapted.

For as it has entirely altered our ideas of him, so has it proportionally improved & amended the service & worship we owe him, [p. 181] it has prohibited *& forbid* as criminals and unlawful all those monstrous modes of worship, that savoured of Cruelty & barbarity, It has prohibited as superstitious & unreasonable all such Rites & Ceremones as obscured the force of Religion & substituted the form for the power of it, It has prohibited as useless & unnecessary all Injunctions that *have* not a direct tendency to <promote> purity & holiness, and tho' under the Jewish Oeconomy <for wise & just reasons> some Ceremonies were preserved *for wise reasons which at present appear trifling & insignificant*, yet under the Gospel Covenant no other Sacrifice is required but the Sacrifice of the heart & affections, no other service but the cheerful service of a ready & willing mind, And to obtain & effect this are certain Religious ordinances enjoined, plain, simple, easy & rational, all designed to improve our good dispositions, to encrease our virtue, [p. 182] to strengthen & confirm our piety & adherence to him, God is a Spirit & they that worship him must worship him in Spirit & in truth,[128] with their Intellectual faculties & powers, with the oblation of their understanding & wills.

And indeed how can we worship him as a pure & perfect Being, & at the same time not endeavour to render ourselves acceptable to him by imitating his Divine & transcendent perfections? How can we adore him as a Just & upright God, & not acknowledge the practice of justice & integrity to be pleasing in his sight? How can we serve him as a merciful kind compassionate God, and yet expect that he will vouchsafe to be favourable to us & accept our service whilst we ourselves [p. 183] are destitute of Charity mercy & pity, or in a word send up our petitions to that God who requires obedience of our <whole> lives, & yet hope only a partial & imperfect observance of his laws to have our requests granted & complied with. In consequence of which it is, that whatever the practice of Men may be, they now universally agree in acknowledging the necessity of virtue & piety to engage the favour & protection of God, The horrible corruption & depravity of former times, enforced by the sanctions of religion is happily abolished, & the unhappy Sinner forced to labour to conceal *their* <his> iniquity & wickedness both from *themselves* <himself> & others <that they may> avoid the lashes of *their* <his> own Conscience & the upbraidings of all wise & understanding Men.

[p. 184] Applic[ation]:

Thus do we see ourselves thro' the mercy & goodness of God rescued from all that misery & wretchedness that accompanied Heathenist Superstition & Idolatry. We acknowledge the unity of a God, we are taught to worship, serve & obey him & him only, we look upon Idolatry as a heinous & shocking Crime, & are justly incensed at the most distant appearance of it.

And yet as ready as we may be to own & profess such opinions, Do we stick to them in practice? If we withdraw ourselves from the allegiance due to God, & *transfer it* <remove this> from him to some other object, what matters it whether a Brasen idol or our own Passions be the Altar to which we bring it, God is equally robbed of his glory, *God is* equally dishonoured, equally offended by [p. 185] us. *But are we not all too apt to set up Deities in our own breasts* But is not such a delusion as this very general & common; Are not our respective lusts & appetites in reality the true & only Deities we often serve & honour, Does not one man etc.[129] [p. 186] Does not one Man make his avarice & covetousness the shrine before which he worships, spend upon the gratifying of it his whole thoughts time & faculties, *employ upon attainment of it those deeds which neglect to be conceived in the service of God* & dedicate those affections to it, which are due to him only.

Does not another erect an Altar to his pride & vanity, feed it with continual & daily incense, bow down before it, incessantly labour to satisfy & please it.

Does not this Person set up Revenge and an imaginary sense of honour as the Idol to which he sacrifices, resign himself up to the service of this passion, disregard the ties of affection, smother the sentiments of Nature, stifle the cheeks of Conscience, neglect the reproofs of Religion to reek his [p. 187] resentment in the blood of his Enemy, *whilst, … are with equal sollicitude & the most superstitious concerns parts with all for the attainment their faceless pleasures, conquers all difficulties with … assiduity.* <Whilst the Greedy Pursuer of lawless> and forbidden pleasures, & employs in destroying *their* innocence, staining purity disturbing the peace of families that care diligence which he owes to the service of God, & the worship of his Creator. So true & <undoubted is the Prophet Samuel's observation> that Rebellion is as the sin of witch-craft, & stubbornness is as Iniquity and Idolatry,[130] *even Idolatry of the most fatal delusive kind, Some Idolaters may plead ignorance, prejudice of education, force of custom & habit, but what apology can we make for our practical idolatry, what defence can we offer for this basest of all Apostacy, what knowledge what assistance what means of improvement do we want?* [p. 188] *At the preaching of the Gospel idols were struck dumb, Pagan Temples were shut, heathen Nations flowed in to the acknowledgement of the <one> only God. And shall we bred up in the pure truths of Christianity set up Altars new to Mammon, become only Idolaters, the only Robbers of the Glory and worship of God.* Let us not then rest upon the purity of our profession alone but contend to express the purity of it by the superior sanctity of our lives & manners, Let us bless God for calling us out of darkness unto light, but let us shew our Gratitude by our actions, Let us maintain etc.[131]

Let us all maintain the honour due to him, preserve our affections disengaged, deliver them up to his will & pleasure, that ever mindful of the Rock that begot us, & of the God that formed us,[132] never casting away our confidence from, nor placing it any where but in him, we may join our hearts & voices to the pompous and pathetic exclamations of the Psalmist with which I shall conclude, Whom have I in Heaven but thee, & there is none [p. 189] that I desire in comparison of thee,[133] Confounded all they that serve graven images, that cast themselves of Idols, worship him all the Gods, Zion heard & was glad, & the Daughters of Judah rejoiced, For thou Lord are high above all the Earth, thou art exalted far above all Gods, Rejoice in the Lord ye righteous & give thanks at the rememberance of his holiness.[134]

Sermon VII

Volume 2 (16)

[p. 221]

Belfast July ye 30th 1749
Ditto April ye 28th 1751
Ditto July the 28th 1754
Ditto May the 15th 1757
Ditto April the 1st 1759
Ditto January the 25th 1761
Ditto March the 4th 1764
Ditto November the 29th 1767
Ditto April the 22nd 1770

[p. 222] In the Seventeenth Chapter of the Acts of the Apostles and at the Twenty Sixth Verse

And hath made of one blood all Nations of Men.

I have lately had occasion to speak of the end & design of St. Paul's famous Discourse at Athens, of which these words are a part, I laid before you the purport and *view he had on it* <definit end of it>, which was to convince that Superstitious People of the folly *and absurdity* of their worship, & <to> induce them to transfer it from Idols to that of the one only God, the creator & Maker of the Universe.[135] This *he* <the> Apostle pursues in the following [p. 223] part of it, & after having founded this important truth upon the visible works of the Creation <he> descends into particulars, & proceeds to shew that as God created the World & all things therein, so did he make of one blood all Nations of Men.

I shall not at present consider these words with respect to the<ir primary> occasion & design *of this*, but shall take them as a General truth from whence some particular & useful Reflections may be drawn, which I intend for the subject of the ensuing Discourse.

1st Consid[eration]

And 1st. God's making all Nations of men intimates, that Men in particular as well as the whole structure and [p. 224] fabrick of the Universe had once a beginning & owe their origin to the immediate Agency of God.

I have already endeavoured in proving the existence of a God to shew the absurdity there is in supposing that things have rolled on as we now see them, in an endless succession of ages without any beginning at all, since we can trace up Arts & Sciences to their first origin, discover the gradual improvements made in each, *date* their birth, *almost fix their period* <progress & encrease>, & that it is not to be conceived if Men had continued for million of ages linked together as they now are, but <that> some Monuments *would still remain* <must have remained> of their sagacity & knowledge, some *traces been left* <hints have> been dropt of their customs employments & occupations in those distant & remote times.

[p. 225] And yet this is the Great argument to which Infidels fly for shelter, press upon them the wisdom beauty & intelligence *that* <which> appears in the form & workmanship of Man, conclude from such plain & visible effects the necessity of a cause, & they elude your reasoning by saying, that all the Generations of Men move on in an endless Circle of effects, one Generation succeeding another without beginning & without end, As if effects could subsist without a cause, as if heaping an infinity of them one upon another superseded the necessity of acknowledging a first Mover & *executor of them & as if* <Creator, or as> perplexing the mind with the abstract ideas of eternity & infinity, could remove the difficulty, & by shifting it from this to that divert our attention from the [p. 226] principal point in dispute, so trifling and evasive are the methods to which Incredulity drives Men to avoid the force of reason & the power of conviction!

But now take the Scripture account of this great work, Suppose one infinite original, eternal being, existing independantly of ever thing else, endued with infinite wisdom & intelligence, & you account plainly & easyly for all these occurrences, The first man took his origin from him, they that came after derived their's from this one, & all were successively & gradually created according to the good pleasure of God the Common Father of them all, the Stock from whence they spring, the Author & Giver of their life breath & all things whose offspring they all are & in whom & thro' whom they live move & have their being.[136]

[p. 227] 2nd Consid[eration]

And as God's making all Nations of Men, shews the absurdity of maintaining an eternal succession of effects without *a* <a first original> cause, so does his making them of one blood demonstrate the little foundation there is for ye conceit of those who fancy there was a Race of Men upon Earth, known by the name of Pre-adamites, existing before Adam, <& consequently a> World stocked with Inhabitants, long before the time of the Creation, as recorded to by Moses, for what is here rendered of one blood is in several Versions rendered of one Man, meaning doubtless Adam, tho whether it be considered one blood or of one Man, it matters little, as in both senses it equally stands for Stock or Root.

T'is true indeed the maintainers of this opinion <ye better to gloss over their scheme> found it upon the authority of Moses himself, *in whom they* <and> think to discover <in him> some [p. 229] hints of an older & more ancient World, *since the efficacy of it as we suppose it to have been in which Adam & his family were living cannot be consistent as they imagine with the fear Cain expressed after the murder of his brother, lest any one that found him should chide him if there were no other Men upon earth besides his son, kinsmen & relations with his banishment to another City which if some such were not then built with his marrying a wife in it there were no families strangers to his which his providing it stocked with Inhabitants, if the peopling of the World arose solely from Adam & his heirs & consequently say they Moses his design was to give us a History of the origins of the Jewish People, not of the origins of the world* <They imagine to see it in the fear which Cain expressed after the murder of his brother Lest any one that found him should slay him,[137] for how could there be reason in this if there were no other Men upon Earth besides his own Kinsmen & Relations, They see it equally in his banishment to another City, in his Improvements while he was in it, in him marriage & alliances, & therefore they venture to say that, Moses his design was only to give us a History of the origin of the Jewish Peoples, not a History of the Origin of the World.>

But how does this appear? *Were the Jews a distinct Nation then?* <Was ye Jewish Policy by which alone the Jew became a distinct people as early as the time of Adam?> Was it necessary [p. 230] for Moses *had* <if he had only> them *only* in view, to relate the Creation of the Sun Moon & Stars? <And> is not his account a History of the beginning of the World to which all Passages in Scriptures refer, to which he himself sets a fixed and determinate sense by calling Eve the mother of all living,[138] & expressly declaring, that there was no man to till the ground, till God formed Adam out of the dust of it, & breathed into him of life,[139] upon which St. Paul has put the same construction when he informs us that the first Man Adam was made a living soul,[140] & to which O[ur] B[lessed] S[aviour] plainly alludes in his answer to the Pharisees question, Is it lawful for a Man to put away his wife for every cause, Have ye not read says he that he which made them at ye beginning made them male & female,[141] & to shew them that the meant Adam & Eve, [p. 231] he immediately subjoins the words of the 1st institution of *marriage* <matrimony as mentioned in ye 2nd Chapter of Genesis>, Therefore shall a Man leave his father & his Mother, & shall cleave unto his wife.[142]

The reason why Men run into such opinions is, that they do not consider the conciseness of the account which Moses gives us, nor reflect upon the time that elapsed between the Creation of Adam & Eve & the banishment of Cain, which according to the best computation happened but a hundred & twenty nine years after his birth, during which period considering the nature of the Climate, the strength of constitution & the long life of Men, the number of the Inhabitants of the World might have vastly encreased, since we read in Exodus that the Children of Israel who went up to Egypt in number 70 Persons [p. 232] & dwelt in it during *one* <two> hundred & *ten* <fifteen> years *could act* <were at their departure from thence encreased to> six hundred thousand fighting Men.[143]

Had we not better then stick to the account given us by Moses than to lose ourselves in wild & unsupported conjectures, & is it to be conceived that the Sacred Historian would not only have omitted informing us of so important a fact as the antiquity of the World, but even used all methods to perswade us, that he was relating the first & original Creation of it, when in reality he never intended to do so.

3rd. Consid[eration]

But 3rd. God having made of one blood all Nations of Men teaches us, that as we have all the same origin, so we are all nearly upon an equality *in* <in respect to> what is <itself> most noble & becoming.

[p. 233] To consider things as they are now modelled, & as the necessities of Society require, there is a plain & visible subordination between Men. Some are placed upon an eminence, invested with authority & power commanding the service & obedience *of others people* <of their fellow Creatures, Others> tho' in a much less conspicuous station, yet thro' the easiness of their circumstances, & the plenty they are blessed with move on in a lower but still a pleasant sphere, whilst many thro' necessity, penury, & want, are obliged thro' constant drudgery & toil, to be instruments & agents in the hands of those above them & to depend upon their own industry & the good will of others for their maintenance & support.

Here is A notable & very remarkable difference <at first sight>, but view men in themselves arising from one common Stock, issuing [p. 234] from the hands of their Creator, born with the same rights, possessing of the same priviledges as we shall see hereafter, & all these[144] accidental deluding vain distinctions *shall* cease & vanish, Did not he that made us in the womb, make them, & did not one fashion us in the womb?[145] Whatever *distinctions* <differences> obtain among us <they> are only the consequences of the present oeconomy of things, <outward and occasional.> Designed to answer the ends & purposes of human Society, a Society which is to last but for a short time & then to dwindle of itself, *a Society* <&> which is no sooner to be at an end, *but* <than> the Great disrobed of their vain pageantry & shew shall be seen in their proper colours, without any false imposing light to mislead our judgements. Without any regard to their pretended superiority over us, without any of that dazzling glittering pomp, *that now surrounds & defends them* <which is now their honour & their defence.>

[p. 235] And what an instructive Lesson does this convey to us? How *should it* <proper to> humble *terrify* & beat down the pride & arrogance of the high & powerful *reduce them* <to engage them> to consider their Inferiors as formed of *the* a *same* <common> mould with themselves *persuade them to behave toward them with a tenderness & meekiness. & sweetness of carriage & deportment that they make their yoke easy & convince them that necessity not choice or a cruel pleasure of tyrannising over others is the cause of the service they require from them And this they might the rather do as they must be sensible* <& thereby entitled to such a mild & gentle treatment, as may make the burden imposed upon them sit light & easie, Ever remembering> that the advantages they enjoy above others, are not fixed & permanent, they fluctuate from one to another. They shift & alter as it is most consistent with the manifestation [p. 236] of God's power & the great ends of his Providence, Families like States have their rise & fall. They who this day prosper & flourish may the next be in a state of dependence and subjection, & those who are now depressed & low may possibly in a short time *find themselves great wealthy & considerable* <emerge our of their obscurity into splendour and affluence.>

A Sufficient reason for them not to repine at the circumstances they are in, not to deem themselves less useful & necessary to Society, because they are less conspicuous, not to be envious or impatient at those above them, but in their respective spheres to discharge their different offices as members of the same body, to *move* <act> together in a regular & even course, & to submit with chearfulness to the inconveniencies of their present situation in sure & certain hope of a happy change for [p. 237] the better, when they shall <reassume their birth right> be raised out of the *obscure cell* <dust>[146] & placed in a rank best suited to their real & intrinsic virtues.

4th Consid[eration].

Are we all made <If God has made all Nations> of one blood, Let us look upon *ourselves* <all men> as Members *of* <of one &> the same family, linked together by the *closest* <sacred> bonds of concord & union, obliged to love one another & <equally> bound to promote & advance <our> mutual welfare & happiness *let the differences that are between us, be what they will.*

It is indeed very natural to be biased in favour of that particular Society of which we are members, to desire & contribute to the prosperity of our friends, or our Country men of our neighbours, preferably to that of foreigners & Strangers when [p. 238] they come into competition, & to feel a sensibility & tenderness for these which we do not in equal degree for others. This is the Dictate of Nature never to be effaced, & which religion that was intended to refine and perfect, not stifle & smother nature, never condemns, for if any provide not for his own & especially for those of his own houshold, he hath <according to this> denied the faith, & is worse than and Infidel,[147] & tho' it enjoins us, while we have time to do good unto all Men, still is it with this caution to do so more particularly to those that are of the houshold of faith.[148]

But yet all Men of whatever nation or degree, however different their Religion, their Customs, their manners, their interests may be, bear a strict & near [p. 239] relation <to us> all have a claim to our kindness and affection. No distinctions of acquaintance, neighbourhood & friendship are to exclude the generous offers of our assistance & support, whenever *a Brother or* < any of our> fellow Creature<s> require<s> & stand<s> in need of it, *but* the single view of Human Nature in distress *is sufficient reason* <calls> for our compassion & humanity *to exert itself*, Every Person in such circumstances becomes bone of our bone, & flesh of our flesh,[149] belongs to our body and is part of ourselves.

The Jews had in this very material point greatly transgressed & violated their law, for tho' *in this* they were taught to esteem the Stranger that dwelleth with them, as one born amongst them, & to love him as [p. 240] themselves,[150] yet in direct opposition to so express a command *they considered* <knowing> all other Men to be aliens from the Common-wealth of Israel & strangers from the Covenants of promise,[151] they considered them upon that account as no way the objects of their kindness & beneficence & even[152] with the Samaritans, their next neighbours, & worshippers of the same God, but differeing from them in some few Articles, they would maintain no dealing or entercourse, whence *in a Parable which I had once occasion to explain* O[ur] B[lessed] S[aviour], shews them under the Similitude of the Man that fell among thieves,[153] how comprehensive the relation is in which *we* <Men> stand to *one* <each> *an* other *how close & intimate it is*, <&> how productive it ought to be of *concord increase support love & agreement amongst us all* <universal concord & harmony.>

But yet do we stick to this in practice? <But is this the light in which we generally place it?> [p. 241] *in* <Does> our entercourse, I shall not say with Strangers & foreigners, but even with each other, with neighbours & kinsmen all *that of those who are truly sensible that they are connected together, formed into one family under one common head* <savour of that love & charity that ought to prevail among those who are formed into our family under one common head?>

In our conversation and discourse how <Are we not too> ready *are we* for the most part to darken & obscure the fame & reputation of others, to discover faults & blemishes in their character, to publish *& blaze* abroad their weakness & infirmities, <&> to set their defects in the most conspicuous and contemptible light?

Do any sollicit our assistance & charity plead the excuses they have from nature to our beneficience, alledge the wretched circumstances they are in, the miseries [p. 242] *under which they labour, the undeserved poverty to which they are reduced, how ready are we to seek for pretences to excuse our uncharitableness & want of bowels* <Are we not too ready to seek for any pretence to excuse our uncharitableness & want of bowels>, to lay the misfortunes *to* <of the poor at> their own door, to invent, exaggerate, enlarge matters, rather than distribute to their necessities by a plentiful & seasonable relief?

Have any by some indiscrete unregarded action executed our anger & displeasure? how ready are we to forget the ties of our former appearances, to break out into indecent expressions of anger & wrath <Are we not ready upon every even the slightest provocation to revenge every imaginary wrong, to forget every past obligation, to reject every proffered submission>, & to turn our former friendship *& acceptance* <& regard>, into a fixed & settled principle of malice and resentment? Are we not in one word, too ready to prey upon each other, to promote our own interest at the expence of that of our brother, to improve [p. 243] his ignorance in his necessity to our private advantage, to lay snares for his deception & even under the specious shew of tenderness & concern for his welfare to advance our own to him destructive and pernicious designs.

[p. 244] 5th Consid[eration]:

5th. God having made of one blood all Nations of Men, shews unto us lastly that he made them all for one & the same end.

To this purpose he has created them in his own image, divided unto them their habitations upon the same Earth, rendered it fruitful & plenteous for their mutual comfort & support, He causes his Sun to *shine* rise, & his rain to descend upon them equally, He maintains & preserves them all by his Providence, calls them to the same trials, exposes them to the same infirmities, visits them with the same afflictions, He forms them with the same natural faculties and powers, gives them abilities sufficient [p. 245] to know their duty, bestows upon them reason & understanding, a sense of good & evil, a Soul active Immortal never to be destroyed, He designs and reserves them all for a future and another State, different from the present both in nature & duration.

It must be allowed indeed, that altho' he never left himself without witness in that he did good,[154] yet in the depths of his Providence he has been pleased to grant greater means of improvement to some Nations than <he has> to others, He first singled out the Jews, whom he honoured with a special Revelation disclosing to them his Nature *more fully*, discovering to them his adorable perfections, appointing & fixing a worship suitable to their circumstances, In succeeding ages he *chose the* ... <extended his favours to other Nations> to whom he spake by his Son, calling them [p. 246] to the profession of a still purer faith, enforcing their obedience by distinct ordinances, alluring them to his service by the most encouraging promises, <&> ensuring to them the most glorious and desirable inheritance.

But whatever *might* <may> be the reasons of this preference, God in the end will manifest his love of all men by an impartial and equitable judgment, summoning them to give an account of their actions in proportion to their knowledge, not requiring where he hath not sown, nor gathering where he hath not strawed,[155] but dealing out his rewards according to their various abilities without grudge or envy, accepting out of every *Nation* <people> him that *works*<eth> righteousness,[156] and <is an>

observer <of> his Laws: And it may even be inferred from many passages in Scripture that a time *will* <shall> come, when [p. 247] those Nations who have long continued in darkness & the shadow of death, shall be admitted into the Glorious light of the Gospel, when Christ the Son of God shall speak unto them In like manner as <he does> unto us, afford them the same assistances, offer them the same motives, that as they have been partakers with us of the same temporal advantages, they may be <sharers> also *of* <in> the same Spiritual *ones* <benefits>, & together with us make one fold under one Shepherd, and be called the City of the Lord the Zion of the Holy one of Israel.[157]

Applic[ation]:

And now since all Nations are the workmanship of the same God, the objects of *the same* <his mercy>, & the care of *the same* <his> [p. 248] Providence, how ought they all to join together in their mutual praises & adorations of him express their grateful sense of the mercies they receive and endeavour to deserve the continuance of them by the sincerity of their obedience, All Kings should fall down before him, all Nations should do him services, the Kings of Tarshish & of the Isles bring Presents, the Kings of Sheba & Jeba offer gifts & all the Nations of the Earth call & acknowledge him blessed.[158]

More Above all, since we have the same destination & sufficient capacities to know & perform our duty, how ought we to advance & promote by our constant care & diligence the end of our present being, unite together in the practice of such virtues, as conduce [p. 249] to this, & never deviate from the chief & principal purport of life, the encrease of the Glory of God & the furtherance of our future eternal happiness; This is more particularly incumb[en]t upon us, who are blessed with such singular distinctions of Graces & knowledge, upon whom the Sun of righteousness shines in it's full splendor, to whom such <exceeding> great & weighty promises are made, & from whom *such* proportionable degrees of virtue and improvement are expected.

Let us therefore walk by one & the same rule, Let us mind one and the same *rule* thing,[159] that pursuing constantly the end of our Creation, we may repay the kindness of our Maker by a right & more proper use of his undeserved favours, & thus engage him to grant us still new & more extensive [p. 250] one's, till we all come to that Blessed State of perfect knowledge & happiness, where we shall rise in Glory as we have done in virtue, grow in splendor as we have grown in grace, become as the brightness of the firmament, and as the Stars for ever & ever.[160]

Sermon VIII

Volume 2 (17)

[p. 251] Belfast December ye 24th 1749
Ditto December ye 22nd 1751
Ditto December ye 23rd 1753
Ditto December ye 19th 1756
Ditto December ye 24th 1758
Ditto December ye 21st 1760
Ditto Sunday before Easter March ye 27th 1763
Ditto on Good Fryday April ye 17th 1767
Ditto December ye 24tht 1769
St. Auoden Dub[lin] April ye 8th 1770[161]
St. Doloughs Apr 28th 1783
Ditto Dec 19th 1784
Ditto Sept 18th 1785
Ditto Dec 22nd 1794 S.C.
Ditto Dec 18 1796 H[oly] C[ommunion].
Rosenallis Sept 26 1802
Mt. Melick Oc[tobe]r 3 1802
Ditto Sept 30 1804
Ditto Sept 28 1806
Rosen[allis] Dec 21 1806
Ditto Dec 23 1810
Mt. Melick April 7 1811
[p. 252] Ardmore 22 Dec 1822
Anacloan 12 Dec 1824
[Lough]Brickland Sunday before Xmas 1824[162]

[p. 253] In the Eleventh Chapter of St. Paul's first Epistle to the Corinthians at the Twenty ninth Verse.

But he that eateth & drinketh unworthily, eateth & drinketh damnation to himself.

The Words now before us originally refer to those feasts of Charity, which among the Primitive Christians generally preceded the Sacrament of the Lord's Supper; For as our Lord's first institution of it was immediately after eating the Paschal Lamb, his followers [p. 254] in conformity to his example established certain feasts, to which the faithfull were admitted in common, & the Poor among them entertained at the expence of the rich & wealthy. But what was at first admirably well intended to preserve unity among Christians, soon degenerated into a vile & scandalous practice; The Corinthians divided into factions & parties came to these feasts with dispositions quite opposite to the original end & design. Some thro' vain-glory eat their meat at home, not to herd with those, whom in the fulness of their sufficiency, they [p. 255] looked upon with scorn and disdaine. Others were on this occasion guilty of the most unwarrantable excess, & even as the Apostle informs us, got drunk at these Religious feasts, whilst Many withdrew entirely from them, & <by> their ill-timed divisions broke thro' the Laws of Charity, & disturbed the peace & union of the Church.

Yet whatever reference the words of the Text may bear to this custom, it is not to be questioned but <that> the Apostle carried his view further, & from this one instance meant to discourse in General of the particular dispositions, which form the character of those that eat the bread & drink the cup [p. 257] of the Lord unworthily, It concerns us all to know what these are, more especially at this time that we are fitting & preparing ourselves for the due celebration of the Lord's Supper, & have just been exhorted in ye most affecting manner to join in this solemn act of our Christian worship.[163]

Give me leave therefore to fix your attention upon this August & Sacred ordinance, & to shew you 1st. Who they are that may be said to eat this bread & drink this Cup unworthily, & 2nd. The fatal consequences of eating this bread & drinking this Cup unworthily, they eat & drink damnation to themselves, or as the original [p. 258] expression literally signifies, & ought indeed to have been rendered, judgment or condemnation, And Let every one among us apply these particulars as they go along, to their own case, allow their reason & conscience to exercise their due power, that this most *sacred*[164] *ordinance* <excellent Institution> may be attended with the reverence which is due to it & so become the happy means of *Keeping* <preserving> souls & bodies unto everlasting life.

1st. Part

First who they are that may be said to eat this bread & drink this Cup unworthily. And this will appear if we consider the nature of this Sacram[en]t, [p. 259] & thence deduce what qualifications render it either fruitless or effectual, vain or profitable.

Now in this act of Religious worship we do these four <2 *3*> things, 1st. We declare ourselves Professors of the Doctrines of Christianity, 2nd. We celebrate the memory of O[ur] B[lessed] S[aviour]'s death, 3rd. We enter into Covenant with God, & 4th. We profess our union & concord with the faithfull in the Church of Christ, from each of which it follows that to eat this bread & drink this Cup unworthily, is to eat the one & drink the other without a proper faith, a lively contrition, an unshaken fidelity, & an unfeigned Charity.

[p. 260] 1st. To eat the bread & drink the Cup of the Lord, is to declare ourselves Believers & Professors of the Doctrine of Christianity.

For as every Religious Society has some customs peculiar to themselves by which they are known, some modes of worship to express their perswasion, So O[ur] B[lessed] S[aviour]'s decision in the Institution of the Sacrament was to establish a Religious Life & ordinance by the careful observance of which his Disciples might be distinguished from all other Men, & furnished with the means of giving an outward testimony of their inward *belief* <faith> of profession, that as with the heart they believed unto righteousness, they might with their mouths [p. 261] make confession of it unto salvation[165] & thereby induce themselves & others to glory by God even the father of our Lord Jesus Christ.[166]

And hence it follows that when-ever we come to the Sacrament of the Lord's Supper, we declare before God & Men, in the presence of Heaven & Earth, that we acknowledged Jesus Christ for our Lord & Master, our Supreme & Merciful Benefactor, that we receive his commands as the Dictates of truth itself & the only & proper rules of our conduct that we are Christians in principle, in practice by choice & conviction that we glory in being so, & are resolved to maintain the profession of his religion, at the hazard [p. 262] of all that is dear unto us in this life.

But if this be one end, for which the Sacrament of the Lord's Supper was instituted, it is easie to see that to eat & drink unworthily, is in this instance to eat the bread, & drink the cup, without a proper & becoming faith, when we barely believe in Christ, but do not know the grounds upon which we do so, neither building our faith upon a reasonable foundation, nor feeling in ourselves the justness & propriety of it's evidence.

When we content ourselves with an empty speculative opinion, not solicitous to express our belief by our works, or to shew the efficacy of our faith by the good *works* fruits of virtue & obedience [p. 263] which it produces where-ever it is genuine & pure, much more when our faith is variable & inconstant, shaken by human hopes or fears, yielding to every temptation, & overset by every appearance of difficulty & danger.

He therefore that eateth and drinketh in this manner, without a faith free from these defects, or in other words, he that cometh to the Sacrament of the Lord's Supper, without a faith, enlightened, productive of good works, form & steady, eateth & drinketh unworthily, not discerning the Lord's body.

2nd. In the Sacrament of the Lord's [p. 264] Supper, we celebrate the memory of O[ur] B[lessed] S[aviour]'s death, This do says he in remembrance of me[167] & St. Paul, as oft as ye eat this bread & drink this Cup, ye do shew the Lord's death, till he come,[168] To this end, & to make the Impression of it more strong & lasting upon our minds, is the bread broke, as a proper emblem of his tortured & crucified body, the wine is poured out as a representation of the shedding of his valuable & precious blood, & each of these Symbols are delivered to each Individual, that every one may apply the merits of his sufferings particularly to themselves, & improve the rememberance of his death to [p. 265] their own benefit & consolation.[169]

But to what purpose is it to remember Christ's death, unless at the same time <that> we take into our consideration the cause occasion & end of his sufferings, reflect with seriousness & humility, that it was to make atonement for our sins, & in the depth of his mercy & compassion, that he offered up his life to God, & that therefore the highest obligation lies upon us to forsake our sins, to detest our former wicked practices, & to endeavour to atone for what we have done amiss by all the acts of a sincere contrition & an active Repentance.

And sure if [p. 266] this be the Duty of those who eat this bread & drink this Cup of Christ's Death worthily, the reverse of this must be the unworthy receiving mentioned in the Text, the case of those cold & lukewarm Christians, who partake of this ordinance with indifference, without any warmth of affection or fervency of zeal, who never examine their own conduct, nor search into the principle of their actions before they presume to come to it, who tho' conscious to themselves that they are guilty of many sins & transgressions yet express no true sorrow & contrition for them, no just sense of their unworthiness, [p. 267] no proper fear of God's displeasure, but on the contrary approach his Altar with as much confidence as if they had washed their hands in innocency,[170] & were clad with the wedding garment,[171] required of those who come to this Heavenly feast.

3d. We not only profess ourselves Christians in the Sacrament of the Lord's Supper & celebrate the memory of his Death, but we also actually enter into Covenant with God.

St. Paul calls the Cup, the Cup of the new Testament in his blood, & this supposes that in this action there are different parties contracting together, whose promises [p. 268] & engagements are mutual & reciprocal, On the one side, God promises his mercy to Men, & Men on the other solemnly engage to fulfil the conditions upon which these promises of mercy are made, If God binds himself to pardon the past sins of penitent Men, they as strongly bind themselves to forsake & abandon them, If he offers to them a powerful Mediator to attone for their transgressions, they <vitually agree to have recourse to him> for grace and mercy with faith & contrition, If he assures them of the aid & assistance of his holy Spirit to support them in their conversion, They equally [p. 269] assure him of their own hearty endeavours to concur with the workings of his Grace, and if God engages his immutable veracity & truth as the pledge of his promises, they engage their bodies, their souls, their eternal salvation, as an earnest that they will inviolably adhere to their vows & Covenant.

But in this as in every other Contract, want of faithfulness & fidelity in performing what we have entered into, must inevitably mar & defeat the end & benefit of it, with which it would otherwise be attended whence it is that I reckoned this as the 3rd. mark of our unworthy receiving.

And under this Class are included not only [p. 270] those who when they sign the Contract which God is pleased to tender to them in this Sacrament, only do it out of Worldly views, without any further intention of reforming or amending their conduct, nor those again whose present Devotion is mere form & shew, who before they come to the Sacrament abstain from the sins they are accustomed to, & then return back to them *again* <anew> with eagerness & impatience, but even those who appear hearty & sincere in what they promise, who inwardly say, what they outwardly express & like St Peter are ready to say to their saviour in the petulancy of their hasty zeal Tho I should die with thee, [p. 271] yet will I not deny thee,[172] but whose vows tho' sincere when they were first made; are not lasting, losing thro' the allurement of the World, & the Various entanglements of pleasure & business, their former weight & authority, & rendering their boastful purposes of future goodness of no longer consequence than the Morning Cloud or than the early dew that goeth away;[173] And how common a defect this is, the frequent vows of this kind which we have all broke, & the many resolutions of amendment which have all vainly formed, can best tell.

Lastly. The Sacrament of the Lord's Supper [p. 272] is the outward testimony which we give our union & concord with the faithfull in the Church of Christ, We being many are one bread & one body, for we are all Partakers of that one bread.[174]

As Members of the same body, we all assemble in the same place, As Children of the same Father, we all eat at the same table, As Disciples of the same Master, we all profess the same faith, As Redeemed by the same Blood, we all are entitled to the same benefits, & all aspire to the possession of the same happiness.

And hence we may infer the last mark of *the* an [p. 273] unworthy participation of the Holy Sacrament, to come to it without Charity, with a heart fraught with rancour, hatred, malice & animosity, Such black & hellish dispositions are indeed thoroughly inconsistent with the performance of any one act of Religion, but in a more singular manner are they incompatible with an Ordinance which was purposely appointed to commemorate the greatest instance of Charity, that ever was known, which carries with it every soothing & relenting consideration, which in itself by it's very nature, answers & baffles all the sophistical arguments, upon which we endeavour to justifie the indulging [p. 274] of our revenge & resentment.

Do we do it because we are conscious that we have been the first injured & offended? Behold in this Sacrament we confess that we have provoked the Lord to jealousie, & yet we come to entreat his pardon; Do we so tenaciously <keep in remembrance> the injuries which we have rec[eived] because they have been many and repeated? Behold in this Sacrament we acknowledge on our <bended> knees that we ourselves are loaded with iniquity, & yet we dare to apply for *God's* mercy; Is *it* the superiority which our rank & station gives us over our Enemy, *that is* alledged as the cause of our hatred of him? Behold in [p. 275] this Sacrament we own that we have offended him in whose presence we are altogether less than vanity itself, & yet we have confidence enough implore his clemency; Are we alledging the ungrateful return we have received for benefits conferred? Behold in this Sacrament we proclaim our ingratitude to God for his unmerited mercies, & yet with the same *mouth* <breath> we intreat the continuance of them, finally Do we colour over our hatred with the specious but common pretence of intending no hurt to our Enemy? Behold in this Sacrament we not only deprecate *his* God's judgments, but loudly plead for [p. 276] his favour, we not only endeavour to avert his punishments from us, but we seek to obtain his best & choicest blessings, What palpable contradiction is there in this, what daring presumption, what inconsistency between a feast of love, such as the Sacrament of the Lord's Supper is, & the principles & affections of an implacable revengeful heart, whence we may venture to affirm that want of Charity & good-will to our neighbours much more hatred & malice towards them is a defect of all other most destructive of the benefits conferred upon us by it & this likeliest to draw down upon us the anger & displeasure of God, [p. 277] Presume not therefore to come to this Holy Sacrament, whilst animosity, malice or a desire of revenge, lye lurking in your minds, least by eating this bread & drinking this Cup of the Lord unworthily, you eat & drink your own damnation, What the import & meaning if this Sentence is I come now to lay before you in the remaining part of this Discourse.

2nd. Part.

I have already observed, that the word here rendered damnation, implies in the original judgment or condemnation, And this I particularly take [p. 278] notice of, because several well meaning Persons have from a dread of eating & drinking their own damnation, abstained entirely from the Lord's Supper, & chose rather to give up the advantages accruing to the worthy Partaker, than to venture upon the dangers that accompany the unworthy receiving of it.

Yet if the Context be attended to, it will clearly appear, that the judgement here denounced respects the Infancy of the Christian Church, & consist in sudden temporal punishments of an unusual kind, inflicted upon the profaners of this [p. 279] Mystery, to add weight & dignity to it, for which reason & to prevent the abuse, which might & which indeed has been made of these words, the Apostle immediately subjoins, that upon account of this profanation many were weak, & sickly among them, & many slept[175] or died, thereby restraining to a Temporal punishment, what at first sight seemed to carry with it the notion of a future & spiritual judgment.

But because God does not punish at present the abuse of this Sacrament with temporal & exemplary punishments, Let us not imagine, that the guilt attending [p. 280] it is trifling & inconsiderable, for as the worthy communicant by taking in this bread & wine, these Holy Symbols, with proper dispositions, receives the pledge & earnest of his salvation, so he that eats & drinks unworthily, draws down upon himself the wrath of God, & seals his own judgment & condemnation.

And this we infer from those aggravating circumstances which render the abuse of this Religious act of worship in a particular manner highly criminal & sinful.

The 1st. is the dreadful Hypocrisie *by* <which> it is carried [p. 281] on. It has a manifest tendency to deceive Men, to represent ourselves to them in a light very different from what we really are, to perswade them, that we are Christians like themselves, convinced of the same truths, professors of the same faith, tending to the same end, at the very time that we are the reverse of what we seem to be, at the very time that we hypocritically pretend to a Sanctity which we have not, & are endeavouring to acquire at the expence of Religion & truth, a Character to which we have no manner of claim or title.

2d. It seeks no less to impose [p. 282] even upon God himself, for it is to him directly do we make these solemn promises, to him do we offer our vows, with him that we enter into Covenant, but a Covenant which we are determined beforehand to break, vows which we never intend to perform; promises which we the very next moment resolve to violate & render void, As if the Great God of Heaven & Earth was not privy to our most secret thoughts, As if the inmost recesses of our hearts lay not open to his all seeing eye; as if the most specious & shewy pretences are of any avail, to screen us from [p. 283] his all knowing wisdom & intelligence.

3rd. To eat and drink unworthily is in reality to frustrate & render ineffectual the most pressing motives which Religion can possibly offer to lead us to it, for in this Holy ordinance they <all> seem united. Here we see the hatefulness of sin displayed in the strongest colours, & the unhappy consequences of persevering in it fully represented & set forth,[176] here we view the mercy & compassion of God in their full <utmost> extent, we perceive the precious blood of his Blessed Son, shed for our redemption, interceding in our behalf, inviting us to a compliance [p. 284] with the laws of God, & promising us upon our doing so, entire pardon & forgiveness. And sure if such strong motives fail of their intended success, where shall we seek for stronger, if the foundation of our virtue be not built upon these, on what can it possibly be laid?

4th. and lastly. The unworthy participation of the Holy Sacrament admits of no excuse, & has nothing to offer in it's defence, the abuse we make of it is wilful & deliberate, we acknowledge the Doctrines of Christianity to be genuine & true, we acknowledge the necessity of Repentance, we have recourse to the means appointed [p. 285] to effect it, & still we live & die in our impenitency, our actions give they lye to our words, & justly sentence us to the severest judgments of God. He then that eateth & drinketh unworthily, eateth & drinketh damnation to himself.

Applic[ation]:

I have now laid before you the different ends, for which the Sacrament of the Lord's Supper was instituted, & the different dispositions which they require from every worthy Receiver, together with the aggravating circumstances, which render the abuse of this [p. 286] Religious act of our worship, highly criminal & sinful. The only application I shall make of what has been said, is to press upon you the indispensable obligation we are under of communicating frequently, & of coming to the Lord's Table when-ever we have an opportunity of doing so, Since it is the very test of our profession, as we are Christians, the peculiar priviledge of the followers of Jesus, & the properest means of joining us together, in the unity of the same Spirit, in the bond of peace.

We may possibly gloss over our neglect of it, with the plausible excuse that we are not duly prepared to receive worthily, but if we be not, where does [p. 287] the fault lye, but in ourselves? Are the dispositions we stand in need of, too difficult to be attained, too far out of our reach to be come at? Are there not sufficient allowances made for the frailties inseparable from our Natures? Or Is anything more required from us in this Sacrament, than a sincere & hearty desire to fulfil the terms of the Gospel, & to practice our Duty in every instance we can.

Let not then any such excuse my Brethren, draw us off from the participation of this Holy Mystery, we are in a particular manner called to it [p. 288] [tomorrow] by the Annual Commemoration of O[ur] B[lessed] S[aviour]'s birth, Let us all endeavour to make the pious design of our Church in setting apart this Season for the completion of this great work answer it's intended purpose, Let us dwell upon the importance & consequence of it, Let us examine ourselves, prove our own hearts, try & sift our own actions, not cursorily or superficially, but impartially, universally & without reserve.

And if there be any among us, who feel any doubts remaining, and languor in their devotions, any defects in their conduct which they wish to correct, Let them not fly from this Sacrament, but rather come to it [p. 289] with the humble expectation of having their faith strengthened, their weakness removed, & their good designs cherished & rendered successful.

May this be the happy consequence of our Devotion at this time, May the Sacrifice of our prayers & praises which we offer unto Jesus Christ come up as a sweet smelling savour[177] in his light, and May our present Communion & Fellowship with him here, be the pledge & earnest of our close & more intimate Communion <with him> in his Heavenly & Glorious Kingdom, here with thee O Father, etc.[178]

Sermon IX

Volume 3 (22)

[p. 37] Belfast on Easter Day April ye 10th 1748
Ditto April ye 7th 1751
Ditto April ye 14th 1754
Ditto April ye 10th 1757
Ditto March ye 22nd 1761
Ditto April ye 22nd 1764
Ditto Sunday after Easter April ye 7th 1771

[p. 38] In the Second Chapter of St. Paul's <2nd >Epistle to Timothy at the Eighth Verse

Remember that Jesus Christ of the seed of David was raised from the Dead.

These words were addressed to Timothy, & intended to be his chief support under the various & infinite difficulties inseparable from his Ministry, I mean not to consider them in the particular point of light, but to *render* <make> them useful to ourselves, By endeavouring to shew 1st. The Strong presumption <which> they carry with them of the truth & certainly of our Saviour's Resurrection, Remember that Jesus Christ of the Seed of David was raised from the dead, & 2nd. The Great advantage *we can draw from such a* <which accrues to us from> a constant & habitual rememberance of Christ's Resurrection *as is here recommended.*

[p. 39] 1st Part.

First I am to endeav[ou]r to shew the strong presumption which the words of the Text carry with them of the truth & certainty of O[ur] S[aviour]'s Resurrection, Remember that Jesus Christ of the Seed of David, the true Messiah, descended according to the flesh from David, as the Prophets declared he should, was raised from the Dead.

And this will appear if we consider 1st the Character *& circumstances* of the Apostle *St Paul who* <who here> recommends the rememberance of Christ's Resurrection, 2nd: the Person to whom *it is* <he> recommends it, 3rd: the manner in which *it is expressed* <he does it>, 4th: the time when, & 5th: the place where, he chose to have *it remembered* <this rememberance presented & maintained>.

1st. I say the Character of the Apostle St. Paul, who <here> recommends the rememberance of Christ's Resurrection.

He we know, was originally a Jew, bred up at the feet of Gamaliel, educated in all the [p. 40] prejudices of the Jewish Religion, & honoured with the favour & confidence of the Chiefs of the Synagogue, His interest led him to espouse their cause, to promote their designs & to concur with them in all their measures, Hence was he from the beginning a bitter Enemy to Christianity, persecuting the Professors of it with a furious zeal, & endeavouring by all means in his power to obstruct the growth & progress of it, following in this the dictates of a mistaken conscience & erroneously taking that for Religion, which in every *case* <instance was> contrary to & destructive of it.[179]

Nor was he even at that time destitute of those qualifications which *properly* constitute the Man of sense & *capacity* <knowledge>, He was free from the charge of Enthusiasm & weakness, of a sound judgement & of a clear understanding, plain artless & unaffected, *not* able to see with his own eyes, & to receive & embrace truth whenever it properly came before him.

And yet this same *Apostle* <Man> with these despositions & under these circumstances, averse as he was to the very name of a Christian, & breathing out [p. 41] threatnings & slaughter against the Disciples of the Lord[180] becomes a zealous Advocate for the faith which he once persecuted, yields a full & entire assent to the truth of Christ's Resurrection, not only is convinced himself of the Certainty of it, but uses his utmost efforts to bring others to a like conviction, persists, not-withstanding the extreme dangers such a perseverance laid him open to, boldly & resolutely to maintain & defend it, suffers all that the resentment of his Enemies could invent against him, rather than give up a point, which carried with it such signal marks of it's evidence, foregoes all Worldly interest, renounces all temporal advantages, willingly runs himself into misery poverty & reproach, & at length testifies the heartiness & sincerity of his profession by laying down his life in confirmation of it.

Now I believe it can hardly be presumed that so thorough & difficult a change as that of a Man's entire temper & principles <can be brought

about by any thing less than the most perfect conviction>, or that St. Paul would have given up his prejudices, his interest, [p. 42] his ease & <even> his life, unless he had had the highest reason so to do, especially as in his case the whole of his Conviction, & consequently of his Conversion depended upon the truth of a simple matter of fact, of the reality of which every Man of common sense may be a Judge which is able to no deception of Collusion, which no Enthusiasm or power of Imagination can force men into the belief of, but which was fairly & candidly submitted to the enquiry of every unprejudiced Person, & made to rest upon the most unquestionable of all evidence, that of his own senses.

St. Paul therefore by becoming a Preacher of Christ's Resurrection, & admitting the testimony of those, who bore witness to it, furnishes us with a strong presumption in favour of the truth & certainty of it, *I come now to the* <& this is confirmed by a> second, *which I affect & which is* much of the same nature with the former, the Character & Circumstances of the Person, to whom the Apostles recommend the rememberance of Christ's Resurrection namely Timothy.

[p. 43][181] And He differed from St. Paul in two instances, each of which particularly tend to evince the clearness & perspicuity of this fact; the 1st was, that he was born of a Greek Father, & a Jewess Mother,[182] unit<ing> in his Person the prejudices & mistakes of both Jews and Heathens, *His need we may suppose early preposessed with their motives tossed and divided between their opposite and contrary principles & upon this account having a greater work to do, to conquor & subdue them all, to distinguish between truth and falsehood & to chuse the safe & true way* <and consequently being rent & divided between such contrary & opposite principles may well be supposed at a greater facility to destinguish between truth & falsehood than even St. Paul was.>

[p. 44] Besides He had this *further* <2d> disadvantage to struggle with *which St Paul had not*, that he was Young, & at that Season of Life, when Passion & Pleasure are sooner attended to, than <solid> argument or Reason, when Men are generally more taken up with the noise & follies of the World, than with serious thought or sober & important enquiries, *& especially* where love of ease, the interest of the World, view of Policy, temporal and present advantages are *generally* <commonly> made the spring & motive of Men's actions;

Is it not then reasonable to conclude that something very weighty & important induced him to take up & perswade which in reality was [p. 45]*contrary to all the visible advantages of this world, Is it to be conceived that a Man uneducated as he was would have gone up preaching on one matter of fact attended with such unpleasant, such consequences, such fatal consequences to his own peace & security if he himself had not been fully convinced of the certaintie of it & if he was it was impossible for him to be deceived or exposed upon a point of this nature where fallacy was to easy to be found out.*

<And sure where there are such obstacles in the way of truth, the evidence that induces us to conquer & subdue them, must be proportionabley strong & clear, where a Man in the very bloom of life breaks thro' all the prejudices of education, acts contrary to his visible advantage, in this World, & for the sake of establishing single matter of fact, exposes himself to consequences the most prejudicial to his own peace & safety as, it's plain Timothy did, the presumption is great in his favour, that he himself, is sincerely convinced of the truth of what he professes to believe, & if he was so in the instance before us, that of the Resurrection of our Lord, it demonstrably follows that the fact itself is undoubtedly true, since it was of such a nature as to render any deception or imposture utterly impracticable>.

From these arguments let us proceed to another & consider the manner in which the Ap[*ostle*] *expresses himself upon this occasion* <Nor does the manner in which the Apostle expresses himself upon this occasion, carry with it a less degree of presumption>, Remember <says he>, or as the words may more literally be rendered, Put them in Rememberance, that Jesus Christ [p. 46] of the Seed of David was raised from the Dead.

For Here we find no Chain of Reasoning no long deduction of arguments, no witnesses called upon to attest the truth & veracity of Christ's Resurrection, The fact *is* <seems to be> taken for granted & the issue of it <to be> left upon the strength of former proofs & reasonings.

And whence does this arise? Is it from want of power and Capacity in the Apostle to explain difficult & intricate points? But where there is occasion for *handling any such* <this>, with what strength *does he explain & demonstrate them* <of argument does he do it>, with what force of reasoning does he support & establish the most mysterious & impenetrable Doctrines, How Great a Master does he [p. 47] appear of Eloquence, Oratory & Perswasion.

Could it proceed from his want of *argum*[*en*]*ts* <proofs> to enforce the truth of it? We see him at other times & upon other occasions, producing a multitude of witnesses to confirm it, bringing in five Hundred Brethren at one time to bear testimony to it, & sufficiently founding it upon the strongest argument which a fact of this nature was capable of.[183]

It remains therefore, that his acting so differently upon the present occasion was entirely owing to the *clearness and perspicaity* <avowed evidence> of the truth itself, It no longer admitted of any doubt, or stood in need of any further support, Timothy was fully convinced of it, The *present Christians had yielded* <Christians to whom he was called to preach it were already satisfied in this point>, [p. 48] the proofs of it were fresh in their minds, & nothing was further necessary than to bring their faith to their Remembrance, & at certain seasons to renew the memory of it.

And this opens the way for another remarkable *observation deducible from the text* <presumption in favour of the truth of O[ur] S[aviour]'s resurrection>, the time when *these words were wrote* <the charge in ye text was given to Timothy>, which was but a few years after this wonderful fact had happened, when the witnesses of it were several of them still living, & the *proof of Christs Ressurection so ready at hand* <nature of their testimony was so well known>, that it was not possible, but their Enemies *could* <must> have disproved the truth of *them* <it>, if it had been capable of being *disputed or controverted* <either controverted or disputed.>

No doubt an Event of this *nature* <kind> [p. 49] whose consequences were of such importance to Mankind, had been narrowly & thoroughly enquired into, & a Space of twenty or thirty Years *since it happened* <during which this enquiry had been carried on>, but have produced abundant proofs of it's falsity, were any such to be had; From the first day of our Saviour's Resurrection to the writing of this Epistle, we may suppose all wits at work to invalidate the Certainty of it, and still it continued firm & unshaken, it's evidence undisturbed, it's authority unremoved; No objection is started against, but what carries it's answer along with it, & no attempts made to destroy it, but what are visibly the low pitiful shifts and evasions of prejudiced, *interested partial cavailing Persons* <and self-deluded Men.>

[p. 50] And if Lastly we add the places, which were purposely chosen for the publishing of Christ's Resurrection, & especially the circumstances of Ephesus, where Timothy is particularly charged to preach this truth,[184] & to preserve the memory of it, we shall find still stronger & more convincing *proof of* <reasons to admit> the genuiness & authenticity of it's evidence.

We do not see it <For it is not> published in a corner, or in the less noted Cities of the World, where People might be tempted to receive it, where Novelty might introduce it, or a yet rude & unexperienced Race Greedyly & unwarily swallow it down, but It is proclaimed at Ephesus one of the most considerable Cities in Asia, addicted [p. 51] to Idolatry above any other, particularly fond of a superstitious & false worship, jealous of every thing that tended to lessen or destroy it, under the Dominion of a multitude of Priests, *all* whose interest led them to support & maintain it, & owing their riches and grandeur to the famed & stately Temple of the Goddess Diana, & the high repute it was in through-out the whole Heathen World.[185]

And yet in the very City does the Certainty & over-bearing evidence of O[ur] S[aviour]'s Resurrection force the assent even of many of it's most obstinate Adversaires, The Temple of the Great Goddess Diana was by this in a manner despised, Her Magnificence lessened & obscured, Her [p. 52] Priests & Officers set at nought, & the Name of the Lord Jesus *was* magnifyed <and exalted above all>, So mightily grew the word of God & prevailed.[186]

Such are the plain & obvious Reflections which the words of the Text naturally offer in favour of Christ's Resurrection, Let us now consider *what practical use and improvement we can make of the constant & habitual Remembrance of it* <of what use & advantage a constant & habitual Rememberance, of it may be to us.>

2d. Part.

And 1st. *A Constant Remembrance of Christs Ressurection* <It> is abundantly useful to strengthen our faith, & establish the truth of Christianity.

[p. 53] It must be confessed, that How sublime soever the Doctrines were, which Ch[rist] <had> preached, How ever Sacred the Character with which he introduced himself into the World, or How ever Great the Miracles which he wrought in attestation of his Mission, *As* <Since> he had been crucified as a Malefactor, exposed to numberless indignities, suffered a shameful & ignominious Death, Had he after this continued a prey to Corruption & remained in the Grave for ever, without appearing upon Earth again, we should find it highly difficult to preserve our faith, & not to be startled at so unfavourable <a circumstance> especially as He himself had given such high & exalted notions of his own Dignity & power.

[p. 54] Even His very Followers & Disciples the constant & continual eye witness of his wonderful works, were themselves dismayed & discouraged during the short space between his Death & Resurrection, giving up in some sense the task they had undertaken, & making this humble &

mortyfying Confession, We trusted, that it had been he, who should have redeemed Israel & beside all this, to day is the third day, since these things *have happened* <were done>.[187]

But what at first shook their faith *& staggered their Resolution*, soon became *to them & us the* <it's> surest & *foremost* <most solid> foundation *of it for what objections strong enough to subvert the faith of* [p. 55] *those who keep in Remembrance Christ's Resurection, who set the argum[en]ts & proofs of it before their minds, who reflect that the very person who preached these Doctrines, who wrought these principles who brought to light such noble & excellent precepts after sealing the truth of them with his own Blood, openly conquored Death, came out victorious & triumphant out of the chambers of the grave and defeated. & loosened the power by which he was held Or what Testimony so glaring as that of God himself, giving a … to Christ's ministry. & declaring him to be his son with power by his Ressurection* [p. 56] *from the Dead.*[188] *With great propriety weight St Paul then lay the whole truth of Christianity upon this single point & make it the Grounds & foundation of our faith. If Christ be not raised then is our preaching vain & your faith is also vain.*[189]

<for after they had seen him according to his own declaration, rising victorious out of the Chambers of the Grave, conquering Death & baffling the power by which he was held, when they saw him shewing himself alive by many infallible proofs during the space of forty days,[190] when by eating with, speaking to & handling of him they undoubtedly knew him to be the same Person who was laid in a Sepulchre certainly & unquestionably dead, there could be no doubt remaining of the truth & divinity of his Mission, the power of such an evidence was not to be resisted, It rose superior to all the arts & stratagems that Infidelity could employ against it, & put Christianity upon such a foundations as to maintain it's ground to this day, & to declare the Author of it to have been the Son of God, with power by his Resurrection from the dead,[191] whence it is that St. Paul lays the whole truth of Christianity upon this single point, whence it is that St. Paul lays the whole truth of Christianity upon this single point, If Christ be not risen, then is our preaching vain & our faith is also vain.>[192]

2nd: The Resurrection of Christ *warns us aga[in]st the Conciousness of our own unworthiness & the inward sense we have of our demenes & dignity* <is a pledge & earnest of our acceptance with God, & the Rememberance of it our firmest support under the sense of our demerits & indignity.>

For if we depended upon our own conduct & the sufficiency of it, to ensure our hopes & expectations, How poor and weak a dependence would this [p. 57] be. The best of us are liable to so many errors *& mistakes*, our virtues so imperfect, our dispositions so languid, *our endeav[ou]rs so fluctuating & inconstant* that little c[oul]d be expected from them, when compared with the purity & excellency of the Supreme Being to whom they are offered.

If we trusted to the sincerity of our Repentance & our present contrition & sorrow for our sins, not to mention how late, how partial, how defective such a Repentance generally is, who could be able to satisfy us, that God would accept this as entire, that such short & temporary obedience would engage him to avert his judgm[en]ts, *to reverse* [p. 58] *his Decrees* to stay his Justice, & instead of punishing for what was past, to reward the present with a great & glorious recompence.

If *we* as the strongest foundation we confided in the merits of Christ's Death & sufferings only, abstracting from the consideration of his Resurrection, How much so ever we owe to *that* <this> our Reconciliation with God, *yet should* <still could> we be but little acquainted with the measure & extent of it, we should be ignorant of it's true worth & intrinsic value & above all we c[oul]d never know it's high price in the sight of God, nor it's full & entire efficacy to procure unto us pardon [p. 59] & forgiveness.

But Blessed be God, who hath begotten us again unto a Lively hope by the Res[urrection] of J[esus] C[hrist] from the Dead,[193] By this we are convinced, that God accepted his invaluable Sacrifice for the propitiation of our sins,[194] By this we see the Sufferings of O[ur] S[aviour] crowned with glory, his obedience rewarded, & the Displeasure of our Creator changed by a pompous act not Complacency & Approbation, & as Christ was openly delivered for our offences,[195] & visibly suffered for our transgressions, so by this do we see him rising again for our justification, sealing unto us our pardon, & removing [p. 60] all our doubts & anxieties.

Here then does every Repenting Sinner meet with comfort & Consolation, Here does he find reason to build his hopes, to expect remission of his sins, & conscious of the sincerity of his Conversion to cry out, Who shall Lay any thing to the charge of God's elect? It is God that justifieth, Who is he that condemneth? It is Christ that died, yea rather that is risen again, who is even at the right hand of God, making intercession for us.[196]

But 3d. *Let us carry in our minds* The *Resuactection*, <The> Rememberance of [p. 61] Ch[rist]'s Resurrection *it will arm* <arms> us against the fear of Death, & the terrors *that attend its approach* <with which the consideration of it is generally attended.>

For if our Faith in Christ be founded upon such undoubted principles as we have seen it is, if *our Perswasion be thus strong & steadfast what is there in Death to fear & dreadful to frighten & alarm us* <our confidence in the truth of his Resurrection be thus firm & unshaken we have sufficient grounds for comfort & support even in the hour of death & at the approach of Eternity?>

Is it <Should> the Loss of what we at present enjoy, *that* fill<s> us with *such* apprehensions, the sudden removal of all that we hold most dear & valuable, *the fashion of this world that is passing away* [197] *all our Glory hon[ou]rs & hopes vanishing in one moment that* causes *this* Confusion [p. 63] within us? The Resurrection of Christ *presents us with* <enables us to fix our thoughts upon> enjoyments highly transcending those we leave behind us, It opens to our view a new & a better State, it discloses <to us> a new Heaven & a new Earth,[198] *the heavenly Jerusalem*[199] whose real *hopes & lasting* <& durable> pleasures <far> exceed all that the most refined & *subtle* sagacious imagination can possibly conceive.

Is it <Should> the Consciousness of our own Imperfections, alarm us? *We have just seen that Christ rising from the Dead secures us against them emputes unto us his own merits, blotts off with his own blood our frailities, weaknesses & defects & inspires us with that confidence & hope which nothing but the works of such a Redeemer could produce within us.*

<The Resurrection of Christ as we have easily seen, secures us against these by applying to us the merits of those sufferings of which it was ye reward & recompence by[200] opening to us the treasures of God's mercy & compassion, by blotting out our frailties & defects & by giving us the reviving hope that our sins shall be done away, & our pardon sealed in Heaven before we go hence, & be no more seen.>

[p. 64] Or should the Black & horrible appearance of the Grave *dispirit us*, the weakness of a perishing frame, the thoughts of a moulding Corruptible body, now to be reduced into dust, the sport & prey of the vilest< & most object> Creatures, <terryfy & dismay us>. The Resurrection of Christ if properly dwelt-upon brightens even this dark & Gloomy prospect, it assures us that as he triumphed over Death, so shall we in like manner triumph over it, that what is sown in corruption shall be raised in incorruption, that what is sown in dishonour shall be raised in Glory, that what is sown in weakness, shall be raised in power,[201] that as we have born the Image of the Earthly, we shall also bear the Image of the Heavenly,[202] that our vile Body shall be fashioned like unto Christ's Glorious body,[203] in a word that Death itself shall be swallowed up in

Victory, & every true & sincere [p, 65] Christian *enabled* <made> to triumph over it in the emphatical words of the Apostle. O Death where is they sting? O Grave where is thy Victory?[204]

But to no purpose is it to carry in our minds the comfortable Rememberance of Christ's Resurrection, to no purpose to feed ourselves with the hopes & expectations naturally deducible <from it> *it does not* <unless> in the Last place it induces us to be stedfast & unmoveable, to abound always in the work of the Lord, & to walk worthy of him who hath called us unto his Kingdom and Glory.[205]

For if the Benefits conferred upon us by the Redemption of the World through Jesus Christ were never intended for those who are the very reverse of their Blessed Redeemer in their lives & conversation. His Great & transcendent love *for me*, so manifestly shewn in *the* his Death & Passion can never *take* <have> those *among us* for it's object, who are merciless, Cruel, uncharitable & unforgiving, His Humility & meekness of Spirit [p. 66] will not allow him to accept the offerings of such as are themselves proud, haughty, vain, over-bearing & imperious, His Mortyfycation & self denyal will never suffer him to delight in those Who *continue* <live> in luxury & Intemporance, & in the incessant gratification of their irregular & violent passions, nor can his Glorious Resurrect[io]n in Contempt of this lower World <permit him> to look down upon us with mercy & compassion, if we mearly grovel upon Earth, if we confine <all> our hopes, *our* <and> enjoyments, *our pleasures* to things of this World, & make them the whole of our wishes and desires.

And indeed <And it is in consequence of this that> all his exceeding great promises, his Glorious rewards & his kind & merciful invitations are only addressed to those, who walk in his steps, who crucifie the flesh with the affections & lusts,[206] & who dye unto him, that they may live again unto righteousness, cleansing themselves from all filthiness of flesh, spirit, & perfecting holiness in the fear of God.[207]

[p. 67] Applic[ation].

Thus *is* <have we before us> both the Certainty of Our Saviour's Resurrection, & the advantage of a Constant Rememberance of it *set before us*, Happy were it for us if we <often> made the one the object of our faith, & the other the object of our *frequent* meditation & reflection, Then should our chief ambition be, to adorn the name we bore by our virtue, our charity, our piety our unfeigned love for God, & undissembled love for our neighbour, Then should no profaneness & impiety, no <lewdness & debauchery>, no unchristian heats & animosities be found among us, Then should we be as much distinguished by the purity of our manners as we are by the purity of our faith & worship, & Then should the Resurrection <of Christ> prove indeed our comfort and our Glory.

May God of his infinite mercy [p. 68] render this Great Event which he himself hath brought to pass, the never failing source of Spiritual mirth & joy to us, & in his son good time [p. 69] vouchsafe to make it so, to every sincere & penitent Christian, render this Great Day which he himself hath made,[208] a Day of spiritual mirth & joy, & in his own good time lead us from the Grave & Gate of death to a joyful & a Glorious Resurrection, for his merits, who died & was buried & rose again for us, even Jesus Christ his Son, To whom etc. etc.

Sermon X

Volume 3 (23)

[p. 70] Belfast April ye 24th 1748
Ditto August ye 20th 1749
Ditto January ye 12th 1752
Ditto November ye 10th 1754
Ditto April ye 24th 1757
Ditto November ye 12th 1758
Ditto December ye 13th 1761
Ditto February ye 5th 1764
Ditto July ye 31st 1768
Ditto August ye 26th 1770 .D.+[209]
Cromlin 1781
Foundling Hospital March 24th 1782[210]
St. Andrews May the 5th 1732 in the Even[ing]
Ditto March the 20th 1783, at Evening Lecture
St. Luke's March the 26th 1783 at Even[ing] Lect[ure]:
St. Dolough's April the 6th 1783
Ditto March ye 14th 1784
Ditto September ye 30th 1787
Ditto April ye 26th 1789 I:L:
St. Thomas's May 3rd 1789
St. Michan's July 1791
St. Dolough September 23rd 1791
Ditto April 14th 1793
[p. 71] Ditto June 21 1795
Ditto February 27th 1797 L:C:
Ditto July 28 1799
Rosenallis September – 1802
Mt. Melick September 25 1803
Ditto July 7 1805
Rosenallis January 12 1806
Ditto May 8 1808
Mt. Melick June 12 1808
Rosenallis June 24 1810
Mt. Melick October 13 1811
Donoughmore July 12 1813
Derry February 21 1819. Evening.
Anaclone April 14 1822
Seagae 4 July 1830
… November 1836

[p. 72] In the Third Chapter of St. Paul's Epistle to the Colossians & the Thirteenth Verse.

Forgiving one another if any Man have a Quarrel against any.

There is hardly any one Duty more irksome & unpleasant in the practice, than the Christian Duty of forgiveness, & of abstaining from revenge & Resentment upon every provocation, Some have made this a powerful objection against Christianity in General [p. 73], & represented that excellent System of Morality, as faulty & defective in this instance, divesting Man in some sense of every noble & generous principle, & introducing in the stead of it, meanness of Spirit, & a low & abject demeanour.

To free Religion from so unjust a charge, I shall in the following Discourse endeavour to enquire some what particularly into the Nature & reasonableness of this Duty, & to this end, I shall offer some general considerations, the better to determine the Nature, extent, & limits of it, that [p. 74] when once these are fixed, I may with greater propriety, press & recommend the practice & observance of it.

1st Part.

And here it is plain at first sight, that the forgiveness of injuries enjoined us by Christianity, does not regard those, who are endued with a Civil & Legislative power, appointed to watch over the welfare & prosperity of that Community, to which they belong, Because without some authority, to inflict punishment upon those, who [p. 75] disturb it's peace & quiet, Society could not subsist, but must necessarily fall into confusion & disorder, Every one in a low rank would become liable to the insult of those above him, & power & wealth might range lawless & uncontrolled thro' the World, whence in Scripture are Magistrates represented, as the Vice-Regents of God upon Earth, deriving their authority from him, not bearing the Sword in vain, but particularly intended to be the Terror of evil doers, & the Revengers, that execute wrath upon them that do evil.[211]

[p. 76] But the Precept now before us, refers to those Quarrels & dissensions, which happen in the common entercourse of life between Man & Man, which often make a breach in families, divide the best and hitherto the most real friends, occasion a variety of enmities & disputes, & thro' the opposition of interests, the whim of tempers, & the factions of Party views, multiply variance & discord, & render all Social communication with each other, highly distasteful & unsatisfactory. And for the more full & distinct knowledge of what is to be properly understood by this Duty [p. 77] of forgiveness, many things are to be considered, because the extent & limits of it depend much upon the occasion, nature, & circumstance of the offences to be remitted. And therefore 1st. whenever we think ourselves injured, the first thing the Christian Precept of forgiveness requires from us, is to consider whether we ourselves have not given occasion to the injury which we have received, & by this rather offended others, than been offended ourselves. Indeed in most private Quarrels & disputes, both parties are in the wrong.[212] There is a Pride & [p. 78] warmth in some Characters, which can brook no manner of opposition, which makes us imagine, that so much deference is done to us from others, that they are bound to bear with whatever usage we are pleased to give them, & if in consequence of our own rude & uncouth manners, they insensibly withdraw them selves from our Company, if they shew some coolness to us upon this account, if perhaps the warmth of their temper, & their impatience under our bad treatment, betrays them into some little harshness or indiscretion, we immediately cry out, [p. 79] as if we had been wronged, & unjustly treated by them. Instances of this are common & frequent in the World, & the Natural reflection arising from hence is, that where this appears to be the case, the Christian Duty of forgiveness, & smothering at once all thoughts of revenge or resentment, is the immediate Dictate of Reason, For what cause have we to cherish hatred or rancour, who have voluntarily brought down upon ourselves, what ever evil we now suffer, who by our own unreasonableness & injustice, have truly trespassed against others, & whose [p. 80] pardon & forgiveness, it is our duty to endeavour to obtain, by a contrary behaviour of mildness & gentleness, Reason & Religion agreeing exactly in this, & no more being required by the latter, than what was equally binding by the former.

And as the occasion of the offence is a necessary consideration, so the nature of it, is 2nd to be enquired into.

For some offences are merely imaginary, & Creatures of our own framing, we are jealous of some particular excellence or good fortune in others, we look with envy & impatience, [p. 81] upon their superiority over us, & fancy they do us an injury, whilst they are only making use of just & lawful means to advance their own interest, whilst the distinctions, which are shewn them, are justly due to their own true & solid merit, & their pre-eminence is in every respect for the good & advantage of Society. Some injuries may again be involuntary, the effect of inadvertency & inconsideration, & to this are many of those offences owing, for which the comfort & peace of Society is *disturbed* so often disturbed, if searched to the bottom, they have their [p. 82] foundation more frequently in Constitution, a bad education, an open & unguarded conversation than in any malicious or ill natured disposition. Some in a word, may be trifling & insignificant, offences without sufficient cause to warrant resentment, A little height in our temper & carriage, a word, a gesture ill construed & ill interpreted, is the only thing, we have to complain of, An insult is perhaps offered to our pride, but no real damage done, no blott upon our Reputation, no Invasion of our property, no lessening of our influence & authority; & is it reasonable to brood over such insignificant injuries [p. 83] as these, & to sacrifice peace, friendship, concord & unanimity to such vain & absurd punctilios. But there may be, & doubtless are several cases, in which the injury, which is offered us is real & considerable, where our honour, our fortune, our Character, every thing which we hold most dear & valuable, is openly & avowedly injured, in such circumstances, Christianity would have us 3rd. overcome evil with good, & endeavour before all things, to bring such Persons to themselves by works of kindness & good nature, melting them down as it were, into sensibility & tenderness; not avenging ourselves of them, but rather giving place unto wrath, feeding them, when they are [p. 84] hungry, giving them drink, when they are thirsty, that such conspicuous instances of undeserved goodness, may work upon their minds,[213] & so bring about the only end, which we ought to have in view, their amendment & our own preservation, which if it can be effected by such means as these, I believe there is no one, but what must allow them to be infinitely preferable to, & highly more eligible, than all the means offered or suggested by violence & force.

4th. As some tempers are strangely perverse, & as Good treatment rather confirms them in their evil disposition [p. 85] than reclaims them from it, so neither does Christianity oblige us, when this is the case to submit patiently to their insults & with a Social Indifference to stand the brunt of their repeated violences & oppressions, which could indeed serve to no other end, than to encourage them to persist in their wickedness, & to extend their ill usage to others, as little deserving of it as ourselves; But what it binds us to is, that instead of being Judges & Executioners in our own cause, we should seek for shelter & protection in the Laws of the Land we live in, & after taking such steps as Prudence & Discretion suggest, that we should leave [p. 86] the whole issue & disposal to God, the all wise & unerring Judge, who can instantly turn that unto good, which our Enemies meant unto evil;[214] continuing even then, such offices of kindness to them, as are consistent with our safety, not rejoicing, when our Enemy falleth, or being glad, when he stumbleth, not suffering our mouth to sin, by wishing a curst to his Soul, lest the Lord see it, & it displease him,[215] but rather supporting him in his distress, commiserating him in his adversity, & endeavour to obtain his Amendment & pardon [p. 87] by hearty & affectionate prayers to God, If thow meet thine Enemies ox or his Ass going astray, thow shalt surely bring it back to him again,[216] & O[ur]

B[lessed] S[aviour] commands us expressly, to bless them that curse us, to do good to them that hate us, & to pray for them, which despitefully use us & persecute us.[217] And when thro' the blessing of God, these measures have their desired effect, & the Offender is *by these means* <thereby> brought to a just sense of the wrong, he has done us, Christianity demands, as the last & most finishing test of our forgiveness, that we [p. 88] should immediately lay aside all rememberence of the injury, we have received never mention to, or upbraid him with his past conduct & behaviour, & at the same time, that we unfeignedly forgive him ourselves, *use* <exert> our <utmost> endeavours to reinstate him again, into the good opinion of others. Those few Reflections I have now made, suffice to shew us, the nature, extent, & limits of this Duty of forgiveness, which has appeared to many so monstrous & unnatural, No doubt the bare stating of it, has great weight & power to reconcile us to it, but as the reasonableness of a precept [p. 89] is not of itself a sufficient motive for Men to act by, when Passion & resentment are in the opposite scale, I shall now offer some strong & forcible arguments to excise us to the practice & observance of it.

2nd Part.

And 1st. It may be proper to consider what great need we have of each other's forgiveness, to obtain the pardon of our own mutual faults & offences. For there are very few of us, but what are apt some time or other to give offence, few are so thoroughly upon their guard, but what some levity or indiscretion may possibly escape them, & justly should [p. 90] we deem those Cruel & unmerciful, who upon every occasion, would convert these into a settled Crime, & make no allowance for the frailties & infirmities of our Nature. But what right have we to demand Charity & indulgence for ourselves, if we refuse the same to others, with what reason can we expect, that men will forgive us our trespasses, if we will not forgive their's, or With what confidence can we hope, that a Vail will be thrown over our slips & miscarriages if we delight ourselves in dwelling upon, & exaggerating those of our Fellow Creatures, tho' perhaps much less [p. 91] considerable, & heinous than our own.

Yet such is the nature of our Passions that Delusions of this kind abound & are common. The most unforgiving are generally the most *likely* <liable> to give offence for where a Principle of settled resentm[en]t dwells there a door is left open for malice & ill nature to enter in & to produce their dire and fatal effects.

2nd. There is as much true honour & greatness in forgiving offences, as there is meanness & baseness in remembering an injury. For consider the unforgiving Person, & examine both the principle, upon which he proceeds, & the motives [p. 92] by which he is influenced, & now will find him acted & wrought upon by the lowest & meanest;

At one time his own, pride the over rated value he has put upon himself, the fancied superiority of his own merit, stifle all thoughts of condescension & forgiveness, At other times a sordid attachment to his interest, a niggardly temper, unable to part with the most trifling advantages for the sake of peace & concord, represent a Reconciliation with an Enemy, as a real loss, & a manifest detriment, Now inhumanity, want of bowels, a cruel pleasure in feeding upon the thoughts of revenge, & the gratifying a spiteful resentment, [p. 93] take entire possession of him, render him unmoved at every generous consideration, exclude all the tender emotions of Human Nature, & reduce him to a callous State of insensibility & utter disregard, for the welfare or good opinion of the rest of Mankind. On the contrary Observe the merciful & forgiving man, & how noble & truly exalted his Character? He possesses Humanity, that amiable & delightfull virtue, in the highest degree, He knows, where of Men are made, their foibles, weaknesses & defects, He loves to consider these with an eye of tenderness compassion, He esteems them <to be> rather [p. 94] the attendants of a frail Nature than the effects of depravity & corruption, His whole department is ever meek, mild & gentle, No animosity or rancour disturb his peace & quiet, He is superior to all the low <arts &> cunning in the World, He neither regards, nor is influenced by them, & his Religion, the true foundation on which such a conduct is built, engages him to submitt all his Worldly & temporal concerns, to the Will & direction of him, who hath the hearts of Men under his rule & Governance, & who can dispose & turn them, as it seemeth best to his Godly wisdom.

And surely in such a case, & where such particulars form [p. 95] the Character, there is more Glory in passing over a transgression,[218] & more greatness & magnanimity in forgiving one offence, than in all the pitiful contrivances of the merciless & revengeful.

And as an unrelenting Temper is contrary to all real honour & Greatness of Soul, so is it entirely opposite to Christianity, & to the Spirit it would inspire us with.

I need not insist much upon this, We all know that the whole Scheme of Christianity is founded upon a principle of mercy & forgiveness, that the Strain of it in general with all [p. 96] its particular laws tend to love & concord to recommend unanimity & good will among Men, to make the love of ourselves the measure & standard of the love we ought to have for others, & even to set the love of our Enemies for the distinguishing mark of our Profession. We are no less acquainted with that eminent instance of perfect mercy & compassion which O[ur] B[lessed] S[aviour]'s example propounds to our imitation, whose whole Life was spent in acts of mercy, bestowed upon Men, that deserved nothing from him, at the worst & vilest treatment, who requited all the evil offices that were done him by new & repeated works of [p. 97] beneficence, who when he was reviled, reviled not again, when suffered, he threatened not, but committed himself to him, that judgeth righteously,[219] & after having patiently endured, what the revengeful malice of ill disposed Persons, could contrive most grievous & afflicting, concluded this life of unmerited kindness & condescension, with fervent prayer to God to forgive the bitterness & savage cruelty of his Murderers. An Example of forgiveness this powerful enough one could imagine, to extirpate every sentiment of rancour & hatred, & to dissolve the most implacable into love & [p. 98] compassion!

4th: But the chief & most argument I shall offer, to enforce the Duty now under consideration, is taken from the sense of that mercy & forgiveness, which we daily experience from God himself, together with the hopes of that remission, which we finally expect to receive from his hands. Our transgressions against God can bear no comparison with, or proportion to those offences, which our Fellow Creatures commit against us; They are constant & repeated, They are voluntary, & our own deliberate choice, contrary more generally to the Dictates of our Reason, & the motions of our Conscience, [p. 99] They carry with them the most striking signs of ingratitude & baseness, & are the most daring abuse, we can make, of the favours & benefits of that God, by whom alone we live, move & have our Being.[220]

And yet black as they are, the bounty & mercy of God bears with them, He wins us over to him by the cords of a Man, & the bonds of love,[221] he allures us to his service by constant, new, & reiterated blessings, He patiently suffers our disobedience, in hopes of our amendment, & when we shew any signs of sorrow & contrition for our faults, he freely forgives them all, & [p. 100] restores us again to his tenderness & affection. And if the Supreme God acts thus mercifully towards us, should we not shew some degree of mercy & kindness in our dealings one toward another? If he looks down with pity & compassion upon such frail Creatures as we are, should we not condescend to have mercy & compassion upon those, who are bone of our bone, & flesh of our flesh,[222] who are of the same nature with ourselves, & to whose imperfections weaknesses & defects we are all equally subject? Or If he against whom we offend daily, be thus *ready* < willing> to pardon & forgive us our trespasses, should we not be ready [p. 101] to forgive those, whose offences against us are only temporary & distant, & when compared to those which we committ against him, trifling & inconsiderable? Accordingly as he vouchsafed to make our acting upon such occasions, the rule & measure of his acting towards us, in the last & final consummation of things, He shall have judgment without mercy, that hath shewed no mercy, with what measure we mete, it shall be measured to us again,[223] whence we are told, that the particular aggravation of the merciless Servant's Crime in the Parable was, not that he had insisted [p. 102] upon having his own, but that he had acted so contrary to the example which the bounty of his Lord had set him, & had refused to shew to a Fellow Servant the same mercy & compassion, which had been shewn to him, for so likewise says O[ur] B[lessed] S[aviour] shall my Heavenly Father do also unto now, if ye from your hearts, forgive not every one his Brother, their trespasses.[224]

Applic[ation]:

Thus have we the nature, extent, Reasonableness of the Duty of forgiveness laid before us, together with some [p. 103] arguments, such as appeared the likeliest to excite us to the faithful & consciencious discharge of it. The subject is in itself of the highest consequence, & the satisfying ourselves, that we heartily forgive, if any one trespasses against us, a point of the highest importance to us we see that upon this turn the hopes of our eternal salvation, & I may add, that without this virtue, all the outward acts *which* of Religion, which we may perform, are of no avail. We cannot deprecate our own sins, we cannot implore God's mercy, We cannot rehearse the Lord's Prayer, We cannot come to the Blessed Sacrament of the Lord's [p. 104] supper, We cannot expect the powerful succour & assistance of God's Holy Spirit, whilst we cherish such revengeful & implacable sentiments. And what Man would chuse to live in such a situation as this, what Man would bare the thought, that perhaps Death may come upon him, when he has thus cut himself off from all Communication with God, rejected the terms & means of acceptance tendered out to sin, & outrageously persisted <to the end> , shew violent, cruel & merciless dispositions.

I shall conclude all with the wise, & at all times seasonable advice [p. 105], of the Son of Syrach, he that revengeth shall find vengeance from the Lord, he will surely keep his sins in remembrance, Forgive thy neighbour the hurt, that he hath done unto thee, so shall thy sins also be forgiven thee, when thou prayest, One Man beareth hatred against another, & doth he seek pardon from the Lord? He sheweth no mercy to a Man, that is like himself, doth he ask forgiveness of his own sins, If he that is but flesh, nourish [p. 106] hatred, who will entreat for pardon of his sins? Remember thy end, & let enmity cease, Remember corruption Death, abide in the Commandments.[225]

Sermon XI

Volume 3 (27)

[p. 229] Belfast July ye 31st 1748
St. John's Dub[lin] February: ye 26th 1749/50
Belfast August ye 5th 1750
Ditto May ye 6th 1753
Ditto February ye 2nd 1753
Ditto August ye 21st 1757
Ditto July ye 22nd 1759
Ditto December ye 14th 1760
Ditto December ye 9th 1761
Ditto March ye 26th 1764
Ditto February ye 9th 1766
Ditto November ye 6th 1768
Ditto August ye 6th 1768
Ditto August ye 12th 1770
Leixlip July 1st 1781[226]
Cromlin August 5th 1781
Magdalin Asylum September 16th 1781[227]
Marine Chapel September 23rd 1781[228]
St. Andrew's Ditto. Ditto. Ditto. In the Evening
St. Kevans September 30th 1781
Ditto Nicholas without February 17th 1782 in the Evening
St. Bride's August 4th 1782
St. John's August 11th 1782
[p. 230] St. Patricks Cathedral September 5th 1782
St. Doloughs September 7th 1783
Ditto December 10th 1784
Ditto December 1st 1786
Ditto May 13th 1787
Ditto June 14th 1789
St. Michans March 1st 1790
St. Doloughs Ditto 7th 1790
Ditto September 16th 1792
Ditto July 20th 1794 S.C:
Ditto September 25th 1796
Rosenallis May 23 1802
Mt. Mellick February 20 1803
Rosenallis July 23 1809
Mt. Mellick July 1st 1810

Rosenallis October 6th 1811
St. Peters August 28th 1814
Ditto June 9th 1816 Evening

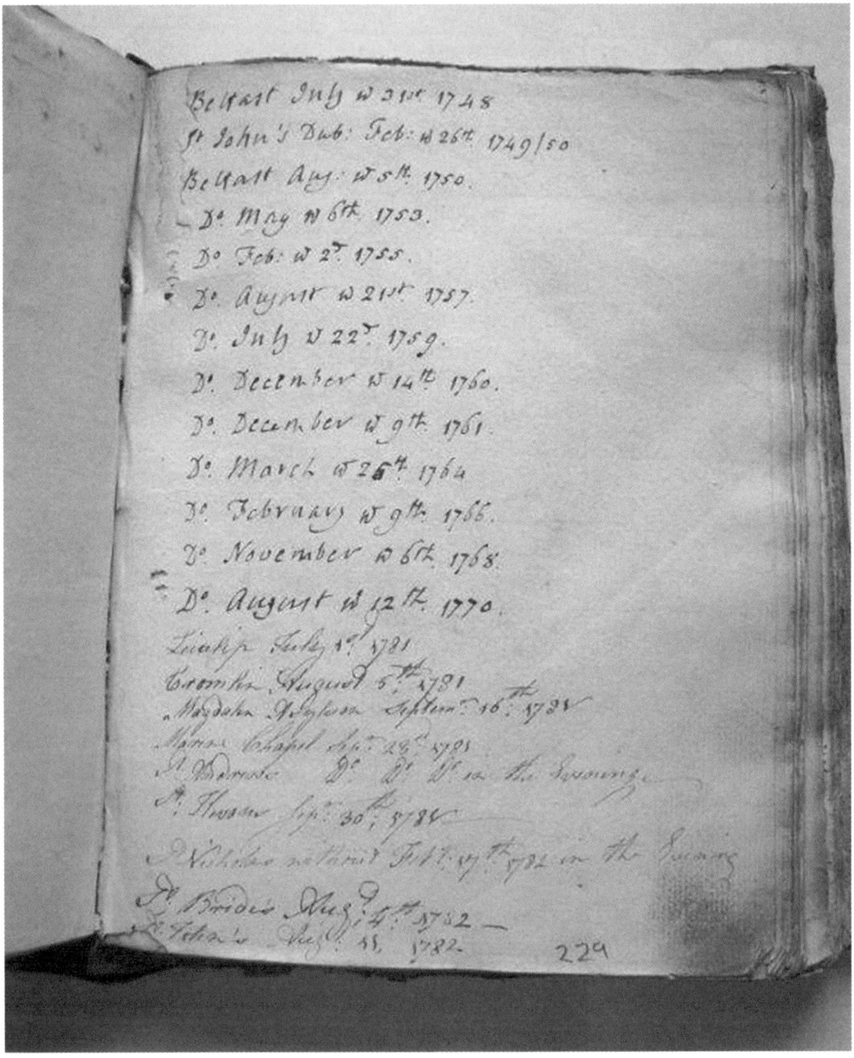
Belfast July ye 31st 1748
St John's Dub: Feb: ye 26th 1749/50
Belfast Aug: ye 5th 1750.
Do. May ye 6th 1753.
Do. Feb: ye 2d 1755.
Do. August ye 21st 1757.
Do. July ye 22d 1759.
Do. December ye 14th 1760.
Do. December ye 9th 1761.
Do. March ye 25th 1764
Do. February ye 9th 1766.
Do. November ye 6th 1768.
Do. August ye 12th 1770.
[illegible] July 1st 1781
Crumlin August 5th 1781
Magdalen Asylum Septemr 16th 1781
[illegible] Chapel Sept 23d 1781
St [illegible] Do. Do. Do. in the Evening
St Thomas Sept 30th 1781
[illegible] Feb 17th 1782 in the Evening
St Brides Aug 4th 1782
St [illegible] Aug 11 1782
229

5 Preaching list for Sermon XI (27) in the hands of James Saurin and his son.

[p. 231] In the Fifth Chapter of St. Paul's Second Epistle to the Corinthians & at the Tenth Verse

For we must all appear before the Judgement seat of Christ, that Every one may receive the things done in his body, according to that he hath done, whether it be Good or whether it be evil.

In the words now read unto you, we have a Summary Description of the last judgement, & an account of [p. 232] the Proceedings upon that great & terrible Day, The Certainty of our appearing in Judgement, The Judge before whom we are to appear The Universality of this judgment, & the Rule & measure of it, are the particulars contained in them, & shall therefore be the different & distinct heads of the following Discourse.

1st Part.

And the first Enquiry is concerning the Certainty of a Judgement to come, We must *all* appear before the Judgement seat of Christ, a Truth [p. 233] which how ever awful & terryfying is too well confirmed both by the Dictates of Human Reason, & the Declarations of Divine Wisdom, to be either doubted or called in Question. For if we look into the Nature of our Actions, we find an essential Distinction between them, arising from the natural & eternal Relation of things by which they become either Virtuous or Vitious, Good or evil. I shall not take up your time in proving this self evident truth, It is impossible for us not be very differently affected at the mention of a Generous or Cruel action, not to feel something [p. 234] applauding the one, & as loudly condemning the other, the Common sense of Mankind join in this, & however various their opinions in other matters may be, concur universally in admitting this first & fundamental principle of all Morality. Now if there be such an essential Difference between our actions, this Difference must be perceivable by the Supreme Being, or in other words, God distinguishes between good & evil, approves of the former, & is strongly displeased with the latter. And tho' there is an infinite disproportion between the [p. 235] Nature of God & the Nature of Man, yet since Virtue & Vice are grounded upon Immutable Relations, always the same in any given circumstances, the effects they produce in God, the approbation or disapprobation of the Action are the same in him, as they are in us, with this very material difference how-ever, that the Degree & quickness of them are proportioned to the Greatness of the Intelligent mind, in which they reside, whence it follows, that in an all Perfect & Almighty Being such as God is, they are not merely ideal &

notional, they do not terminate in a vain & fruitless speculation, they [p. 236] must be expressed by suitable rewards to the virtuous & suitable punishments to the Vitious. But the present Oeconomy of things, & the State of Man here on Earth, does not admitt of an immediate distribution of Good & evil, The Constitution of things is such, that did God render to every one according to his works upon the direct committal of them, the freedom of our actions would be greatly obstructed, & such a restraint put upon them, as would transform them into acts of mere compulsion & necessity. Hence <it> is that *reason why* we see the Virtuous often under oppression, whilst the Vitious [p. 237] prosper & triumph, & Hence are we enabled to infer this Conclusion, that what God does not do under the present Dispensation of things, he most certainly will do in a future & subsequent Period, & consequently that there shall be a signal & pompous Judgment to demonstrate the infinite rectitude of his Nature, & his invariable & immutable love of equity, order & regularity, This was the method, which the Royal Preacher pursued, He saw under the Sun, the place of judgment that wickedness was there, & the place of righteousness, that inquity was [p. 238] there,[229] He considered all the oppressions that are under the Sun, & beheld the tears of such as were oppressed, & on the side of their oppressions, there was power, but they had no Comforter,[230] & the *method* <way> he took to solve this objection, was a just one, I said in my heart, God shall judge the righteous & the wicked.[231]

2ndly. This truth is still further confirmed unto us by attending to what passes within ourselves, & to the principles of self-approbation, or [p. 239] self-condemnation, which we carry about us, & by which we must justly deem ourselves accountable Beings. We feel an inexpressible anguish & sorrow after the perpretation of some actions, which all the power & art of Men, all the Sophistry of Passion, all the Cunning of Appetite, can neither present, nor remove, & this for actions not cognisable by Human Judicature, not liable to Human Censures, not visible to any Human eye, but known only to ourselves, & to our own hearts. On the other hand we experience a pleasure, a satisfaction, a sincere & heartfelt joy, [p. 240] at the Consciousness of having done good & beneficent actions, tho' no present reward is expected for them tho' others are not acquainted with them, & tho' nothing contributes to impart this satisfaction to us, but the intrinsic satisfaction to us, but the intrinsic worth of the action, we have been happily engaged in.

And for what reason should God fix such a principle in our breasts, unless it were to make us sensible, that we are answerable to him for every thing we do? To what end this inward sentence, this Decree of our own Conscience, unless it be an intimation from [p. 241] God himself, that there is a Tribunal highly superior to any here below, before which we are to be brought, where this voice of Conscience shall be found to have spoke to purpose, & there Whispers of our own Hearts to be neither vain nor Delusive.

Yet strong as those arguments are in themselves, they are the result only of deep thought & reflection, & therefore would be very far from being thoroughly satisfactory to the Generality of Mankind, who want both capacity & leisure to consider them properly, had not the Divine Goodness graciously condescended [p. 242] in the 3rd place, to make a full & perfect Discovery of this great & important truth in the Revelation of his will by Jesus Christ.

It had indeed been hinted at in his former Dispensations to men, more obscurely at first under the Patriarchs, & the administration of Moses, by degrees opening to the World thro' the Ministry of the Prophets, & at last appearing in full splendour under the Gospel of our Lord & Saviour Jesus Christ. The words of the Text are express upon this head, & St. Paul preaching at Athens, & instructing that Superstitious [p. 243] People in the first principles of Religion, makes this a fundamental point, that God had appointed a Day, in the which he would judge the World,[232] & in another place declares, that God would bring to light the hidden things of darkness at his coming,[233] which by way of eminence is styled the Day the Great Day, that Day of the Lord.[234]

It were to no purpose to pursue this subject any further, We profess our solemn belief of it daily, with our mouth in the Recital of our Creed, & therefore taking it for granted that [p. 244] we are thoroughly convinced of the certainty of a Judgement to come, I shall proceed in the 2nd place to consider, who the Judge is, before whom we are to appear, We must appear before the Judgement seat of Christ.

2d Part

The right of judging originally was in God, He as our Creator and Father, our Supreme Lord & Governor to whom we owe all submission & obedience, had doubtless a power to bring us to his Tribunal & to call us [p. 245] to an account for our behaviour here, but this authority he has delegated to our Saviour Jesus Christ, as an Act of that Regal power, which he is now exercising over those, whom he hath redeemed by the shedding of his own blood, The Father judgeth no Man, but hath committed all Judgement unto the Son.[235]

And admirably well-qualified is this Sacred Person for so solemn & important an Office, As Partaker of the Divine Essence, he knows the inmost secrets of men's hearts he can view the principle, upon which [p. 246] he acts, No motive ever so remote that can escape his notice, No thought ever so concealed but what he knoweth <it> altogether,[236] And as Cloathed once with Human Nature, he is sensible of our frailties weaknesses & Imperfections, he has a compassionate condescension for our frequent slips & offences, & as he himself was in all things tempted, like as we are, not without sin,[327] he can best be touched with the feeling of our infirmities, & make proper & suitable allowances for them, So adorable is the Mercy of God in Thus appointing our Redeemer to be our Judge, with whom every [p. 247] Good Man is sure to meet acceptance, every Sincere Penitent pardon and forgiveness.

3^{d} Part.

The 3^{d} particular contained in the words of the Text, is the Universality of this Judgment, intimated by this expression, We must all appear.

There is then no Distinction of rank or Dignity to take place, every condition is to be upon a level & every Man to stand before his God, with no other support but what the integrity of his own heart can give him, The [p. 248] Great & Mighty disrobed of their vain pageantry & grandeur, shall be jumbled & confounded with the lowest & meanest of Men, whilst those estimated only by their real & intrinsic worth, shall appear with equal confidence before that God, who is no Respecter of Persons, & who in every Nation, & in every condition, accepted him, that feareth him & worketh righteousness.[238]

For tho' the Distinctions of this World be indeed highly useful to answer the ends & purposes of Human Society, yet is it manifest [p. 249] that those are *but* <only> accidental & arbitrary differences, fitted to the present State of Mankind, & absolutely to cease with this, but still an equality is preserved in other respects, sufficient to shew the end & Destination of all Men to be the same. Hence are they all alike made dependant upon God, all alike subject to his laws, all furnished with means of instruction to direct their conduct, all inwardly conscious of having done good or evil, all equally flattered with the hopes of a reward, or allarmed with the apprehension of punishment, This [p. 250] evinces that the Design of God was to create Men for a future existence, & since a General Judgement is preparatory to this, that what proves the necessity of it with regard to some, equally does so with regard to all.

And this is confirmed by Revelation, St. John in his Prophetic Description of a future Judgement, declares this expressly, I saw says he, the Dead, both small & great, Stand before God, And the Sea gave up the Dead which were in it, & Death & Hell delivered up the Dead, which [p. 251] were in them,[239] O[ur] B[lessed] S[aviour] assures us, that the Son of Man shall sit upon his Throne, & before him shall be gathered all Nations,[240] & St. Paul charges Timothy before him, who is ordained to be the Judge of quick & dead,[241] which expression of Quick, being some what of a doubtful signification, & capable of being misunderstood, the Apostle in his Epistle to the Thesselonians gives the meaning of it to us himself, by explaining it of those only, who shall be found living upon Earth at the time of our Lord's second Coming, & who being expressly [p. 252] said to be caught up together in the clouds to meet the Lord in the air,[242] prove beyond doubt, that all the Inhabitants of this World shall be indiscriminately dealt with, & none of them exempted from that General & universal Judgement, which is to be the end & final Consummation of the present frame & Constitution of things.

And this brings me to the last particular to be spoken to, the Rule of this Judgement & the measure to be observed in it, that every one may receive the things done in his [p. 253] body, according to that he hath done, whether it be good, or whether it be evil.[243]

4th Part.

And a Rule of the greatest exactness & equity this is, tending to demonstrate, that God doth not require where he hath not sown, nor expect to gather, where he hath not strawed,[244] but that he deals out good or evil to his creatures in proportion to the good or evil of their actions, & so make their happiness or misery here-after to depend entirely upon themselves [p. 254] & their own endeavours.

Our Actions, our Behaviour in our respective Stations & circumstances, our whole Conduct, the most secret thoughts, as well as the most new Actions, all the words of our mouths, all the Devices of our hearts, sifted & enquired into, in proportion to our knowledge & the means of Instruction attended unto us, are to be the Subjects of this trial, & to determine our eternal boon, to happiness or misery, As many as have sinned without law, shall perish without law, & as many as have sinned in the law, shall be judged by the law,[245] They who had nothing to [p. 255] direct them but the Law of Reason, shall be accountable for their actions no further than as they were conformable or not to that Law, whilst those who lived under a Higher

Oeconomy, whilst Christians who heed the greatest assistances & the best means to improve in virtue & Moral goodness, shall be proportionally examined & their good works be more conspicuously rewarded, or their vices & transgressions more severely & exquisitely punished.

And with what Ineffable joy shall they be filled, who upon this tremendous occasion shall find their conduct agreeable to & approved by God, who in this solemn assembly, where all the Glory & power of [p. 256] the Divine Being shall be so *beyond expression* <astonishingly> displayed, shall see the Severity of a Judge melted down into the favour & compassion of an Indulgent Father, who in the presence of Angels, & Archangels, & of all the triumphant Host of Heaven, shall receive Commendation & Applause, & in consequence of this be put in full & future possession of a happiness so *complete* stable, that no Accidents from without can possibly interrupt it, so real & perfect as to transcend the highest stretch of our Imagination, so durable & lasting, that the power of time <itself> can neither Lessen nor exhaust it.

But if such be the joy arising in the virtuous & Good Man's [p. 257] breast, what Intolerable Anguish must possess the hearts of those unhappy Men, to whom all this Pomp, this Glory, this Splendor of the Divine Being appears full of terror & dismay, who can neither look up to God for pardon, nor within themselves for excuses & pleas in extenuation of their guilt, who felt the stings of their Conscience confirming the Voice of their incensed God, & the whole Army of Heaven, joining in & bespeaking their condemnation & punishment, They would then willingly stray unto the Mountains to fall on them & to the Rocks to hide them,[246] & by crushing them to pieces, to reduce them to their [p. 258] primitive nothing, but the Scheme of God's providence require's that they should continue lasting Monuments of his Justice & of the fatal effects of transgression & disobedience, I beheld saith St. John in *his Prophetic description of the last judgement* <the 6th Chapter of his Revelations>, I beheld, when he hath opened the sixth Seal, & lo! there was a great Earthquake, & the Sun became black as sack cloth of hair, & the Moon became as Blood, And the Stars of Heaven fell unto the Earth. Even as the fig tree casteth her untimely figs, when she is shaken of a mighty wind, And the Heavens departed as a [p. 259] Scrowl, when it is rolled together, & every Mountain & Island were moved out of their places, And the Kings of the Earth, the Great men, & the Rich Men, & the Chief Captains, & the mighty Men, & every sound man & every free Man hid themselves in the dens, & in the rocks of the Mountains, And said to the Mountains & rocks, Fall on us, & hide us from the face of him, that sitteth on the Throne, from the wrath of the Lamb, For the Great day of his wrath is come, [p. 260] who shall be able to stand?[247]

Applic[ation]:

The Inferences from this Discourse are many & obvious.

Is there a time appointed for the judging of the World? Then Let us refer to this Great Day all our doubts & scruples concerning the Wisdom of Providence in the Administration of things below, whatever Irregularities we any imagine we see in it's conduct, whatever probable contradiction we may think to discover in it, or what ever advantage the promiscuous distribution of good & evil may furnish [p. 261] the Adversaries of God's Providence with, a Universal Judgment is at hand to set all things right, to vindicate his ways, to give to every Man a just & due recompence, & to fix the Immutable Attributes of God's equity & Justice upon the strongest & most unexceptionable grounds.

Is there a Day appointed for the Judging of the World? Then Let us judge nothing before the time, Instead of peircing with an indiscreet & uncharitable curiosity into the views & secret motives of other Persons actions, & rashly censuring what we neither can, nor do know, Let us leave them to the Determination of him, who judgeth righteously, & patiently [p. 262] wait till he himself vouchsafe to bring them to light, in the Day, <u>when he shall judge the Secrets of Men by Jesus Christ</u>,[248] They will then appear in their true & proper colours, without prejudice to mislead or private Interest to warp our judgment, & what now draws down our censure & reproof shall perhaps be found consistent with the strictest prudence & to deserve our highest praise & commendation.

Is there a Day appointed for the judging of the World? Then Let us bear with patience the troubles & afflictions of this life. Tho' Slander & Detractions at present wound & torment us, tho' Misery oppression wrack & consume us, or Sorrow [p. 263] & Adversity be our bitter & wretched portion here, the Time is coming, when our Integrity & Virtue shall be publickly acknowledged & made known, when every one that is <u>ryghteous, shall eat the fruit of his</u> own <u>doings</u>,[249] when a Just & Good God shall condescend to look himself into our real characters, & to assign to every one of us the proper & becoming station.

Lastly and Chiefly. Is there a day appointed for the judging of the World? Then Let us often bring this Great, this important Transaction to our Rememberance, suppose ourselves standing before God's Tribunal, summoned to give an account [p. 264] of our Actions & to <u>receive according to that we have done, whether it be good or whether it be evil.</u>

And if this was our Case, Could we stand with confidence, Could we answer with assurance; when Examined concerning the use, which we have made of the good things of life, Could we shew them to have been used with moderation or dispensed with discretion? Could our riches & wealth be shewn to have cloathed the naked, relieved the oppressed, & comforted the afflicted? Could our influence & authority be seen directing to virtue, discountenancing vice, giving shelter & protection to the Virtuous, or [p. 265] Could, every Talent we have received appear to have been exercised to the purposes for which it was intended, the Glory of God & the Good of Mankind.

When examined concerning the use which we have made of our time, Could we shew it to have been managed with care & spent with prudence, Could we say that we have considered it as the only season allowed us to work out our own salvation, & consequently that we have been as frugal managing of it, as the value & importance of such a treasure required.

When in a word called upon to give an account of our Improvement under the many Religious advantages, which we enjoy, Could [p. 266] our Hearts bear witness to us, that they have produced the designed effect? Would our lives & Conversation shine with a Lustre proportioned to the clearness & perspicuity the light afforded us to walk by, & Should we be as much distinguished from all others by the purity & holiness of our manners, as we have been by the purity & perfection of the Religion which we have professed.

The Consideration of a judgement to come practically improved by this manner, would fill & prepare us for it, & by giving us a true knowledge of ourselves, it would furnish us with desirable opportunity of amending our conduct, & of improving daily in virtue [p. 267] & goodness.

The Universal Judgement of the World may indeed be very far off, but the Day of account for each Individual is very near many, & at no great distance from any of us, Death fixes our eternal doom instantly, Beyond the Grave, there is no Device, no knowledge, no atonement for sin, It then concerns us to work the work of him that sent us, while it is day,[250] that when it shall please God to take us to himself, we may stand before him with joyful & well grounded hope, & so receive from the mouth of our Judge this comfortable & enlivening Sentence, Well done thou Good & faithful Servant, enter thou into the Joy of the Lord.[251]

Now to God the Father & son & Holy Ghost be ascribed all power, might, majesty & dominion now & forevermore.[252]

Sermon XII

Volume 3 (28)

[p. 268] Belfast on Christmas day 1748
Ditto on Christmas day 1750
Ditto on Christmas day 1753
Ditto on Christmas day 1759
Ditto on Christmas day 1762
Ditto on Christmas day 1767

[p. 269] In the First Chapter of the Gospel by St. John & at the fourteenth Verse.

We beheld his Glory, the Glory as of the only Begotten of the Father.

It hath been objected to the Religion of Christ, that the Author of it was a Person of a low & mean appearance, that he had no form or comeliness, no beauty that we should desire him,[253] that he was void of all outward pomp & glory, without wealth to recommend *him*, without Worldly honours to support him, or any dazzling distinctions to engage the attention of Men, & therefore that he little appeared like a Messenger sent down from Heaven to reveal the will of God, & to publish to [p. 270] the World the glad tidings of a new & a more excellent dispensation.

Against an objection of this kind so pernicious in it's consequences, I shall endeavour to arm you by enumerating some of the most *emminent &* striking particulars *that* <which> constitute the Glory of Christ, not a Glory, like that which the World falsely calls so, & by attending to which, our judgment is misled, but a Glory suited to, & befitting him *that* <who> was the only Begotten of the Father, full of Grace & truth. Come then my Brethren, with silent wonder & admiration, behold upon this Day the Glory of your Redeemer, See it issuing forth out of the mists & clouds, *that* <which> intercept it from your view, till at last it appears in perfect splendor, carrying with it both conviction & improvement.

[p. 271] But before I descend to a particular account of the Glory of Christ, it is proper to explain what is meant by this expression, the only Begotten of the father, as it seems to denote some thing peculiar to Christ, by which his Birth is distinguished from that of all other Men, & to so singular & eminent an appellation, he has a just & undoubted claim, preferably to all the Sons of Men, both upon account of his Human, & of his Divine Nature. With respect to his Human Nature, he was wonderfully & miraculously born, He derived his Being from a pure & spotless Virgin, The Holy Ghost came upon her, & the Glory of the Highest overshadowed her, therefore also was that Holy thing, which was born of her [p. 272] called the Son of God,[254] His second Birth was equally extraordinary, when his soul & body were after death vitally re-united, & made a living substance, according to that which is written, that he was appointed the Son of God with power by his Resurrection from the Dead,[255] & being after this highly exalted, he as a son entered into his father's house & became Heir of all things.[256] With respect to his Divine Essence, he has still a higher right to be called the only begotten of the Father; For he is of the same Nature with God, being the brightness of his father's Glory, & the express image of his Person, In the beginning was the word, & the Word was with God, & the Word was God,[257] he partakes of the Incommunicable Attributes of God, being [p. 273] coeval with & from all Eternity like unto him, I am Alpha & Omega, the first & the last,[258] which are expressions peculiarly ascribed to God himself by the P[rophet] Isaiah, I the Lord the first, & with the last I am he, I am the first, & I am the last, & besides me there is no God,[259] to which O[ur] B[lessed] S[aviour]'s description of himself particularly refers, I am Alpha & Omega, the beginning & the ending, saith the Lord, which is, & which was, & which is to come.[260] His Power is equal to that of God, All things were made by him, & without him was not any thing made that was made,[261] for by him were all things created, that are in Heaven, & that are in Earth, visible & invisible, whether they be Thrones, or Dominions, or Principalities, or Powers, all things were created by him & for him & he is before all [p. 274] things, & by him all things consist.[262]

[p. 275] His knowledge is boundless & infinite like that of God, He needed not Saith St. John that any should testyfy of man, for he himself knew what was in Man, & all things are naked & opened unto the eyes of him with whom we have to do,[263] And to Sum up all, His Presence is said to be as extensive & immense as that of God, Where two or three are gathered together in my Name, there am I in the midst,[264] upon all which different accounts it is that this Divine Essence is honoured & adored with the same worship that is paid to God, himself & all Men are required to honour the Son, even as they honour the Father.[265]

Well may we then expect to find this Divine Person endued with Glory with a Glory as of the only Begotten of the Father, full of Grace & truth, What the different [p. 276 blank, p. 277] particulars are which constitute & form <this Glory>, is the next & principal thing I mean to speak to.

2d Part.

It would perhaps be more consistent with the Design of the Evangelist to refer the Glory here spoken of, to the *simple* <particular> instance of O[ur] B[lessed] S[aviour]'s Transfiguration on the Mount, in presence of St. Peter, St. James & St. John, when the fashion of his countenance was altered, his raiment became white & glittering, and Moses & Elias appeared to bear witness to his authority & mission.[266] But *however this may be* <whether it were so or not>, I shall for the present consider the Subject in general, & shall endeavour to illustrate O[ur] B[lessed] S[aviour]'s Glory in the *five* <2 or 3> following instances>, *1st. In that series of Prophecies & Predictions which preceded his appearance, 2* 1st. In the particular & extraordinary Circumstances which accompanied his Nativity, 2nd. In the Greatness [p. 278] & power of his Miracles, *4th* 3rd. In the *glory* <lustre> of his life & Conversation, & Lastly in the Glorious Victory <which> he obtained over Death & the Grave by his Resurrection & Ascension.

1st. The Glory of Christ is visible in that series <continued chain> of Prophecies & Predictions, which preceded his appearance.

How numerous so ever these were, how early their Publication, how frequent & repeated Christ was the end of them, Christ their chief & only object, To him says the Apostle, give all the Prophets witness,[267] & in him do all their words & Predictions center; From the very Infancy of the World to the day of his appearance, one Prophet followed another, publishing his birth, proclaiming his Glory, displaying his dignity & power, The whole Jewish *nation* Dispensation had him, & only him in view, Their numerous Ceremonies feasts & ordinances [p. 279] their various Rites & Customs, their different Sacrifices & Lustrations for sin, were obscure yet striking intimations of that Redeemer, who was to come into the World, & who for many ages was the desire of all Nations,[268] & justly considered as the Consolation of Israel.[269]

Hence did this knowledge spread & gather strength by degrees, & the expectation of a Messiah gain new force in proportion as they drew near the appointed Period, Then do these Inspired Men fix the exact time of his Coming, determine the place of his Nativity, declare his family & Parentage, explain the Nature of his Office, the Blessings of his Ministry, & the Glorious State of his Spiritual Kingdom, & this in such sublime strains of unaffected Oratory, as exactly correspond with the Dignity of the Subject they had before them & fully shew the Divine power by which they were *wrought* <dictated>.

[p. 280] Now what true & real Glory was <there> in this! *To be the object of Men's best & most ardent desires, to be celebrated as the principal instrument of good to Mankind, to employ the pen of Men & of Angels, during a Succession of ages, is surely one instance of the Glory of Christ, worthy of the only Begotten of the Father, &* highly becoming him who was the brightness of his Father's Glory & the express image of his Person.[270]

Nor were the Circumstances which attended his appearance & which were mentioned as the *2d* 1st instance of the Glory of Christ, less remarkable, than the Prophecies & Predictions *that attended* <which preceded> it.

For as if Nature was then at work to produce something most wonderful & surprising, A multitude of Prodigies appeared, A Messenger of a High Nature, John the Baptist one of whom it was [p. 281] expressly said, that a Greater was not born of a Woman, was purposely sent & commissioned to usher in his appearance, Prepare ye the way of the Lord, make his paths straight, Animated with the Spirit of Elias he publishes his Supreme Dignity & honour, He that cometh after me, is mightier than I, whose shoes I am not worthy to bear,[271] A Star of an unusual make & splendour awakes the attention of Skilful & intelligent Men, & brings them from distant parts of the World, to worship & adore him, whom they falsely thought was intended for an Earthly Monarch,[272] And whilst this Infant lay in obscurity, wrapped up on swaddling cloaths lying in a Manger, neglected & unobserved, do a numerous Host of Angels sing aloud his praise, & proclaim the glad Tiding of his Birth in this noble & pious Hymn, [p. 282] Glory be to God in the Highest, in Earth peace Good will towards Men,[273] And that God himself might shew his complacency in this Supreme Being, & thereby add to his Majesty & honour, when he was entering upon his Office, & solemnly taking upon himself the Ministry, unto which he was appointed, by submitting to the Sacrament of Baptism, as he was coming out of the water, the Heavens were opened, the Spirit of God descended on him as in the form of a Dove, the emblem of innocence & meekness, & the Voice of God himself was heard saying, This is my Beloved Son, in whom I am well pleased.[274]

Could any Circumstances be thought of stronger than these, to illustrate his Glory & the Superior Dignity of his Nature? Was there ever a Birth accompanied with more real pomp & Lustre, or Is any Glory [p. 283] like unto his Glory.

But *3d* <2nd> Christ Jesus manifests his own Glory & Majesty in the Infinite & boundless power, *that* <which> attended his Miracles.

What a Miracle is, we all know, Any Action *that* <which> exceeds the power of Nature, or *that* <which> cannot be brought about by the known laws of *it* <Nature>, bespeaks one *that* <who> is Superior to Nature, & who can control & over rule it at pleasure, & in this respect how Great is the Glory of Christ!

All Nature appears subject to his command, He rebukes the winds & the Sea, & they instantly obey his voice, He restrains, subdues, conquers, the most inveterate & obstinate Diseases, He restores the blind to their sight, the dumb to their speech, the lame to their feet, & what no Human power could possibly do, what the force of Imagination [p. 284] could never persuade one to believe, nor the strongest Enthusiasm effect, He raises up to life, those who had been for some days *dead* <grave> & *already* <who> carried about them *the* <visable> marks of putrefaction & Decay.

And these wonders did he *effect* <perform>, & these prodigies accomplish, not by any borrowed authority, but by a word of his mouth, by the touch of his Garment, by the slightest intimation of his pleasure & good will, Other Prophets had a delegated authority by which they acted, but Christ acts of himself, the Divine Energy joined to & accompanying his Human Nature, enabled him to exert a power superior to every thing besides, & to excite the wonder & astonishment of Men, by the constant repetition of new & extraordinary Deeds.

4th 3rd. Let us view the Glory of Christ in his Life & Conversation, & in that [p. 285] assemblage of the most eminent & transcendent virtues which *composed* <formed> & adorned his character.

If the possession of some virtues tho' mixed & blended with several frailties & imperfections, gives a Glory & Lustre to Human personages, How *full of* Glor*y*<ious> must he be, who possesses them all pure & unsullied, who carries them to the highest degree of improvement, they *are capable* <can possibly admit>, & who never defaces or obscures them by any indiscreet or unguarded step.

Is there a Glory in condescending to the wants & infirmities of others, in endeavouring to remove the mistakes of the prejudiced, to correct the errors of the rambling, & to fetch them home *to the flock of God* <to the Shepherd or Bishop of their souls>, Behold the Blessed Jesus, breathing the most affectionate Charity, descending from the height of his power to adapt himself to the necessities [p. 286] of Men, employing his time in works of Compassion & pity, his preaching in promoting the valuation of Mankind, his ease & quiet in the advancement of their temporal & eternal happiness.

Is there a Glory in making the honour of God, the end of all our actions? Behold the Blessed Jesus maintaining, advancing, furthering the growth & encrease of it, What constancy in his publick & private Devotion, what exalted sentiments of the Deity, what strains of the highest & most enlightened piety appear in all his Discourses.

Is there a Glory in submitting one's self to the will of God, in patiently enduring what he is pleased to inflict upon us, & in owning & acknowledg*e*<ing> ourselves under his power & Dominion? Behold the Blessed Jesus in the midst of the greatest trials, [p. 287] preserving a mind ever calm & serene, betraying no signs of murmuring or impatience, encouraging himself from the consideration of the justice & wisdom of God, *& resolving* leaving the issue of things to his determination & disposal, O Lord not my Will but thine be done.[275]

In a word. Is there a Glory in *being eminently trancendently virtuous, in* uniting in one's self every virtuous & Religious perfection? Behold the Blessed Jesus in entire possession of them all, exhibiting to the World the brightest pattern of Virtue that had ever been seen, adding one Grace to another & to each virtue the highest Lustre they were susceptible of.

5th. But in Vain had the Glory of Christ by the Heavenly Host, [p. 288] in vain had numerous Miracles *confirmed & illustrated it* <bore witness to it>, in vain had his bright example shone thro', & enlightened the World, if he had remained in the power of his Enemies, & an ignominious Death <had> been the close & conclusion of his Life, whence as the last indication of the Glory of the only Begotten of the Father I mentioned the Conquest he obtained over Death, & the powers of the Grave by his Resurrection & Ascension.

The low State of Humiliation, in which his Suffering & Death had shewn him, seemed indeed but little connected with the former Scenes of power & authority, in which he had been so remarkably conspicuous, To see him, who a while before over-ruled Nature with an unlimited power, now arraigned before an unjust Tribunal, the butt of Calumny & malice, suffering whatever Cruel & blood [p. 289] thirsty Men could contrive most ignominious & painful, was without doubt the matter of amazement to all his faithfull Servants, & might well stagger the hopes of the most confident & zealous.

But when they saw him after a few days, rising up to Life again, in spite of all their endeavours, bafling & disappointing all their contrivances, controlling by his power the effects of Death itself. When they saw him for forty days, standing in the midst of that People, who a while before had laid him in a Sepulchre, undeniably & unquestionably dead, shewing himself alive to them & many infallible signs. When in the issue of things, Some of them saw him visibly ascending into Heaven, the Clouds opening to receive their Lord, & all of them perceived the effects of his Glorious Ascension by the miraculous powers & gifts he shed down [p. 290] upon them, What new & additional manifestation was this of his Glory & Majesty? What could possibly alter this darken & obscure it or leave any doubt remaining, but that he was the Son of God with power, the only Begotten of the Father, whose Glory they all beheld of Grace & Truth.

Applic[ation]:

And now If the Glory of our Redeemer is such as we have seen it is, How absurd is it to take exception at Christianity merely <upon> account of the apparent meanness of him, who preached it.

For if the Doctrines of Christianity [p. 291] be in themselves reasonable, & every way worthy of the God who published them, if the Precpets it enjoins, the Observance of conduce as much to the happiness of every Individual, as they do to the welfare & advantage of Civil Society in general, If the motives & sanctions, by which they are bound upon us, be of that infinite weight & importance, as to make the most lasting impression upon every considerate & thinking mind, Is the nature of them changed, or the truth & usefulness of them the less, because they are not ushered in with all the Parades of Human Greatness, or the exterior splendour of Worldly pomp & Glory, Such dazzling appearances are of no value [p. 292] in the sight of him who is no respecter of ranks or Persons,[276] who purposely chooses the weak things of the World, to confound the things that are mighty,[277] & who puts the inestimable treasures of his Wisdom & knowledge in Earthen Vessels, in order to shew the Excellency of their power to be of him & not of Man,[278] that so, no flesh should glory in his presence, but that all should own & acknowledge, that however Christ crucified may be unto the Jews a stumbling block & unto the Greeks foolishness, not unto them which are called, both Jews & Gentiles, Christ is the power of God, & the Wisdom of God.[279]

[p. 293] 2nd. If the Glory of our Redeemer be such, as we have seen it is, Let those unhappy men justly fear & tremble, who slight & condemn it, who view it with coldness & indifference, who are neither awed into Obedience by the splendor, nor deferred from sin by the Greatness & irresistible power of it.

For whatever the season of levity & passion, or the principles of a vain Philosophy may suggest to them, not a second Coming of the same Omnipotent Being, is speedily to be looked for when the immensity of his power, will no longer be employed, as it was of old, in the operations of new Miracles to effect their Conversion, but in the punishment of their transgressions, not as here to fore, in Invitations to mercy but in Denunciations of Wrath, [p. 294] not in proclaiming pardon, but in consigning them over to Death & condemnation.

And when that tremendous Day comes, will they dare to face that power, which they have so wantonly set at nought? Will they *then* dare to appear before that pure Holy Being, who loathes & detests their iniquity? Can they see him coming down from Heaven, in flaming fire, to make vengeance on them, that obey not the Gospel of Jesus Christ, & not cry unto the Mountains & unto the Rocks, to fall on them, & to hide them from the face of him, that sitteth on the throne, & from the wrath of the Lamb, for the Great day of his wrath is come, & who is able to stand.[280]

[p. 295] *given over to eternal Death and condemnation*[281]

3rd. If such be the Glory of our Redeemer, Let *those who profess to believe in him* rely *upon his* in full confidence upon his mighty aid & support; The same power which he shewed upon Earth, the same Glory which rested upon him, the same holy & virtuous Dispositions *that* <which> added so distinguished a Lustre to his character; subsist still, & are the pledge & earnest of the performance of his Gracious promises to us, tho' for a time he should seem to hide his face from us. Tho' Afflictions should try our patience, or doubts stagger our faith, Tho' Errors should overspread the truth, & superstition & Bigottry deface his Church, yet he that promises is faithfull; he <who> will not suffer us to be tempted above that we are able, who will lead us out of the furnace of Affliction, *he will* guide us with his council, after that receive us up in to Glory,[282] The heathen may furiously rage together, & the people imagine vain things, The Kings of the Earth stand up, & the Rulers take counsil [p. 296] together against the Lord & against his Anointed, but He that dwelleth in Heaven, shall laugh them to scorn, the Lord shall have them in derision.[283]

Finally and to Conclude. If such be the Glory of Christ, Let us be very careful to observe the vows <which> we make, & the engagements which we lay ourselves under to him.

This Day is generally a Day for pious purposes, & hearty resolution of amendment, the Sacrament of the Lord's Supper, of which we *intend* <are going> to be Partakers, employs at present our thoughts & attention, It engages us to look back upon our past ways, to reflect upon our past mis-carriages, to bewail our unworthiness, to implore the pardon & forgiveness of God; upon our sincere & Speedy amendment.

And no doubt such Religious meditations as these are some of the chief ends which tho' Communion of the body & blood of Christ was splendid to answer, no doubt they are the proper dispositions of those, who attend upon this solemn & awful Act of worship.

[p. 297] But still much of our work is left unfinished, much is wanting on our part, to carry these good purposes into execution, & to shew our sin-cerity by fixed & settled habits of virtue & goodness; *If we believe (& we have seen that we know the most undoubted to do so)* If we believe that Christ was endued with infinite power, during his appearance upon Earth, & still continues invested with the Highest Majesty Dominion, we must believe *him* <that he is> able to know & judge of the sincerity of our hearts, We must believe *him* <that he is> able to know, whether we fulfill exactly the engagements we enter into, we must believe that he is able & ready to punish & afflict us, if we do not.

Let us *therefore* cherish such a thought, & by cherishing, let us endeav-our to *render* <make> it useful & profitable to ourselves, Let us vow an entire & unfeigned obedience to God, but in vowing it, Let us use our utmost efforts to *make it* perfect & compleat <it>, Let us as the Redeemed of the Lord walk worthy of the vocation where with we are called;[284] This is the way *to make* <for> [p. 298] our present Devotion to come up as a Memorial before God. This is the way to secure to ourselves the blessings if that Dispensation under which we live, and This & this only is the way, to render ourselves worthy of being one day, admitted into the presence of that Supreme Being, whose Glory & Radiancy we now see, thro' a Glass darkly, but which we shall then see face to face, whom now we only know in part, but when we shall then know, even as we are known,[285] whom Clouds & Darkness may possibly now hide from our eyes, but who shall then appear to be the true light, that lighteth the World,[286] & the lasting Glory of his People Israel.[287]

To which Blessed Saviour & etc.

Sermon XIII

Volume 3 (29)

[p. 299] Preached at Belfast Upon the Peace in 1749[288]
Ps 30. 11–12

[p. 300] In the Thirtieth Psalm at the Eleventh and Twelfth Verses.

Thou hast turned for me my mourning into dancing, thou hast put off my Sack-cloth & guided me with gladness.

To the End that my Glory may sing praise to thee & not be silent; O Lord my God I will give thanks unto thee for ever.

We are this Day solemnly assembled by the Wisdom & authority of our Governors to celebrate the goodness of Almighty God in his seasonable deliverance of these Nations from the Dangers & Calamities with which they were threatened; All Ranks & Degrees of People are now summoned to send up their praises & thanksgiving to Heaven & to acknowledge with one heart & voice the mercy of God in putting an end to the Ware in which we [p. 301] were engaged, & removing those just & dreadful apprehensions, with which this Messenger of God's wrath is always attended.

In pursuance then of such a Design I shall at this present time endeavour to lay before you the different Calamities & dangers to which we were exposed during the continuance of the late War, & by setting our present situation in opposition to these, endeavour to shew you our mourning turned into dancing, & our sackcloth laid aside for the pleasing girdle of gladness, that from this consideration our Glory may sing praise to God, & not be silent, & every Individual among us join with David I in this devout Ejaculation, O Lord my God I will give thanks unto thee for ever.

[p. 302] 1st Part

First. I am to Lay before you the different Calamities & dangers to which we were exposed during the Continuance of the late War, & by setting our present situation in opposition to *our past and preceeding one* <these>, endeavour to shew you our mourning turned into dancing & our sack-cloth laid aside for the pleasing girdles of gladness.

And Here it may perhaps be thought absurd & improper to talk of mourning and sack-cloth to the Inhabitants of this Kingdom, whom God was graciously pleased during this time of trouble & confusion to cover with his shield & buckler, & to exempt from the immediate distresses of War, whilst he so plentifully inflicted them *in full measure* upon their nearest & most intimate neighbours.[289] We have been preserved unmolested & undisturbed. [p. 303] No Enemy has been ravaging our Country, no cry of force & oppression has been heard in our Streets, no destroying Angel has been sent to smite us in our houses. And this contrary to the expectations of the most sanguine, against all human appearances, in a Kingdom full of Men, whose principles make them avow our destruction, & whose zeal generally carries them beyond the bounds of prudence, even beyond a regard to their own interest & advantage.

But as true as this is, & as fitt a subject for our continual praise & thanksgiving, the Danger however remote was gradually advancing towards us, & the Flame that was wasting our neighbouring Kingdom would soon have spread amongst us & involved us in the same destruction; One Interest unites us to them, Our safety is inseparable from theirs. A common Cause engaged our [p. 304] attention & solicitude, The Invaluable Blessings that were at stake as much concerned us as they possibly could do them, & therefore we may well consider ourselves as sharers in the same dangers & calamities, & the miseries & distresses that were impending upon them, as equally impending upon us. Let us then *enquire what these were & the different reasons we had to mourn & put on sack cloth during the continuance of the Late War* <take a view of these>, that by *comparing our part with* <setting> our present situation <in opposition to them, ye better> we may see our Lamentation turned into dancing & our sackcloth laid aside for the <pleasing> Girdle of Gladness.

The 1st. I shall mention was the disturbance of our Domestic peace & quiet by an unnatural Rebellion which for a long time roused our fears & filled us with unspeakable anxiety & anguish. The Rememberance of this is still fresh in your minds, & the memory of it too new to need any repetition. A number of unhappy [p. 305] deluded Subjects drawn from their

Allegiance to [p. 306] *their King* < a Prince> by whose bounty & goodness many of them were supported, regardless of the solemn ties of honour Conscience & Duty by which they were bound, unmoved at the consideration of the miseries they were bringing upon their Country, conspired to destroy it, & at the time we least expected threatened us with immediate destruction. A few weeks produced a most dreadful scene, Citizens against Citizens, Country men against Country men, Brothers against Brothers, unsheathing the sword & mercilessly dipping it in the blood of each other, Foreign Powers exciting & feeding the Rebellious disposition of the People, & taking advantage of the *slavery* <baseness> of some & the treachery of others to promote & advance their ends, Cities & Towns opening their Gates to receive the Enemy, & by a strange & unaccountable infatuation, hugging & in appearance pleased with [p. 307] the Chains that were tendered out to them.

In this urging extremity we saw our Armies obliged to leave the most advantageous posts, upon the preservation of which depended the wellfare and being of States & Nations to fly to the relief of their oppressed Country, We saw our friends & Relations exposed to the malice & Cruelty of these implacable Men, contending with a rigorous season & a relentless foe, We saw our Illustrious Prince undauntedly standing in the Breach, hazarding his valuable Person to the chances of a Civil war to< preserve> our liberties & restore our quiet.[290] We saw our whole happiness depend upon the success of one Battle,[291] & the fate of these Kingdoms turn upon one & a single Blow.

Then was it that every heart was truly pained, & every eye dim, fearfulness & trembling came upon us, & an horrible dread over-whelmed [p. 309] us till that ever memorable Day, in which God himself appeared on our side and stretched out his powerful arm to our assistance, in which he enabled one Man to chase a thousand,[292] & a hundred to set ten thousand to flight,[293] in which he put his hook into our Adversarie's nose & his Bridle into their lips, & turned them back by the way in which they came;[294] A day which <at once> crushed Rebellion in *its head which enabled us* <the midst of it's highest expectation> to finish & compleat the work we now commemorate,[295] Which restored ease and tranquillity to our troubled & affrighted hearts, which furnished us with means to[296] whereby factions & Seditious Men are deprived of all opportunities of exercising their restless & turbulent dispositions *by which* <whereby> the counsils & devices of the wicked are destroyed & defeated, and our Domestic peace and quiet happily placed beyond the reach & power of our inveterate & most envenomed foes.

[p. 310] *Finish & compleat the work, whose Success we this day commemorate, which deprives factions & Rebellious Men of all opportunities of exercising their turbulent dispositions, which destroys the counsil & devices of the wicked, & gives us rational promising hopes of having our Domestic quiet secured & placed beyond the reach & power of our inveterate and envenomed foes. <finish & compleat the work, whose success we this day commemorate, which deprives factions & Rebellious Men of all opportunities of exercising their turbulent dispositions, which destroys the counsil & devices of the wicked, & gives us rational & promising hopes of having our Domestic quiet secured & placed beyond the reach & power of our inveterate and most envenomed foes.>*[297]

2nd. The Dangers with which we were threatened, & the grounds of our mourning will appear still greater if we consider the nature of the Enemies with whom we were at war, Enemies the most powerful upon Earth, Masters of wide & most extensive Countries, Absolute & arbitrary in their Government, supporting large & numerous Armies in different parts of the World, *their* <furnished with> Generals experienced in the Art of war, & shewing as much policy & cunning [p. 311] in the Cabinet, as they did Valour & bravery in the field, & *their country abounding* <abundantly provided> with Men *ready* <willing> & *sufficient* <able> to recruit & repair their losses.

With these advantages they carried on their Designs with incredible swiftness, they put themselves in possession of several strong & important Places, they over-ran Countries with whom we are nearly & closely allied, they baffled the opposition that was made to them, & for a long time One Messenger succeeded <to> another with unexpected & unwelcome tidings.

T'is true indeed this Prospect gloomy as it was, was in some measure cleared up, by the consideration of the Natural strength of these Kingdoms & of their then circumstances & situation; *Our Armies at one time headed at one time by the Monarch in person,*[298] *at another by their* [p. 312] Armies numerous & considerable were on foot, inspired with the high concerns with which they were intrusted, they exerted their utmost strength & power, maintained the Reputation their fathers had acquired, & gave such proofs of their courage & intrepidity, as more than once extorted the applause & admiration even of those who fell a sacrifice to them. The*ir* Sword was drawn, not in quest of Dominion, not to gratify ambition, not to conquer by violence, but to maintain the noble cause of freedom <& Religion> & Liberty against the Invaders of both, to deliver innocence from slavery & bondage, to fulfil the most sacred & solemn engagements, And a King happily reigned over us, whose fatherly care for his People we safely might rely in, whose generous & Princely heart tenders our preservation as nearly as we do our own, who now governs these Nations with a sceptre of righteousness, & during a reign of twenty years continuance inviolably preserves every Immunity every priviledge of the lowest & meanest of his Subjects. [p. 313] *Brave & beloved Prince were encouraged by these illustrious examples to exert their utmost power & upon all occasions exerted it accordingly, maintained the Reputation their Fathers had acquired, & gave such proofs of their Courage & intrepidity as more than once extorted the applause & commendation even of those who fell a sacrifice to them; The People chearfully assisted them with their endeavours their fortunes & their lives, A council composed of the Greatest & most considerable Men in the Nation ever remarkable for their zeal in defence of it's liberties & freedom sat at the Helm, & took all methods which wisdom or prudence could suggest to ward off the Dangers then impending upon us.*

But<Yet> as *proper* <favourable> as these <appearances> were, how uncertain was the success how vain all these implements of war, *if* <unless> God himself *had not* forwarded our endeavours, *if* <unless> he himself [p. 314] *had not gone* <went> forth with our Armies, and *crowned* <furthered> our designs with his choicest Blessings, There is no King that can be saved by the multitude of an Host, neither is any mighty Man delivered by much strength, An Horse is a vain thing for safety, neither shall he deliver any by his great strength,[299] It is of the Lord's mercies <that> we were not consumed. That Providence which so often interposed in our behalf, that wrought Deliverances in these Kingdoms hardly to be paralleled in any other, was still ready to save & protect us, It's right hand & it's Holy Arm opened unto us a way to escape, It procured unto us that extraordinary Success in two Naval engagements, by which we were enabled to wound our Enemies in the most sensible parts, to cut off the very Sinews of War & in the midst of their conquests to force them to sue & beg for peace.

[p. 315] And by this bountiful interposition of Heaven was the face of things altered & an end <put> to the progress of the Enemy. Our mourning was turned into dancing, & our Sackcloth into Garments of joy & gladness. The Adverse Power retired into his own Country within the limits prescribed to it by him, who bounds the violence of the Sea & commands it to come hitherto & no further, & there to stay it's proud & mighty waves; Our Allies resumed their former influence, the ballance of power was *preserved* <maintained>, & the Interest of Liberty & freedom secured by the Election of a Prince to a High & exalted Dignity whose Glorious Ancestor rescued our liberties & laid the foundation of the Blessings we have ever since enjoyed, whom the Archers sorely grieved & hated, but whose bow abode in strength, & the Arms of whose hands [p. 316] were made strong by the hands of the Mighty God of Jacob.[300]

3rd. From this General view of things let us proceed in the 3rd place to consider the many Calamities & disasters, which befell particular Persons & families among us.

For war is a Judgement from God big with the most dire & dreadful consequences, and what a numerous train of evils did the late one bring along with it? What Destruction & profuse shedding of much precious & valuable Blood? How many thousand of our Countrymen has it bereaved us of? How many families whose wounds are still open & bleeding yet? How many disconsolate Widows & afflicted Mothers whom the sword of the Lord has rendered so? What wracking separation of the most intimate Relations to attend the [p. 317] calls of their Country, uncertain of ever meeting again, & parting to engage powerful Enemies & what was equally to be dreaded to combat deadly & poysonous Climates?

What Immense Sums were yearly required to support Armies abroad, what lessening by this of the Industrious Man's fortune & what enhancing the price of necessary & useful Commodities? What prodigious Debts was the Nation obliged to contract, which if long continued might have endangered it's Credit? What considerable check did it put upon Trade, on the freedom encrease & growth of which depend the riches the wealth the very being of these Kingdoms, *and* <for> tho' some particular branches of Trade might thrive & prosper upon the War <& some private Persons perhaps be yet in General enriched by it>, in General what losses were sustained *by it*, what diminution of reasonable [p. 318] profits from the extraordinary charges for security & defence, what hazards of falling into the hands of an Enemy & seeing the hopes the support the expectation of a Family lost at once & destroyed for ever.

And now change the scene & set our present situation in opposition to our past & preceeding one, *All* <Such> anxious & uneasie fears cease & vanish, & comfortable and pleasing reflections take place of melancholy & desponding thoughts.

The Warrior returns to his family, & enjoys the greatest of all human Blessings domestic peace & quiet, beats his swords into plow-shares & his spears into pruning hooks, The Honest Farmer sits contented under his vine & under his fig-tree,[301] expecting the fruit of his labours, & certain [p. 319] to gather in his Harvest without lett or molestation, The People no longer oppressed with burdensome & expensive taxes feel their load daily lessening & learn by this that the Publick good not the paltry Interest of Private Men occasioned the hardships under which they groaned. The Fair Trader send*s* his Ships to the most distant parts to the World, *may* bless<es> his Country & enrich<es> himself without the dread of losing by the activity & diligence of an Enemy what his just labour & toil give all orders & Degrees of Men are *enabled* <at liberty> to follow the Duties of their respective Callings, & under the Guardianship of peace & plenty to promote virtues to encourage arts & sciences, to make [p. 320] useful & laudable Improvements.

But the *Last & the* Greatest Danger we were in from the Continuance & Progress of the War both foreign & domestic in which we were involved, & the Last I shall mention was the Loss of our Religion & the Destruction of the Protestant Faith.

How valuable this is, how worthy of all our care & anxious concern, how inseparable the Profession of it from all real & solid comfort, need not be proved in this place & upon this occasion; You my Brethren are thoroughly sensible of the value & importance of it. You expressed upon a late trying occasion your just abhorrence of any attempts to over throw or destroy it. You generously <stood forw[ard] offered yourselves to stand up> in defence of it. You gave [p. 321] convincing proof that no private interest, no Worldly consideration could prevail on you to remain idle & unconcerned whilst the pure Protestant faith was openly attacked & it's destruction intended & contrived.[302]

For what would have become of it, had the Designs of our Enemies succeeded, & God in his justice & for the punishment of our sins suffered them to take effect what would have become of it, had the Rebellions made their way, had a Popish Bigotted Prince ascended the Throne of these Realms, & a Popish Ministry <Faction> presided over the Counsils of this Protestant Nation; If we judge from what our Fathers formerly experienced in a like case,[303] we surely [p. 322] can not conceive any thing more dreadful & terrifying, When Popish Superstitions were established by Law, & Civil Courts directed to rule over the Consciences of Men, When Conformity to the Idolatrous practices of the Church of Rome *was* in all points was made the only means to preferment in Church or State & the least deviation from them became the object of the Secular Power, was punished with Imprisonment persecution & death, & only to be *attoned for* <removed> by the greatest of all evils, Apostacy from the truth.

What would have become of our Religion, had the Enemies of our Country prevailed, & the Schemes of foreign Powers to reduce us under their yoke [p. 323] met with the desired success; They are enslaved to these erroneous principles, destructive of all peace, and contrary to all Reason, They desire to propagate them where-ever they have any influence. They stick at no means to bring about what they so zealously tho' falsely think their duty, Witness their unparalleled Persecutions of the Protestants in the last Century, and their sacrificing to this darling Passion a Million of Good and industrious Subjects, Witness the Contrivances of the same Spirit in the Bloody Reign of Queen Mary, and the Tragical Scene of the Rebellion in Ireland, with the intended Conspiracy upon the fifth of November.

[p. 324] What in a word would have become of the Protestant Religion through-out the World, had it once been destroyed in these happy Kingdoms, whose most radiant Glory it is to be the Bulwark of Protestantism & it's strongest security, & *bulwark* defence, under whose wing alone it can truly spread & flourish & to whom every Protestant State looks up for support, saying with Samuel to King Saul, On whom is all the desire of Israel? Is it not on thee & on all thy Father's House.[304]

But Blessed for ever Blessed be God who has preserved this Religion amidst all these impending dangers, & founded it upon a rock, who [p. 325] graciously continues to us the free exercise of it without dread & terror, who leaves us still at liberty to make use of the valuable priviledge of coming into his House, of attending his worship, of reading his Sacred word, of professing the best & purest Religion cleared of all the errors & superstitions with which it had for a long time been clouded & obscured, & who by baffling the hopes & disappointing the views of it's Enemies, gives us the pleasing prospect of seeing it prosper & flourish under the <mild &> auspicious Government of a Protestant Prince, blessed with a numerous Progeny formed after his example, educated in the same Civil & Religious Principles & early instructed to transmitt the [p. 326] Blessings we enjoy to our latest Posterity.

Applic[ation]:

And now to apply these Considerations to ourselves. What returns of the most lively gratitude & acknowledgement do they require from us? O Lord my God I will give thanks unto thee for ever. How ought we to celebrate & adore that mercy, by which we are thus bountifully & providentially preserved? How are we to look up with a fervent & pious zeal to the Author & Giver of these Great & singular benefits, acknowledge ourselves unworthy of all his boundless favours, and resolve them into the effects of his bounty & goodness alone.

But is meer Gratitude & thankfulness sufficient? Can the bare tribute of our lips fulfil these obligations, and Should not our highest concern be to manifest [p. 327] the sincerity of our Praise & thanksgiving by the most pure & upright Conversation.

For *had* <was> the hand of God still *continued* upon us, & his judgments making nearer approaches to us, Was our Liberty still in our Religion attacked & tottering, Who among us would not bow down his Head as a Bulrush,[305] who would not form the strongest & most entire purposes of amendment, who would not part immediately with his most darling sinful affections, & by the signs of the most hearty & unfeigned repentance endeavour to stay the Justice of God & remove his impending Arm.

This we have every one of us done in those Days of solemn Humiliation, which were yearly appointed upon this occasion and shall such promises & resolutions of [p. 328] amendment be forgot, now that the messengers of Divine wrath are recalled, & the engaging emblems of compassion & mercy are substituted in their stead? Shall such former vows be broke, & our transgressions once more oblige God to visit us again with his judgments, & to effect by some sorer punishment what the Sword & the Dreadful attendants of war could not perfect & compleat.

For is the End & Design of these mercies to encourage us to persevere in security & indolence? Is the Liberty & peace we are restored to, intended to give us a freer opportunity of continuing in sin without *dread* <curb> or *fear* <restraint>? Is the Plenty we enjoy, designed to engage us to live in luxury & sensuality, in voluptuousness & intemperance? Is the Freedom we possess a Reason why we should turn [p. 329] it into Licentiousness, make use of it to arraign the Government under which we live, to sow the seeds of faction & discord, to raise ourselves superior to <all> laws, to be accountable to none & guided by the suggestions of a blind & ambitious Passion? Is our Religion thus preserved & fixed upon such strong foundations, that we may continue to abuse it by our impious writings, our Atheistical Discourses, or what is equally destructive of it, our impure & unrighteous lives, our profaneness & immorality, our gross Contempt & neglect of all it's ordinances & injunctions.

Let us then turn unto God with a lively & hearty Repentance, endeavour to shew ourselves worthy of the Blessings we receive, & engage the Continuance of his favour & protection to us and [p. 330] our Country.

Let us send up our Prayers to him in behalf of that Prince whom his hand has placed & his Providence established upon the Throne of these Kingdoms, Give the King thy judgments O God & thy righteousness unto the King's Son,[306] that his Dominion may be from sea to sea, & from the River unto the ends of the *Earth* World, that in his days the Righteous may flourish, & abundance of Peace so long as the Sun & Moon endureth,[307] &

that his Corruptible & Worldly Crown may late be exchanged for an Incorruptible Immortal one that never fadeth.[308]

Let us pray unto God to perpetuate the Succession in this Illustrious House to endue the Descendants of it with [p. 332] Let those who like fire-brands pluckt out of the burning,[309] have escaped the fury of the Enemy, bless adore and reverence the hand that preserved them, pour out their souls before God in hearty praises & thanksgiving, and continue ever mindful that God was their strength & that the High God was their Redeemer[310]... the generous Principles of their Ancestors & to make them the Lasting Blessings of a free and a Happy People.

[p. 331] Let those who like fire-brands pluckt out of the burning have escaped the fury of the Enemy, bless, adore & reverence the hand that preserved them, pour out their souls before God in hearty praise and thanksgiving & continue ever mindful that God was their strength, & that the High God was their Redeemer.[311]

[p. 332] Let us who have been so remarkably distinguished by the singular favour & protection of God unite together in our earnest prayers to him, that he would be graciously pleased to give us a right and proper sense of the Greatness of his mercies, that continually sheltered under [p. 333] his wing, covered with his shield, upholded by his mighty hands, we may be rendered happily triumphant ever all the Disturbing of our peace here on Earth & so join our hearts & voices to those of the Prophet David in these strong & emphatical words with which I shall conclude.

The Lord is my strength & song, & is become my salvation, The Right hand of the Lord is exalted, The Right hand of the Lord doth valiantly,[312] He maketh wars to cease unto the end of the Earth, He breaketh the bow, & cuteth the spear in sunder, & burneth the Chariot in the fire,[313] Thou art my God & I will praise thee, Thou art my God, & I will exalt thee,[314] O Give thanks unto the [p. 334] Lord, fore he is good, and his mercy endureth for ever.[315]

Sermon XIV

Volume 4 (40)

[p. 306]

Belfast October ye 25th 1747
Ditto August ye 6th 1749
Ditto August ye 12th 1753
St. Andrew's Dublin March ye 17th 1754
Belfast Febr[uar]y ye 27th 1757
Ditto January ye 14th 1759
Ditto November ye 30th 1760
Ditto September ye 5th 1762
Ditto October ye 14th 1764
Ditto July ye 26th 1767 L.D.
Ditto July ye 2nd 1769
Ditto April ye 5th 1772
Rosenallis Oct[ober] ye 20 1805[316]
Mt. Melich Aug[ust] 10 1806
Ditto June 26 1808
Mt. Melich March 25 1810
Rosenallis Mar[ch] 17 1811

[p. 307] In the Twentieth Chapter of Exodus at the Fifth Verse.

Visiting the Iniquity of the Father upon the Children unto the third & fourth Generation of them that hate me.

There is *hardly any one but what is struck with the seeming* <something which savours much of> Cruelty & *injustice of* the *sentence decreed in the text* <in the words I have now read unto you>, That a Father's guilt should be visited upon his Children, & the punishment *of it* fall upon those who had no share in the transgression, <that occasioned it>, is a truth, *which at first indeed savours of cruelty* <very harsh in itself>, *&* <which> if superficially considered, & *easilly appeared* <hastily ascribed> to God, [p. 309] *may be of a most dangerous consequence* <has a manifest tendency>

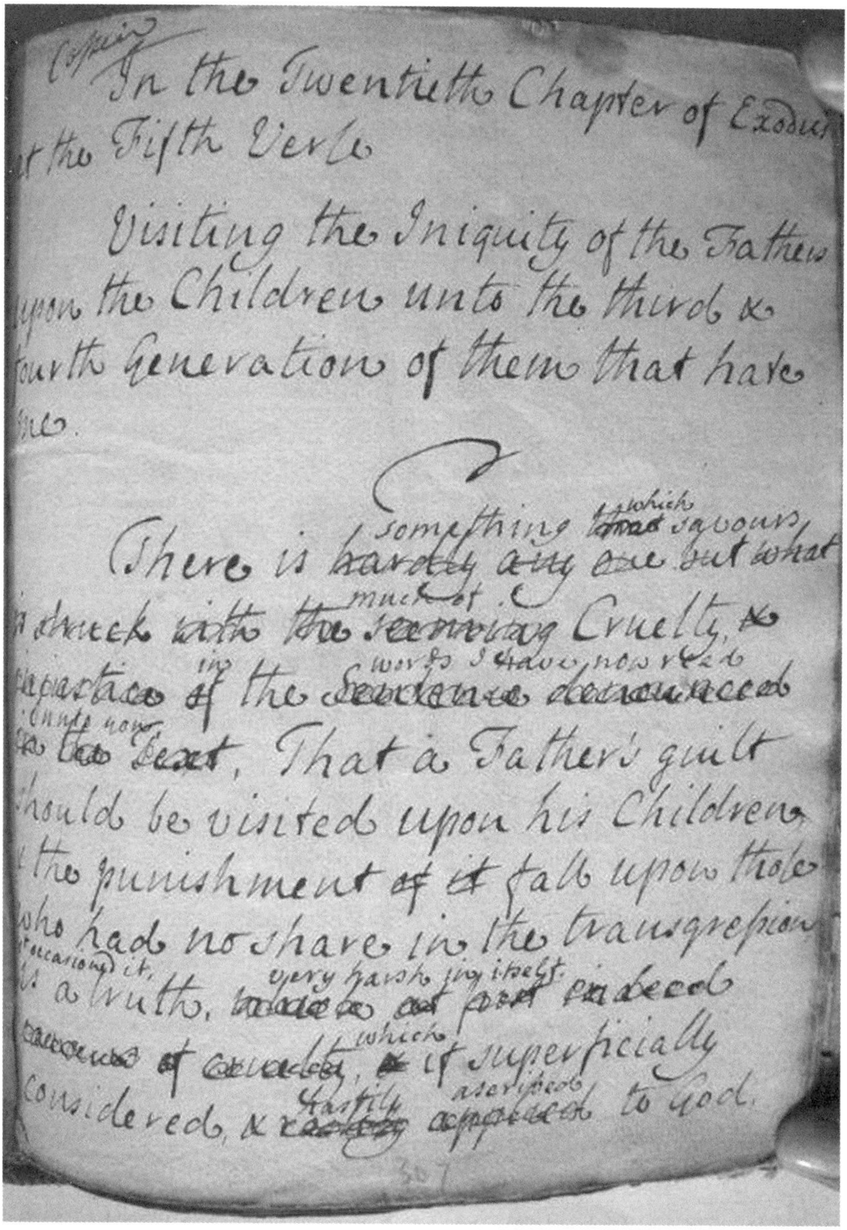
In the Twentieth Chapter of Exodus at the Fifth Verse

Visiting the Iniquity of the Fathers upon the Children unto the third & fourth Generation of them that hate me.

There is hardly any one but what is struck with the seeming Cruelty, & injustice of the Sentence denounced in the Text, That a Father's guilt should be visited upon his Children & the punishment of it fall upon those who had no share in the transgression. 'Tis a truth, which at first indeed savours of cruelty, & if superficially considered, & rashly applied to God.

6 Opening page of Sermon XIV (40) with Saurin's later revisions to the text.

to deprive him of one of his most essential & immutable attributes & <to beget in us unbecoming notions of his supreme justice & goodness>, to cast upon his Moral Government of the World, this false & injurious reflection, The Fathers have eaten sowre grapes, & the Children's teeth are set on edge.[317]

My Design in the following Discourse is *to consider [&] to remove this objection* <to endeavour to remove an Imputation of this sort> & by[318] offering some plain considerations, drawn both from the nature of the thing, & the connection of the words, to shew how consistently with justice God may be said to visit the Iniquity of the Fathers upon the Children, *& then to* <after which I shall> make some [p. 310] practical applications of the Doctrine to our own use & improvement.

1st Part.

And here whatever be the *nature* meaning of the Sentence denounced in the Text, we must certainly understand the punishment consequent thereupon to be merely Temporal, *for of this kind generally were threatened against the Jews, who* <because the Jews to whom it is principally addressed>, were <generally> restrained & kept in order by the terrors of a present <& immediate> punishment, nor is Almighty God so severe a Master, as to make our eternal salvation to depend upon so precarious & uncertain a thing, as the virtues or vices of our Fathers, in which we ourselves have *had no share* <never been so concerned>, Every Man's own [p. 311] conduct & behaviour in life is to determine his eternal doom; However wicked & profligate a Father may have been, the Virtues of his Children are held in equal *esteem* <estimation> before God; At the hour of death, & in the Day of judgement their own hearts, the sincerity of their <own> endeavours shall be the only thing considered, The Soul that sinneth, that only shall dye, the Son shall not bear the iniquity of the father, neither shall the Father bear the iniquity of the Son, the righteousness of the righteous shall be upon him, & the wickedness of the wicked shall rest upon him.[319]

Nay so far is God from making the sins of fathers to fall upon their [p. 312] Children in a future State, that he has even promised to forgive Fathers their own sins, upon their true & sincere repentance, If the wicked will turn from all his sins, which he hath committed, & keep all my Statues & do that which is lawful & right, he shall surely live, he shall not die, All his transgressions that he hath committed, they shall not be mentioned unto him, in his righteousness that he hath done, he shall live,[320] & if he deals thus mercifully with the Sinner himself, it is not to be imagined that he will deal rigorously & cruelly with this young & innocent offspring.

And as the Punishment can only be of a Temporal nature, so does the Commandment seem to limitt it to one kind [p. 313] of sin chiefly, which is the great & heinous sin of Idolatry, for if we consider the Context we find *it* <this> to be the peculiar punishment of those, who make unto themselves any graven image, or any likeness of any thing which is in Heaven above, or in the Earth beneath, or in the water under the Earth, for I the Lord thy God am a Jealous God visiting the iniquity of the fathers upon the children unto the third & fourth generation of them that hate me,[321] that is of them *that* <who> basely offer themselves & dumb Idols, the duty & veneration they owe to God, & who by such acts of vain worship express their contempt of his Divine Majesty, & the *lesser regard* <low opinion> they *have for* <entertain of> his *authority* <nature> & essence.

[p. 314] But tho' this be the plain & obvious meaning of the Commandment, Reason & the nature of things oblige us to extend the punishment contained in it some-what further, for as odious as the sin of Idolatry is, there are many others of as black a die in themselves, as fatal in their consequence, & which no doubt are as hateful in the sight of God, Such is a Determined Spirit of Infidelity, an avowed Apostacy, & renouncing of God & Religion, An Habitual course of debauchery & licentiousness, A Life of continual injustice rapine & extortion, & *which* <what> is the Sum of all impiety, an entire Contempt of God, manifested by oaths, Imprecations & perjuries, Vices of this kind are in Morality, what Idolatry is in Religion, with this difference [p. 315] that acts of Idolatry may be palliated & excused by some, as the unhappy effects of education prejudice or inconsideration, whilst Vice stands condemned by the stings of our own Conscience, & the rebukes of our own hearts, & therefore as Idolatry exposed Children to be visited for their father's iniquity unto the third & fourth Generation, so may settled habits & confirmed acts of Iniquity, induce God to deal with us after the same manner without any Impeachment of his goodness & justice in either case.

For 1st Providence has established *certain* general Laws, in consequence of which certain temporal evils unavoidably follow upon the committal of *certain* <some> actions, unless prevented by the interposition [p. 316] of God *&* <or> over-ruled by a particular act of his power. Thus according to general laws, prodigality Luxury & vice bring a Man to poverty, consume & eat up the fortune *that* <which> was entrusted to him for the *welfare* <support & sustenance> of his Children, & reduce an innocent &

harmless family to *distress & poverty* <penury & want>. A Life of voluptuousness & sensuality is the fruitfull Parent of numberless diseases, which descend to a Man's posterity, & entail anguish & pain, even upon a remote & distant generation. This is the genuine consequence of such actions, in the same manner as health, peace of mind, severity of conscience are the almost infallible result of Honesty, Industry temperance & sobriety.

And can it be expected that God should interpose upon every such [p. 317] occasion, that he should break thro' known & established Laws, & for the preventing of such evils, that he should act in an extraordinary & miraculous manner, If he should do this in one instance, it might be asked why he should not in another, & if he should do it in every case, what confusion & disorder would ensue? what subversion of the nature of Moral actions & what encouragement to Fathers to persevere in sin, if upon account of their Children's innocency, they had the temporal punishment of their actions remitted to them & were themselves freed from *all the* <those *immediate* evils>, *that attend* <which are the immediate attendants of> a vitious & irregular conduct.

Vice indeed of all sort is an open renunciation of our Duty & allegiance to God, a manifest & publick rebellion against [p. 318] the Lord & King of Heaven & Earth, & therefore may as well subject the Children of vitious parents to punishment, as disobedience to a Prince subjects the Members of a family to the forfeiture of its head <& to attain of pure tho' unmerited evil> according to the well known practice of *every community* <States & Communities> whose wisdom of justice in this *case* <respect> is never called in Question.

And this instance is the more to the purpose as Idolatry among the Jews was actually a Rebellion against God, who had more than once declared himself their King, who had instituted a Civil & Religious Policy, & who when he visited the sins of the fathers upon the children, did no more than punish their treason, and exercise an act of his Regal authority & power.

[p. 319] 2nd . *The Visitation of the Fathers sins*< Visiting the iniquity of the Fathers> upon the Children, is extremely equitable because the example of a vitious father often leads Children to the practice & imitation of the same sins.

For The authority of a Parent carries such weight with it, & is enforced by such endearing & engaging motives, that where it is employed, in countenancing of vice & Immorality, there is required a high degree of virtue in a Child, to resist the power of so evil an example, It is natural for him to think well of that particular course of life, which he sees that Person take, of whose tenderness & good-will he has a constant & daily experience, & to lose by Degrees that aversion which all Men have for sin, till Constitution Passion or the powerful influence [p. 320] of example stifle & efface it.

And this holds true more especially in the case of Idolatry, to which the words of the Text originally have a reference, for Children born of Idolatrous Parents, & constantly witnesses of Idolatrous acts are from their infancy prejudiced in favour of that particular form or manner of worship, in which they are educated, it's shocking absurdities make no impression upon their minds, they keep up without further enquiry an intimate correspondence with the Gods of their fathers, & in the Prophet's language, forsake the fountain of living waters to drink out of broken & corrupt cisterns, which their fathers have hewn out, & which hold no water, or such only as is poysonous & hurtful.[322]

[p. 322] When therefore God visits the sins of fathers upon *those* <the> Children *only* <who> partake of their vices who follow the same impious & wicked course, his infinite justice sure cannot be impaired, nor the ways of his Providence be deemed unequal, they are both criminal, & consequently both may be punished. There is no reason why God should dispense with their punishment, & the expression is very proper to call this a Visitation of the fathers sins upon the Children, since it is the*ir iniquity, the evil example they have set before them that has brought them to misery & occassioned that load of trouble under which they now labour* <prevalency of their evil example which has led that portion of them into the snare, & brought upon them that portion of misery,[323] which they may now endure.>

But as true as this is, it admits of many exceptions, A *Child* <Person> may be endowed with such natural principles of honour & integrity, as may secure him even against [p. 323] the deluding example of a vitious father & yet notwithstanding his <own> steady & inflexible virtue he may & frequently is a Sufferer on account of his father's transgression, To obviate therefore the ill impression which this might make upon our minds, I shall add this third & very weighty consideration.

3rd. That whatever misery God inflicts <upon a Child> in consequence of the father's iniquity, it is always intended as a punishment to the Father only, but with respect to an innocent & virtuous Child, it changes it's nature, & shews itself to him under the appearance of a trial & probation, the trial of his patience, & the probation of his virtue.

I say, it is intended as a punishment to the father only; And a punishment [p. 324] of a heavy nature it is indeed; For what Reflection can be more striking to a father, if he has any remains of tenderness & fatherly affection still glowing in his breast, than to consider himself as the *sole* <only> cause *& occasion* <*source*> of that misery <*& trouble* under> which his Children labour, to see those who were entrusted to his care, who depend upon him for every improvement in nature & grace, who were taught by the powerful Dictates of their very Being, to look upon him as their best & most accomplished pattern, To see these Persons struggling against temptations, into which his own bad conduct has *led* <brought> them, exposed to numberless difficulties, which he himself has *caused* <occasioned>, liable to infinite dangers into which he himself has run them, To depart this World with a pungent sense [p. 325] of this, and with the mere pungent reflection that he is accountable to God here after for every false step, which their <unhappy situation> may force them to take, is certainly as dreadful a punishment as a Man can *possibly* undergo in this life, & the most sensible image of what he is to expect *& fear* in the next.

But with regard to *a* <his> virtuous and innocent Child, the case is very different, He indeed is liable to misery & wretchedness but his misery & wretchedness <like all other kinds of adversity & affliction> is productive of the greatest & most solid advantages, It gives him an opportunity of manifesting the greatness of his religious courage & resolution, It excites him to a more sincere & diligent discharge of his duty, It displays his patience & resignation to the will of God, It obliges him to a constant [p. 326] watch over himself, & the irregular inclinations of his heart, It makes him*self* feel the comfort of God's Holy Spirit in the inward satisfaction *that* <which> arises from his own good actions, & what is an advantage of a much more exalted nature, It acquires to him a new & a higher claim to that infinitely glorious reward of Immortality, which is to crown the patience of those *that* <who> endure temptation, & <who> submitt to the dispensations of Providence with fortitude & chearfulness.

It is this infinite reward of Immortality & glory, which gives an undeniable answer to all objections of this kind. Take a future State within your view, Consider your present existence as preparatory to another, & all the Good Man's troubles are accounted for; Virtue may be oppressed, but the time is coming, when [p. 327] it shall recover it's genuine Lustre & beauty, Innocence may be tortured, but the time is coming, when it's misery shall be done away, it's present sufferings <shall be> rewarded with an eternity of happiness beyond what any Human mind can either conceive or imagine.

And in this manner do we see the great objection against the Justice of God drawn from *Gods* <his> visiting the sins of the fathers upon the Children, in a great measure answered & removed, Upon a closer examination it vanishes & falls to the ground, & thus it fares with all objections of this kind, A false glimmering light dazzles us at first, we greedily run away with the least *shew* <shadow> of an argument, till sifted & enquired into, it only serves to set [p. 328] the opposite truth in a stronger view, & to make it more palpable & evident.

And should not the repeated experience we have made of this, engage us to be more reserved & <diffident in our judgement> & to suspect all those arguments of weakness & insufficiency, *that* <which> in any degree impeach the wisdom & equity of God, What we know of him, is founded upon avowed & unquestionable principles, the opposite arguments *on the contrary* are drawn from things <of> which we are no competent Judges *of & sure*, <but> if that which we <no> certainly & undoubtedly know, manifests his Justice & goodness, it is the height of madness & absurdity from every appearance of difficulty <or inconsistency> to suffer that faith *& confidence* to be staggered *that* <which> is founded upon the strongest & the most *unquestionable grounds* <incontestable proofs>.

[p. 329] Applic[ation]:

From what has been said, we may deduce <1st> the indispensable obligation all Parents are under so to order their own lives & conversation, as constantly to set before their Children a shining & uniform example of piety & virtue.

A Regard for the Dignity of their Natures, & their own Interest requires this from them at all times, & in all the circumstances of their lives, but when they reflect that their Children's welfare & happiness, for which they express the most hearty & <generally the most sincere> concern, depends in a great measure upon themselves, & the examples they set before them, that young & tender minds are susceptible of any impression, & frequently that the first setting out influences [p. 330] & determines their whole future conduct, how terrible & strong is the motive in the heart of a fond & generous Parent.

He doubtless thinks no pains too great, no costs too high, to furnish their minds with curious Sciences, or to improve their bodies with ornamental & graceful exercises, & should he be less careful & less solicitous to motivate their heart, to settle in them strong & lasting principles of

Morality & Religion, & to manifest to them by his own practice & example, the usefulness & advantage of such a course of life? Without this the severest lectures, the sharpest reproofs, or the most rational Discourses upon the attractive beauty of virtue, or it's conformity to the Nature of Man, are of little *use* <avail>, for how can a Child be perswaded to love Justice, temperance or mercy, whilst he daily sees the very Person [p. 331] who preaches these up to him living in open violation of them, acting the most unwarrantable & iniquitous *things* <parts>, or committing the most violent & shocking oppressions.

But when Precept & Example accompany each other, when a Man shews his family the advantage of what he recommends to them in his life & practice, when he himself is ever Religious, meek, charitable just & temperate, Nothing but an obdurate depraved heart, can withstand the power of so engaging an example, the yet innocent & tender mind imbibes the same virtuous principles, his affections are strongly prejudiced in favour of what is truly laudable, & thus early trained up in the way he should go, he will not depart from it, when he is old,[324] but will continue steadfast & immoveable[325] in a course of virtue, repaying all the pains [p. 332] *that* <which> have been bestowed upon him by all the returns, which Gratitude & Duty can possibly offer to a benevolent & virtuous Parent.

2nd. From what has been said, we may learn what is the proper duty of those unhappy Children, who actually feel the sentence denounced in the Text, & <who> suffer in this World for the sins & iniquities of their Fathers.

They are to remember that their Father's ill conduct, does no way free them from that respect & regard which Children *whose circunstances of life* <in every station & at every age>, owe to those from whom they have received their Being, that whatever faults they may be guilty of, or to whatever excesses liable; they should honour their persons, tho' they detest their vices, reverence the Father, tho' they loath the Sinner.

And as they are continually exposed [p. 333] to the dangers of an ensnaring corrupt example, it is more peculiarly incumbent upon them to be constantly upon their guard, to conceive the highest hatred for those sins, *which … become familiar to them* <under whose baneful influence they unhappily live>, & in opposition to these to place their own good example into suspicious a light, as may in some measures prevent the ill effect of their Parents vices, *retard* <lessen> the *consequence* <power> of their Fathers bad example.

And who can tell whether so bright an instance of virtue may not touch the part of a depraved Father, whether in the close of life & the decline of age, the virtue of a Dutifull Child may not excite some sentiments of sorrow & repentance in the breast of a sinful Parent, *whether he may not be won over by the attracting example of his Childrens wise conduct* & whether God may not <upon their account> be prevailed on *by their virtue* to mitigate [p. 334] the punishment of their Fathers transgressions as he visits the iniquity of the Fathers upon the Children, so to extend the Children's virtue upon the Fathers. *Or if this should not be the case & all their endeavours should prove affected nor shall they undoubtedly draw the blessing of God upon themselves & their children, they shall add grace and dignity to their families, they shall sanctify themselves, these severe trials of Providence shall make the final end & issue of things terminate in their own good & in the salvation of their Incarnated souls*

Lastly. Let those who have the happiness to owe their birth to virtuous & good parents *learn to* prize & esteem the gracious gift of God, Let them improve the opportunity afforded them of instruction & example to the advancement of themselves in virtue & [p. 335] goodness, Let them be ever ready to receive advice & to hearken to counsil & reproof, Let them be meek & tractable, dutiful & obedient full of filial love & affection, Let them rejoice in the virtue of their Parents, & let their hoary heads be ever their Glory Crown of rejoicing; Then shall the Skies drop down righteousness upon them, & the Lord shall shew loving kindness,[326] yea the Lord shall shew mercy unto thousands of them that love him, even unto their Children's Children.[327]

Now to God the Father & etc. & etc.

Sermon XV

Volume 5 (46)

[p. 98] Belfast January ye 15th 1748/9
Ditto October ye 22nd 1752
Ditto December ye 28th 1755
Ditto January ye 15th 1758
Ditto July ye 29th 1759
Ditto August ye 3rd 1760
Ditto May ye 2nd 1762
Ditto July ye 10th 1763
Ditto November ye 11th 1764
Ditto January ye 24th 1768
Ditto July ye 30th 1769
Ditto January ye 5th 1772
St. Doloughs May ye 18th 1783
Ditto May ye 9th 1784
Cromlin May ye 14th 1786
St. Doloughs October 8th 1786
Ditto April 20th 1788
Ditto May 6th 1792
Ditto January 4th 1793/4
Rosinallis March 6 1803
Mt. Melich May 22 1808
[p. 99] Rosenallis October 6 1805
Mt. Melich December 1805
Ditto May 24 1809
Rosenallis September 17 1809
Cork St. Peters June 28 1812
St. Peters Dublin February 6 1814 S:C:
Ditto January 15 1815 in the Evening
Donag[h]more July 30 1815
Derry June 20 1819 Evening
Burt July 11 1819
L[ough] B[rick]Land 19 February 1826

[p. 100] In the Fifth Chapter of St. Paul's Epistle to the Ephesians and at the sixteenth verse.

Redeeming the Time

The Subject I am now to discourse upon from the words just read unto you, is of a very important & interesting Nature, It regards the use we are to make of our time, the *method* <manner> of redeeming it when we have been so unfortunate as to *lavish it away. The words of the Text were originally intended as a prudential advice to Men in the times of persecution & trial when a higher degree of prudence & circumspection was necessary either to prevent the Dangers they were in or to make them subservient to some use & good purpose, whence immediately after the precept to redeem the time the Apostle adds this reason because the days were evil* [p. 102] *But the wisdom & propriety of it holds equally strong in all the circumstances of life and concerns us all and is of infinite concern to each of us in particular etc*[328] *for if any fault may be deemed universal and general that of squandering away our time idly & to no purpose may justly be called so* <lose & misspend it and tho' It was at first addressed to Men under persecution & trial, from whom greater degrees of prudence & … were required, yet is the mercifulness of it the same in all the circumstances of life, for if any fault might be deemed unusual & general, surely this squandering away time idly & to no purpose may justly be called so.>

I shall therefore in the following Discourse offer these four things to your consideration, as relative to the point in hand, & capable of being made useful to the right management of our time, 1st. That the Time at present afforded us, is given unto us to work a Great & an important work, 2dly. That most of us have misspent this Time, & applied it directly contrary to the end for which it was given us, That therefore 3rd. We are to redeem the Time past by improving the time to come, & Lastly That the Reasons to induce us thus to redeem the Time are infinitely strong & cogent.

[p. 103] 1st Part.

First, That the Time we at present enjoy, is given unto us to work a great & an important work, namely to fitt & prepare ourselves for a new & a better Oeconomy by contracting in this State of Discipline *& trial*, such habits of Virtue *& goodness* as may entitle us to the favour of God & the Rewards of a Blessed Immortality here-after.

And in the proof of this I need not be particular, as I *lately* <often> had occasion <in my last Discourse from this place>[329] to prove more at large that our present State was *only* a State of exercise & Discipline, that whilst we continued upon Earth we were only Strangers & Pilgrims travelling in a foreign Country and at a Distance from our own home, that *no ends could be answered upon any other supposition than this by our existence here below* <our present existence could answer no wise & good end, unless we supposed it to have been given to us by way of probation or trial>, that our [p. 105] faculties & Intellectual powers *are* <were> vastly too infinite & immense *for the little use they are of to us*[330] that there *is* <was> no proportion between what they *are* <were> in themselves, <their extent & capacity> & the advantages we *drew* <derive> from them thro' want of leisure & opportunity, that far from answering any great purpose, they often served to make us miserable, *& necessarie at one* <some> time restraining us from *such* gratifications & pleasures, *as that* would be attended with satisfaction & *real advantage* <delight>, at another leaving us at a loss for objects adequate *or commensurate*, to our boundless Capacities, & generally disappointing & *leaving* <forsaking of> us when we *stand* <stood> most in need of their assistance, & Lastly that a Good & Gracious God *can* <could> never be supposed to take any pleasure in the unhappiness of his Creatures, or to furnish them with powers purposely to render them miserable, & by raising the Dignity of their Nature to sharpen & quicken the sense of their [p. 106] wretchedness & misery.

These particulars I say I have *very lately* <often> spoken to, & shall therefore without further entering upon them, infer this conclusion, that the present time is only a time of probation & trial, a season for exercise and improvement, that the faculties we are possessed with, are designed to teach us the knowledge of God, of his infinite perfections of *our* <the> great & weighty obligations to be deduced from them, that we are sent into this World to prepare ourselves for the more full & perfect enjoyment of God in another, & by several rubs & obstacles in our way to manifest our adherence to his Laws & Commands, Hence in <Sacred> Scripture is the Space of our existence here called our Day, & the present time the time of our Visitation, & Hence are we exhorted to work out our own Salvation in the fear [p. 107] & trembling[331] as the work of the utmost concern & which requires our greatest Diligence & attention.

But if this 1st Consideration be true, that the present time is allowed unto us to effect & accomplish our Salvation the 2nd is easyly to be demonstrated that most of us have misspent this Time, & applied it directly contrary to the end & design for which it was given us *which is the next particular I am to speak to.*

2nd Part.

For to secure the salvation of our Souls *be our principal business here many things are required to be done by us before we can compass the end. Is not the knowledge of religion absolutely necessary, the acquiring of such useful saving knowledge of God and of the terms & means of* [p. 109] *acceptance with him & may give us just proper notions of ourselves & of our present destination & Calling. But how few of us app[ly] themselves to such a study, how few labour to attain the knowledge of religion few that lay out their time, their parts, their leisure upon this, how few of us are acquainted with its principles & doctrines or give themselves any trouble & uneasiness about them.*
<we must know & understand ye means by which thy salvation is detained, we must endeavour to acquire the Knowledge of Religion, of ye nature of God, of Religion, of Ye Character of Jesus Christ, of ye Redemption brought by him as may only one hand destroy all vain presumption a the generality of people live[332] on is other prevent all despair & diffidence, But how small is the number of those who have bestowed or do now bestow any part of their time upon the study of Religion, live in the profession of a Religion which they do not understand, believe principles which they know nothing of, entertain hopes for which they can give up reason they can assign no ground.>

To obtain salvation *are* we <are> indispensably obliged to subdue every inordinate affection, to curb & restrain every Inclination to sin, to keep a proper Empire and Dominion over our Passions, & to subject them all to the Government & Guidance of our Reason? *But how few of us act in this manner, how few who think at all of bridling & moulding their vicious and irregular dispositions, how few who* <But how few are they who have thought, or do not think of bridling & subduing their vitious & irregular inclinations, we for the most part> look [p. 110] upon the Committal of Sin as a matter of *any* <no> great consequence, *How few who do not* <we securely> indulge *themselves* <ourselves> in the habitual practice of some one vice, & preserve in a Course of disobedience & transgression, *in some one instance or other* <without much thought or concern>.

To obtain Salvation we are indispensably obliged to put on <certain> Virtues & dispositions *suited to the Nature of the Great Author of our salvation*, to accustom ourselves to the practice of such Graces here, as we are more fully to improve ourselves in here-after, & to live in some measure upon Earth as Men constantly mindful of their future eternal Salvation; But how few of us <did or do> carry such thoughts in *their* <our> minds, *how faint are generally* our endeavours after Virtue, *how weak our attempts after it, how imperfect the* <are generally faint & weak our> good dispositions *we acquire, how languid & cold the means* <mixed & imperfect, & the means we make use of to secure> the <future> welfare of our souls languid cold & ineffectual.

[p. 111] *we make use of to secure the welfare & happiness of our souls.*
In a word To ensure salvation we are to be pious, devout, Religious, heavenly minded *we are*, to seek the Kingdom of God & his righteousness,[333] to live soberly righteously & Godly in this present World, looking for the blessed hope & the Glorious appearing of the Great God, & our Saviour Jesus Christ;[334] But is this the end of our labours, this the improvement & use we generally make of our time? Like Martha we are careful & troubled about many things, whilst the one thing needful[335] is neglected & overlooked, & spend our strength & spirits in wearisome & fatiguing pursuits, till the Scene is closed up, & shews our Life to be a*n empty and* <meer blot>, a heap of inconsistent [p. 113][336] & absurd actions, the very reverse of *what it* every thing it might & was intended to be.

This then being *the* <our> Case *of the generality of People,* the Apostle's advice to us to redeem the time is very seasonable & proper, What the true import of this Precept is, & in what manner lost time may be redeemed, comes now in the 3rd place to be more particularly *to be* enquired into.

3rd: Part:

The Expression redeeming is in itself very strong & emphatical, It denotes properly the recovering or *repurchasing with* <regaining upon> a valuable *price* <consideration> some thing that had been lost <&> which <was> once *was* in our power, & in this sense Christ is said to have redeemed us from the Curse [p. 115] of the Law,[337] that is, to have recovered us from the condemnation under which we lay and thro' the powerful merits of his Death, to have restored unto us the favour & beauty of God, which we formerly enjoyed, but which by our manifold sins & transgressions we had *justly but unhappily* <unhappily> forfeited.

And this Expression when applied to lost & mispent[338] Time intimates, that we are to use our utmost endeavours to improve the <present> time <and that time> to come, so as to make some amends for the time that is past & by a double portion of diligence & activity in that part of it which is still in our power, to make our future conduct attone & compensate for all past errors & offences.

Now if we consider what were the chief & principal Causes that occasioned our losing the time past, we shall by preventing the like for the

<time to> come, literally & properly redeem & recover it, & these we shall find [p. 116] to be one or other of those that follow.

1st. Inadvertence or want of Consideration. For where is the Man who would consent to spend his time in a continued round of senseless & empty pleasures & amusements, if he considered what he was, what the end of his Being, what the Design of those noble & exalted principles with which he is endued. Could he bear the thought, that that precious time he enjoyed, given unto him to advance his ultimate and final happiness by the wisest & most rational means, was squandered away in foolish & impertinent occupations, in pampering perhaps his body, in satisfying his luxury & vanity, in ministering to his Pride & folly; Could he who considered that he was reserved for the highest & noblest purposes, that he was designed for the enjoyment of God in a State of Glory, [p. 117] that he was sent into this World to contract certain virtues & aptitudes to render him capable of happiness & felicity. Could he I say voluntarily & cheerfully consume his time & the space of his existence here upon idle & unworthy pursuits, debate his Being by grovelling & mean desires, & act a part far below the original Dignity of his Nature.

Since then want of considering properly the work we have to do, & the time we have to do it in, has been one great cause of our losing the time past, *Let us now ende[avour]* <the best & surest way> to redeem the time to come *by* <is> scrupulously & inviolably <to> reserving<e> a considerable portion of it for this necessary & important concern to allow ourselves some moments in each day, to put these serious Questions to ourselves, Why are we sent into this World? Is it to take our pleasure wantonly & idly in it, or to answer a Great & important end? If it be, Do we by the Schemes we [p. 118] now lay down the projects we now form, the principles we now proceed upon, Do we advance this end <and> thereby promote our chief and only business, the future advantage of our Souls in another & a better State.

2nd. Time past has been lost by too immoderate a pursuit of the Goods & advantages of this World, I say too immoderate a pursuit, because our well being here absolutely requires that we should spend some time in the search & acquisition of *some things* <them>, the necessities of Society demand it, we are naturally formed with dispositions prompting us to it, & without this Society would degenerate into savageness & barbarism.

But if some of our time may be laid out in this manner, sure it doth not follow that our whole time may be so with equal safety & expediency, if we may pursue the advantages of the World to a certain degree it is very far from a just consequence [p. 119] that we may grasp at them without measure & without *measure* bounds.

And yet upon this fatal rock do we generally split, Divided between the interests of a Family, the business of particular Callings the Cravings of Ambition <& covetousness what generally attends it is Crav[ing]s of our avarice & covetousness> we plunge ourselves so deep into the hurry & confusion of the World & labour with so much anxiety to secure to us the advantages of it, that we have neither leisure nor opportunity to think of anything besides, & thro' want of time & power are frequently obliged to forget & disregard the end of our Being.

Consider the Man whose heart is set upon the acquisition of wealth & riches, & now will find his mind & all his affection continually engrossed by this one thing, computing every probability of loss or gain from each of his undertakings, wracking his mind with the invention of new [p. 120] methods to encrease & enlarge his Store, & heedlessly lavishing away his time upon this & this alone.

Consider the Man of Ambition, & his thoughts <& time> roll on in an incessant course of new devices to rise to the height he desires, still bent upon some higher degree of honour or power, he continually labours to attain it, & the satisfying of his pride is the sole purport of all his undertakings.

Consider Men in General their present views, pursuits & designs & they all tend *in* to some Worldly good or advantage, some yoke of oxen to be proved, some farm to be viewed, some merchandise to be attended, employs their whole time, & prevents their listing to matters of a higher & more important concern.

If then we would redeem the time we have lost in this manner, *Let us* <we should> improve the time to come by directing it to different & opposite purposes, *Let us* <we should> desire [p. 121] the advantages of the World, but desire them with Discretion, & pursue them with moderation that using them so as not to abuse them, we may ever be mindful of the true end of our Being *&*, ... *to advancement steadfastly &* ... <& refer all our actions to this as to their true & proper center>.

The 3rd Cause *of our losing the time past was thro'* <to which I shall ascribe the loss of time past, is> the strength of our Passions & the demands of vitious & irregular Appetites.

And what great wasters & consumers of time are these, whether we are finding out ways & means to supply them with gratification or actually do gratify & indulge them.

What a large portion of precious & valuable time does the Drunkard and Intemperate waste upon his Revelling & debauchery, how many long days & nights are consumed in this work, what a part of such a Man's existence [p. 122] is lost before he can recover his oppressed Spirits, & get the better of the preceeding Day's extravagance & excess?

What profuse & lavishing throwing away of time do those present us with, who seem born for no other purpose than to sit down to eat & drink, & rise up to play,[339] who continues whole months & years at such dangerous amusements, & make their happiness to depend, nay the very being of their families upon their fortune & success in this wasteful & expensive exercise?

What waste again of time & opportunity in the Man of pleasure rioting in disorder, & rambling in search of sinful & forbidden enjoyments?

And is this the case of any here present, the Apostle's admonition will teach them, how to redeem the times [p. 123] lost by such means, The night is far spent, the Day is at hand, Cast off the works of darkness, & put on the armour of light, Walk honestly as in the day, not in rioting wantonness, not in strife & envying, but put on the Lord Jesus Christ, & make no provision for the flesh to fulfil the Lusts there-of.[340]

Lastly <if> Time past has <not> been lost thro' active & excruciating cares, *not* <nor> thro' the *strength* <Demands> of Passions & appetites *but thro' a total ignorance of the right & true way to spend it properly* <yet, is it often squandered away for want of knowing how to spend it properly.>

To whatever Cause this be owing, Certain it is, that it becomes the occasion of much loss & expence of time, Hence do we see numbers of Persons those especially whose [p. 124] circumstances in life are easie & comfortable by spending their days in entire idleness, sluggish standing without concern or care. Others obliged for want of employment to wander up & down in quest of something to say or do, thence *preying* <praing> with an inquisitive eye into the affairs of others, meddling with what they are no way concerned in, & travelling up & down to impart their observations to others, which generally consist in malice slander detraction and evil speaking.

To redeem time thus lost, it were to be wished that each Person would seek for employment in the exercise of some honest Calling, which might take them off from that idleness & which is the consequence of it, that slander & ill-nature they accustom themselves to, or if they are above this that they would betake [p. 125] themselves to some profitable entertainments to fill up these empty spaces of their life, such as reading useful conversation & *looking* acquiring that important knowledge, the knowledge of one'self; Above all that they would be careful to prevent the like mischief in their Children & Dependants by accustoming them early to labour & diligence, by giving them a taste for improving studies, & teaching them the true way to avoid that great & real evil the weight & burden of time.

4th Part.

And now that we have seen, wherein the Redeeming time consists, we shall not be at a loss in the 4th place for reasons strong & cogent to induce us to do so, if we consider that this time is extremely short, that with this it is [p. 126] extremely uncertain & lastly that the loss of it is irretrievable & attended with terrible & dreadful consequences.

1st. Our Longest Days are extremely short; This we are all convinced of, the astonishing & amazing swiftness, with which our Years successively glide on, is sufficient to perswade us, that the longest Period of existence we can promise to ourselves <here> is even as nothing, so soon passeth it away & we are gone.[341]

What Time have we then to lose? Which of us can tell whether in the Years he may still live, he shall enjoy that strength & vigour of mind necessary to finish the work he has to do, Old age generally brings on infirmities both of body & mind, often impairs the faculties of the Soul, obstructs & impedes their [p. 127] exercise & function, Is this then a proper season to begin & perfect a work for which our whole life was designed & intended, shall we refer it to that Period, when perhaps we shall find ourselves unable to work, deprived of all the means & powers to effect or even to think of our Salvation.

If indeed we could promise to ourselves as long a continuance have, as the frame of Human Nature will allow, short as this is, there might be some colour of reason for us not to husband time with such caution & circumspection, but when we reflect that this Time is extremely uncertain in itself, that no dependence can be laid upon a month a day or an hour, that our Life is subject to & depends upon a thousand accidents, & that for one who comes to a vigorous old age, & lives out his whole days, there are Millions [p. 128] cut off in their very bloom, when their hopes seemed best founded, & their prospect of living most clear & unsullied. How is this sufficient to engage us to be thrifty & prudent to manage time with the nicest discretion, that part of it which is now past is irrevocably lost, what is to come is extremely uncertain, the present *then* is the only opportunity we can be certain of, & the only thing we can properly call our own, let it not then slip from us unimproved & unemployed, least in the 3rd place we find the loss of it attended with the most dreadful & terrible consequences.

For in that case we defeat the end of our Being, we answer no one purpose in life, for which life was bestowed upon us, we live for a number of Years to no other end than to treasure up unto ourselves [p. 129] wrath against the day of wrath & Revelation of the Righteous judgment of God.[342]

And how dismal must the State of that Man be, who in the close of his life has no other reflections but these to comfort & support him, who come to the period of his present existence has nothing to offer in his behalf but empty & unavoiding sighs & groans, who cannot purchase one moment more to quiet*en* his Conscience & appease his offended Judge, who <when he> looks back, *upon* <sees> a Life *past* <spent> in perfect opposition to the will of God, & *who now* <when he looks forward> sees abused & misspent time succeeded by a Dreadful Eternity, from which there is no escape, *nor* <or> appeal.

O then that we may know in this our day the things which belong to our [p. 130] peace, before they be hid from our eyes,[343] that when our Sun sets, & our Worldly enjoym[en]ts vanish & disappear, we may thro' time sanctified & improved pass to a glorious & Blessed Eternity, Which God of his infinite mercy Grant etc. etc.

Sermon XVI

Volume 5 (47)

[p. 131] Belfast January ye 29th 1748/9
Ditto September ye 2nd 1750
St. Anne's Dublin October ye 28th 1750
St. Michael's Ditto November ye 25th 1750
New Church Co Down July ye 26th 1752
Belfast April ye 8th 1753
Ditto December ye 15th 1754
Ditto October ye 3rd 1756
Ditto May ye 7th 1758
Ditto January ye 27th 1760
Ditto July ye 19th 1761
Ditto may ye 1st 1763
Ditto March ye 24th 1765
Ditto August ye 2nd 1767 L.D.
St. Audeon's Dublin March ye 20th 1768
Belfast September ye 24th 1769
St. Dolough's December 18th 1785[344]
Ditto October 7th 1787
Ditto May 17th 1789
Ditto March 27 1791 L:C:
Ditto November 3 1793 L:C:
[p. 132] St. Doulough's June 26 1796 L:C:
Ditto June 11 1797 L:C:
Ditto June 9 1800 L:C:
Rosenallis Otober 2nd 1803 L:C:
Mt. Melick November 20 1803
Ditto May 25 1805
Rosenallis July 20 1805
Mt Melick June 7 1807
Rosenallis November 15 1807
Mt Melick April 9 1809
Rosenallis September 3rd 1809 L:C:
St. Peter's January 2nd 1814
Donaghmore August 6 1815
St. Peter's Jan 28 1816 Evening
Donaghmoure October 12 1817
Derry January 10 1818 Evening
Anaclone 9 June 1822

Anamore 12 January 1823
L[ough] Brickland 13 March 1825
Ditto 21 May 1826 Evening S[ervice]

[p. 133] In the Twenty Eigth Chapter of the Book of Job & at the Twenty Eigth Verse

Behold the fear of the Lord, that is Wisdom.

One Great Art used to prevent the Growth & influence of Religion, is to represent the Professors of it, as destitute of all true wisdom & knowledge, Persons of a credulous disposition, apt to take up opinions without rational grounds, & to persist obstinately in them, merely for want of judgment, & capacity to know better. This Artifice is daily & too [p. 134] successfully employed, Infidels openly recommend themselves to the World under the Pompous & deluding Title of Free-thinkers, & of Men, who are happily loosed from the fetters, which keep the Vulgar enslaved, & thro, an uncommon degree of penetration, have raised themselves *superior* above the prejudices of the rest of Mankind.

To these then is the Observation in the Text very seasonable & proper, Behold the fear of the Lord, that is Wisdom. It was originally designed to answer a very important Question, Where shall wisdom be found, & where is the place of understanding,[345] & it tends to lead us to this Conclusion, that they who fear [p. 136][346] the Lord are the only wise & understanding men, the only persons who can lay claim to the honourable appellation of wise & inteligent & to seek for wisdom where alone *it is to be sought for* <they can expect to find it>.

These words now before us require two things to be done for their better Illustration, 1st To explain what is meant by the fear of the Lord & the 2d To shew how this fear of the Lord is our truest wisdom

1st Part

By the Fear of the Lord we are to understand such a servile dread of God as represents him to us under [p. 137] the Character of a severe & rigorous master, armed with infinite power, always ready to punish his Creatures, & inflicting the most grievous judgments upon every Delinquent, without mercy & without measure.

Such notions of the Supreme Being, rather tend to discourage Men from his service, than to allure them to it, destroy all hope & trust, all joy & pleasure in the contemplation of his Nature, & reduce us to the unhappy State of Slaves & bondmen, without any generous principle <from> us within to excite us to the practice of virtuous & good actions, whence in Scripture, we oftner see God described under the endearing emblems of mercy & compassion, than under the [p. 138] dreadful & awakening Images of irresistible power & might, And in the usual dispensation of his Providence, have more frequent instances of his tenderness & mercy than we have of his severity & justice, at one time finding him willing to bear with our repeated transgressions, at another to promote our Conversion by the most engaging & effectual means, & even in the midst of his judgments, to give us some Intimation, that they are the Corrections of a Father, & not the scourgings of an Absolute Monarch.

But the Fear of the Lord here recommended as the highest Wisdom, consists in such a just & reasonable apprehension [p. 139] of the superior Excellency of God's Nature, as begets in us due & proper sentiments of reverence, submission & awe, as raises within us a hearty desire of pleasing, & consequently a dread of displeasing this perfect & supreme Being, as kindles in our breasts the most intense love & affection for him, & thereby diverts us from every thing <which> we judge, may offend or displease him, It is like the Reverence of a dutiful Child towards a Venerable Parent, fear tempered by love & the highest esteem, or as the respectful regard of Virtuous & Good Men for great & worthy Characters, In a word, the fear of the Lord, is nothing else but a sense of Religion in General, as [p. 140] it actuates, enlivens, inspires all our actions, as it becomes the spring of every thing we do, the motive & principle upon which our whole conduct is built. Since then the fear of the Lord, or in other words, how Religion is Man's truest & only wisdom.

2nd Part.

And this it will be no difficult matter to evince, if we consider 1st. That Religion teaches us the knowledge of such things, as are of the highest concern & importance *to us* <for us to know>, 2nd. That it teaches [p. 141] us the true way to prevent the greatest & most real evils of life, & to soften and alleviate those, which it is beyond our power to prevent, & 3rd. That the practice of it is attended with inestimable advantages, & is the means of attaining the chief & only good.

1st. Religion teaches us the knowledge of such things, as are of the utmost concern & importance *to us* <for us to know>. And here I do not intend to lessen the value of such Human Sciences, as stand unconnected with Religion, there are many of this sort, highly useful & important upon the attainment & improvement of which, our wellfare & happiness in Society greatly depends. But where [p. 142] are the Human Sciences, *upon* <for> which men acquire the character of Wise & intelligent, that can <in point of importance> be compared to the Knowledge, which a thorough acquaintance with the principles of religion naturally gives us. They have for their object the things of this World, their use & advantage is confined to, can not be extended beyond, & must end & determine with these, whilst the knowledge we acquire by Religion, takes in Eternity within it's view, & the usefulness & advantage of it reaches beyond the Duration of time itself.

For it is Religion that teaches us that there is a Supreme & Intelligent Being, who presides over, & directs all things, that by his power we were <at> first [p. 143] made & have since been preserved & protected, that by him we are endued with *Immortal* souls, which have reason to preserve or be annihilated <of a Spiritual and Immortal Nature>, that to him we are accountable for our actions, & according as they have been conformable or not, to the Rules he has laid down, to be entitled to a reward, or to a punishment here after.

It is Religion that informs us, to what end the noble faculties of reason & understanding are given unto us, that such Divine & excellent powers are designed for a more perfect & lasting existence that the present, that one life is only a State of trial & probation, to fitt & prepare us for another, that at the [p. 144] end & close of it, a day of Retribution takes place, in which every man shall reap the fruit of his own good actions, & plentifully receive the full reward of his virtue.

It is Religion that teaches us how to calm the fears & apprehensions of God's Judgments, by informing us, that how great so-ever our sin's & offences may have been, yet if with Penitent & contrite hearts we return unto him, & as assiduously persevere in the ways of righteousness, as we did once unhappily deviate from them, our former sins will be thoroughly done away, & our title to the favour & acceptance of God <be> fully & unreservedly restored unto us.

[p. 145] It is Religion <again> that teaches us where to seek for succour & assistances to undertake & perfect the great work of our Conversion, that gives us the strongest assurances, that Gods Grace will second our own endeavours, & his Blessed Spirit render our progress in Virtue both pleasant & easie. <Finally> It is Religion that teaches us the danger of Impenitency & hard heartedness, that if we absolutely persist in a course of Sin, live in the actual breach of God's laws, & due without making any atonement for them by our repentance & reformation, we have nothing to expect from God, but his highest indignation & wrath, we are [p. 146] no longer to depend upon the assistances of his Grace, but are to be left to ourselves & to the punishment threatened to unrepented Guilt.

These are some of the General truths, which Religion teaches, & is there any thing more necessary to be known, whose consequences are of greater importance to men & in the knowledge of which they are more *nearly* <nearly> concerned, upon which account it is, that the knowledge of Religion has ever been held in the highest esteem by all Good Men, & that the Character given of it by them <is> perfectly answerable to it's usefulness & importance, Thus David, The Law of the Lord is perfect, [p. 147] converting the Soul, the Testimony of the Lord is sure, making wise the simple, the Commandment of the Lord is pure, enlightening the eyes, the Fear of the Lord is the beginning of wisdom, a good understanding have all they, that do there after, the Praise of it endureth for ever,[347] And Moses's advice to the People of Israel was to keep the judgments & statutes of the Lord their God, for this says he, is your wisdom & your understanding in the sight of the Nations, which shall hear all these Statutes, & say. Surely [p. 148] this Great Nation is a wise & understanding People.[348]

But 2ndly. Religion not only teaches us the knowledge of such things as are of the utmost concern & importance to us, it also teaches us the best way to *prevent* <avoid> the greatest & most real evils of life & to soften & alleviate those which are beyond our power to prevent. For if we examine narrowly into the source of all those evils, which abound in the World, we shall find the greatest part of them to be owing to the want of Religion & the little Influence, which it is generally suffered to have upon our life & conduct.

[p. 149] To what can this Man ascribe his loss of Health, that real & substantial blessing of life, but to his neglect of the precepts of temperance & sobriety, & to his refusing to bridle his Passions according to the commands of religion. No defect in his Constitution, no weakness in the original texture of his body, no innate unacquired infirmity occasions the rack & torment under which he groans, but his present Diseases are his own doing, & the consequences of his own Irregularity.

To what does another owe his poverty & misery, but to his idleness & sloth in not exercising according to the commands of Religion, the talents which God has given him, to his [p. 150] extravagance & prodigality in wasting disorderly the measure of goods dealt out unto him, to his pride & vanity in raising himself above his Station, & affecting to view with those, whose more easie circumstances in life make a different conduct consistent with the strictest prudence.

To what is it to be imputed that Men's labours are not always attended with the desired success, but because they do not pursue the method which tends to draw down the Blessing of God upon their endeavours, because they lay foundation of their house upon oppression, extortion & grinding the face of the poor, because the means they employ are fraudulent and [p. 151] iniquitous, & the path they walk in, the very reverse of that, which religion traces out for them.

To what do we owe the most intolerable of all the evils of life, the pangs & remorse of Conscience but to a sense of Guilt & an inward Conviction that we have acted contrary to the Law of God & the Injunctions of Religion. It is this, which fills the mind with unspeakable anxiety & anguish, which renders a Man fearful of himself, fearful to look into his own actions, fearful to listen to his own reason & the upbraidings of his own heart, It is this, which poysons the most flattering enjoyments of life, which creates misery & wretchedness in the midst of every thing intended to [p. 152] make us happy, which turns our silver into drops, & cankers our best & choicest possessions, according to the observation of King Solomon, The Spirit of a Man will sustain his infirmity, but a wounded Spirit, who can bear?[349]

Thus does Religion prevent & root out the principle of many great & real evils in life, & as for those which have not their foundation in vice & appetite, & consequently do not proceed from ourselves, it mitigates & softens them. It shews us their proper use tendency & design. It furnishes us with motives weighty enough to excite our patience & submission under them, & thereby frequently *makes* enables us [p. 153] to draw comfort & satisfaction, even from the most unfavourable & unpromising circumstances, the daily experience of Good Men evinces the truth of this, & the shining Examples of fortitude & resignation which virtue in distress from time to time, has exhibited to the World, are a standing proof of the power of Religion to support a Man under the pressure of the greatest misfortunes.

If then it be true wisdom to use the fittest means to prevent real evils, or to lessen the force of those, which we are not able to ward off, If that Man be truly wise, who stedfastly pursues the only methods, which can bring about these desirable ends. He who follows the Dictates of Religion, [p. 154] who makes these the foundation of his conduct, who inviolably adheres to & never swerves from them, He I say is wise & intelligent, & in this sense again, the truth of the observation in the Text is manifest, Behold, the fear of the Lord, that is Wisdom.

3rd: Lastly. Religion is our truest wisdom, because the Practice of it is attended with many considerable advantages, & is the means of attaining the chief & only Good. The advantages, pleasures & unspeakable satisfaction arising from the performance of all that Religion requires, how much so-ever [p. 155] they may be ridiculed & made the objects of raillery by those, who have never desired nor sought for them, are yet so real & solid, so satisfactory in themselves, so infinitely happy in their consequences, that they abundantly out-weigh whatever difficulties, they may be attended with, & fully manifest the Wisdom of him, who makes Religion his choice & the Rule he steers himself by.

For what pleasure & advantage do we derive from a lively & firm perswasion, that we are ever under the Government & Guidance of a Wise, a bountiful, & a Gracious Being, that all things are ruled & directed by him, & consequently that what-ever [p. 156] befalls us, is the result of infinite wisdom & goodness, & therefore must be intended for our own good & to answer some useful purpose.

What advantage do we draw as well as pleasure from the constant practice of the outward Acts of Devotion & piety & the regular Intercourse which we keep up with God by Prayer & the participation of his Sacraments, entering as it were into a kind of familiarity with him & receiving in return the encouraging pledges of his love & favour. What heartfelt satisfaction from the exact & punctual discharge of the Moral Duties which Religion enjoins? Now much more true & real complacency, in relieving the distress of the afflicted, in undoing the [p. 157] heavy burden, in letting the oppressed go free, in breaking the yoke of the weary, in conciliating difference, in making up strife & contention, in introducing concord & harmony, in fulfilling the different acts of mercy, compassion & Charity, than in all the noisy & empty pleasures of the vitious & Libertine, These never clog, nor satiate, they are never attended with anxiety or remorse, they leave no bitter sting, no uneasie rememberance behind them.

What constant & never failing delight does the Religious Man draw from the testimony of his Conscience & the natural Reflections from a well spent life? To look back upon his own actions, to see them conformable [p. 158] to the will of God, to have his own heart to bear him witness, & his own Conscience to applaud & commend him, is a spring of joy & delight, incessantly flowing with good, hourly overspreading such a Man's life with serenity & contentment, & daily furnishing him with new matter where-on to exalt & rejoice.

But if the Religious Man be truly wise in thus securing his present peace & happiness, how much more so is he, if we add this more important & weighty advantage, that at the same time, that he is doing this he is providing for his future eternal welfare, & laying the foundation of endless & never ceasing joys.

[p. 159] For when all is said & done, let the circumstances of Men be what they may, their present enjoyments ever so great, their fortunes ever so large & ample, their alliances ever so conspicuous & flattering, a time must shortly come, when all these dazzling distinctions shall afford them no assistance, when disrobed of these, they shall be left to themselves, with no other comfort, but what the Intimations of their own hearts & the sense of their own integrity can give them. And who shall then appear truly wise but he who has early provided against that time, who has laid up a fund of good words against the day of Visitation, & who with his [p. 160] lamp burning & his Loyns girded can meet his Lord with the confidence of a faithfull & Diligent Steward.

Applic[ation]:

Thus is the Religious Man wise in acquiring the most useful knowledge, procuring to himself the greatest good; But if this be wisdom, the reverse of all this must be the highest folly & the extremest rashness, The Man who gives up Religion, gives up at once all the comfort & satisfaction of life, lays himself open to all the disasters & accidents of this World, has no inward [p. 161] principle to support him under these, no outward stay upon which to rely, but his only expectation is, that there is nothing beyond this World & his only hope that he is to be annihilated & reduced to his original primitive nothing.

And is this the mighty advantage which these Men would put us in possession of, this the service they do the World? To rob Men of their best & most flattering wishes, to deprive them of every source of comfort & consolation, & to leave them to struggle against the evils of vice by the meer strength of their own Reason. It is indeed highly probable, that they are [p. 162] conscious to themselves that by undermining Religion they are doing a manifest injury to Society, but their Passions are so strong & their inward fears so alarming, that it becomes their interest to believe Religion with it's threats & promises to be the meer Invention & Contrivance of Crafty Men, & thus do they go on, deluding their own selves, & taking an handle from every appearance of an Argument to silence their fears & get the better of their apprehensions & terror, till sickness & the approach of Death fix their attention & force them to be considerate for then do the hardiest Opponents of Religion generally [p. 163] alter both their opinions & languages abjure most sincerely their former impious tenets, & heartily wish it was then in their power, to secure to themselves in their last hours the comforts of Religion, & the encouraging support it affords.

Let not then the Endeavours of Wicked Men to draw us all from the practice of Religion ever prevail or prove effectual, Let us arm ourselves against them by a steady & invariable adherence to all it's precepts & injunctions, This is the only way to judge of Religion & of the usefulness & importance of it, & to convince ourselves, that [p. 164] what-ever others may pretend to, or what-ever they may glory in, yet to <u>fear the Lord is wisdom, & to depart from evil is understanding</u>.

I shall conclude with the lively description which Solomon gives us of Religion under the name of wisdom.

<u>Happy is the Man, that findeth Wisdom, & the Man that getteth understanding, For the merchandise of it is better than the merchandise of silver, & the gain there of than that fine Gold, She is more precious [p. 165] than Rubies, & all the things thou can'st desire, are not to be compared unto her length of days is in her right hand in her left hand riches & honour, Her ways are ways of pleasantness, & all her paths are peace. She is a tree of life to them, that lay hold upon her, & happy is every one, that retaineth her, sleep therefore sound wisdom & discretion, So shall they be life unto thy Soul & grace unto thy neck, Then shalt thou walk in thy way safely, [p. 166] thy foot shall not stumble, when thou liest down, thou shalt not be afraid, yea thou shalt lye down, & thy sleep shall be sweet</u>.[350]

Sermon XVII

Volume 5 (48)

[p. 167] Belfast on Easterday March ye 26th 1749
Ditto March ye 29th 1752
Ditto March the 30th 1755
Ditto April the 15th 1759
Ditto April the 3rd 1763
Ditto April the 3rd 1768
St. Keavans Easterday April ye 11th 1784[351]
St. Doloughs Sunday after Easter April ye 18th 1784
Ditto on Easter Sunday April ye 16th 1786
Ditto on Ditto April 12 1789
Ditto on Ditto April 24 1791
Ditto on Ditto March 31 1793
St. Michans Sunday after Easter 1793
St. Dol[oughs] Easter Day 1795
Ditto Ditto 1798
Ditto Ditto 1800
Rosenallis Ditto 1803
Mt. Mellick Sunday after Easter 1803
Ditto Easter Sunday 1805
Rosenallis Eas[ter] S[unday] 1806
Ditto Ditto 1809
Ditto Ditto 1811

[p. 168] In the Fifteenth Chapter of St. Paul's First Epistle to the Corinthians at the Fifty fifth Verse.

O Death where is thy Sting, O Grave where is thy Victory?

The Fear of Death is a Natural Principle implanted in *every* <the Human> Breast by the Author of our Being to answer several wise & *useful* <good> ends, *To* <It> makes us bear with the severest dispensations of Providence, rather than *to* defeat the *use & tendency* <usefulness & advan-

tage> of them by putting an end to our *present* <own> existence, *To* <It> spurs us up, to action & *engages us to to go chearfully thro' that mass of toil & care, which the maintenance and preservation of life alone and renders easy & acceptable* <prevents our weariness, & dignity under all that toil & labour, to which we are incessantly exposed. *To be* <It is> a <powerful> restraint upon our [p. 170] unruly Passions, & a fence against the Violation of the Laws of God and Man.

But the misfortune is that these ends are often perverted & the natural principle like some others is carried to extremes that the fear of Death is often <frequently> suffered to embitter the comfort & happiness of our lives, that we allow it to fill us with unspeakable anxiety & anguish that we become <in some sense> slaves to this natural principle & thro' fear of Death are all our life-time subject unto bondage.

But the misfortune is, that the ends intended by this principle are too often perverted, *to the embittering all the compass of life & to the reducing us to a state of … and bondage* & that instead of confining them within the bounds which Reason & Religion *have* prescribe*d to them*, we suffer them to embitter all the comforts of life & to reduce us to a continued State of slavery & bondage.[352]

Against this excessive & unreasonable fear of Death does the Apostle *endeavour to* caution us in the Chapter out of which the Text is taken; And the method he proceeds upon is to establish the *Great & important* truth of *Christ's* <O[ur] B[lessed] S[aviour]'s> Resurrection, which he shews us to be founded upon all the arguments *that* <which> a fact of this Nature could possibly admit of, upon his own testimony, upon that of the [p. 172] twelve Apostles, & upon the joint evidence of above five hundred Brethren at once[353] whose authority in this case was so much the more to be regarded, *that* <as> the Nature of the fact <which> they attested, submitted as it was to the<ir> senses *of so many Persons*, for the space of forty days, could not allow them to be deceived in it, nor the hardships Persecutions & distresses *that* <which> were the immediate consequence of their attesting it, *to have us at liberty to think that they intended to deceive us* <to think that they ever intended to deceive or impose upon the World>; whence the Impression <which> these arguments make upon the Apostle is so strong, as to induce him to break out into this Confident boast, that since Christ was truly risen, Death had now lost it's sting, & the Grave it's Victory over Man & the powers of Human Nature.

The Inferences to be drawn from O[ur] B[lessed] S[aviour]'s Resurrection are so important & many, that they cannot well be comprised within [p. 174] the Limit of one Discourse, I shall therefore select the particular one now before us for the subject of our present mediation & from the Comfort which Christ's Resurrection affords us <in this aspect>, shall endeavour to lessen since it is impossible to eradicate entirely the natural dread we *are in* <have> of Death, *to consider the arguments that such a consideration offers, to sustain & support us at the approach of it & tho'* we cannot with the Apostle wholly triumph over it <we may> at least prevent <in some measures> it's triumphing over us.

To this end I shall enquire into the true causes of the Dread & fear of Death & attempt to remove them by adding under each of these the comforts & Encouragements <that> naturally flowing from Christs Resurrection,

And in order to this Let us enquire into the Grounds & foundation of this fear of Death, *that by setting in opposition to these the comfort & encouragment which naturally flow from the Ressurection of Christ, we may decide then of their power & from these sources of trouble & anguish into occasions of confidence and joy* <& see how far a firm belief of Christ's Resurrection deprives them of their power & naturally lends to them these sources of stress & anguish into sources of confidence & joy>.[354]

1st Cause

And the First Cause of the fear of death *that* <which> I shall mention is *Great doubt & [p. 175] uncertainty with relation to what is likely to happen to us here-after & to be the consequence of our own Death* <the doubt we generally entertain of the certainty of a future state>.

For as We are made up of a Soul & of a body, it concerns us much to know, what is to become of these two different Substances, whether the Soul dyes with the Body or whether it survives it's dissolution; the desire we have of Immortality, the consideration of God's infinite and adorable Perfections, the consciousness *we have* of the merit or demerit of our own actions, had us indeed to *expect that there may be a future State & that our souls may be immortal* <the expectation of a future State>; But then this is not sufficient to remove all doubt & diffidence, there still remains some anxiety, some scruple, we stand wavering between this hope and the fear of annihilation, we are alternately moved by these two Passions, & unaccountably wracked in our last moments by this uncertainty, till <we raise our thoughts to> the Resurrection of Our Lord & Saviour Jesus Christ <which effectually> strengthens [p. 176] our faith, confirms our hopes, fixes & settles all such dubious & wavering thoughts.

For if we believe that J[esus] C[hrist] was raised from the dead, if we once admit this principle, & it is so fully proved, that none can reject it without giving up at once all matters of fact of which they have not been eye witnesses, it follows as an undeniable consequence, that the Religion which he preached, the Doctrines which he taught & the truths which he published were genuine & authentic, *since God would never perpetrate such a story as his Resurrection from the dead to be expressed upon an Imposture which had amanifest tendencey to lead them into such mistakes & therefore we may yield an undoubted assent to evry thing he taught* <carrying with them the stamp of God himself & confirmed unto us by the Greatest & most undoubled authority>.

But among those truths which he published we find the Certainty of a Future State & the Immortality of our Soul, not slightly [p. 177] mentioned or cursorily hinted at, but in some *measure* <sense> made the whole of Christianity, the end which it always has in view & to which it always refers, These are propounded to us as the foundation of all our hopes, the anchor of our Souls *strong* <sure> & steadfast,[355] the motive of all our actions, the enlivening principle of every thing we do, These are settled by the Gospel not only as all other truths of the like importance, upon the strongest & most convincing arguments, but <they are> also in a particular manner *compiled &* illustrated to us *& by* in the Resurrection of J[esus] C[hrist] from the Dead.

For if his Body was suffered to see Corruption, & to be laid in the Grave, his Soul returned unto him, *that* <who> gave it, It descended not into the Chamber of the Grave, but continued in the hands of God, till united again to his body, he entered into his Glory as our fore-runner ...[356] <to prepare a place for us that where he is, there we might be also>.[357]

[p. 178] *And of the same importance is it to us to* <Nor is it of less importance to us, to> be informed minutely of the fate *& destination* of our bodies after Death, & to know upon some very certain principles, whether they continue in the Grave, or whether they are one day to be joined again to our Souls. And to such a knowledge the faint Glimmerings of Reason could not carry us, for how are the Dead raised, & with what body do they come up,[358] was thought by the wisest Men a Question of itself sufficient to expose the impossibility *& absurdity* of the Resurrection of the body, *Could* <Can> the putrid & dispised particles of matter be united & gathered into one body? *Could* <Can> bodies *that* <which> have been mouldring in the Grave, be brought to life again, or Dead & dry bones live?[359]

But the Resurrection of Christ is a full & compleat answer to such an enquiry, & demonstrates at once the possibility and certainty of our own

Resurrection, <It demonstrates> [p. 179] the possibility, for cannot the same power *that* <which> brought O[ur] B[lessed] S[aviour] to live after he had been three days in the Grave, raise up our dead bodies, & restore them to life again, What was possible then is equally so now & the same Divine Energy *that* <which> exerted itself in Ch[rist']s Resurrection, may effect & bring about ours, however long we may have remained in the Grave, & visibly carried about us the marks of putrefaction & dissolution.

And the certainty of it, it equally proves not only as it is founded upon immutable & invariable promises, but as it immediately follows from the close & intimate union between Christ & us, for as we are all his body & members in particular,[360] so since Christ our head be risen, shall we the Members rise together each in our order, that as we have been planted in the likeness of his Death, we may be also in the likeness of his Resurrection[361] for as in Adam all dye ever so in Christ shall all be made alive.[362]

[p. 180] And now Let but the condition of a dying Christian dying with this comfortable assurance be present to our minds, *Let but the Comfort arising from the Consideration of O[ur] B[lessed] S[aviour]'s Ressurection be substitued in the place of those dreadful Phantoms which out imagination is apt to form to itself* and in how different a *view* <light> does Death appear! Death to such a Person, & with such an inward conviction is only a passage to a far more desirable existence, where he expects to have his longing after Immortality, crowned with Immortality itself, *both in his Body & soul,* his thirst after knowledge gratified *&* ..., his faculties restored & employed for ever without satiety & without disgust, No gloominess intercepts, his view, no mists of doubt or dissidence obscure his prospect full of faith he peirces beyond the Grave & <with St Stephen> sees Heaven open & Jesus standing at the right hand of God, & supported [p. 181] by this he is enabled to resign *his soul* <himself up> into the hands of his Creator *to defy the terrors of death, to shake & overthrow our confidence in the emphatical words of the Apostle Death is swallowed up in victory & Death where is thy sting & grave where is thy victory?* <in sure & certain hope that tho' worms destroy his body, not in his flesh shall he see God, whom he shall see for himself & his eyes shall behold & not another>.[363]

2nd Cause

The 2nd Cause of *the* <our> Fear of Death *arises from* <is> the sense *& Conciousness* we have of our own <sins> & infirmities *imperfections and defects.*

And this seems to follow naturally from what has been already said, For if there be a Life after this, & a future State of rewards & punishments, the Retribution *that* <which> is then to take place must be in proportion to the virtues & vices of Men, They who are contentious, & obey not the truth, but obey [p. 182] unrighteousness, are to expect only Indignation & wrath,[364] whilst honour Glory & Immortality are to be the just hire of those who seek for them by their constant & patient continuance in well doing.

But how few of us are there whose *Consciences* <Lives> can bear that strict scrutiny & trial which a consideration of this infinite importance must necessarily occasion, how few whose past conduct does not upbraid them with neglects & omissions of various kinds, how few who can witness to themselves that they have laboured to the utmost of their power to conform to the Laws of God, how few who do not shudder at their *many* <manifold> infirmities, their defects, their transgressions, their unfruitfulness under the means of Grace, *their neglect & disregard of the opportunties tendered to them* & consequently how dreadful the Reflection that the hour is now [p. 183] come to give an account of all these thoughts words & actions & according as they have been conformable or not to the Rules & Directions of Religion to be doomed by an irreversible Decree to endless happiness or endless misery.

Even supposing <that> in the examination of our *lives &* conduct, we should find but little reason to dread the displeasure & judgments of God, no habitual practice of wickedness to allarm us, no settled principles of disobedience, no voluntary willfull daring transgression, yet How weak of itself is such a dependence, unable to ballance all the misgivings & terrors *that yet* <which> still remain. The best of us are liable to so many errors & mistakes, our virtues so imperfect, our dispositions so languid, our endeavours so fluctuating & uncertain, that we could build but little dependence upon them *especially* when *compared* <above all we compare them> with the purity & [p. 184] excellency of the Supreme Being to whom they are offered, & by whom they are to be accepted & rewarded.

Or should we trust to our sorrow & sincere Repentance for what we have done amiss, not to mention how late, how partial, how defective such a Repentance often is, how could we be sure that God would accept some transient sighs & groans instead of obedience, that a short & temporary sorrow for many great transgressions, would avert the threatened judgments & obtain to our present submission *as short as it is,* the reward *that* <which are only> promised to a*n endure* <constant> perseverance in the practice of Virtue & godliness.

We may indeed as the strongest foundation of our confidences rely upon the merits & sufferings of O[ur] B[lessed] S[aviour] & expect from that mercy by which we are redeemed, the pardon & remission of our sins; But how much [p. 185] so ever we owe *to his Death and Passion* our Reconciliation with God <to the Death & Passion of Christ> yet had *Christ* <he> continued in the Grave, we should still have some doubt of it's true worth & intrinsic value, we could not *tell* know it's utmost price in the sight of God, nor fully understand the whole efficacy of it to procure unto us *his* favour & *approbation* <acceptance>.

But Blessed be the God & Father of our Lord Jesus Christ which according to his abundant mercy hath begotten us again unto a lively hope by the Resurrection of Jesus Christ from the dead,[365] By this *does* did God declare that he accepted the invaluable sacrifice of his B[lessed] Son as the propitiation for our sins, By this we *see* understand the terms upon which we may expect & expect with undoubted assurance the rewards promised to a [p. 186] perfect obedience. By this we see the displeasure of our Creator changed into Complacency & Approbation, & the hearty & sincere sorrow of a Penitent Sinner graciously received & amply rewarded, And as Christ was openly delivered for our offences, & visibly suffered for our transgressions, so by this do we see him rising again for our justification, sealing unto us our pardon, & *calming our remorse & anguish of ours* <by this one act speaking peace unto the penitent soul>, Who shall Lay any thing to the charge of God's elect? It is God that justifieth, who is he that condemneth? It is Christ that died yea rather that is risen again, who is also at the right hand of God making intercession for us.[366]

3rd Cause

The Last Cause I shall mention of the Dread & terror with <which> Death is generally [p. 187] encompassed is the Loss & Removal of every thing we enjoy in this Life.

Death deprives us of our most valuable possession, dissolves the closest & most intimate Relations, looses the bands of the strictest & most inviolable friendships, puts an end to all the Greatness of this World, determines & that for ever our present pleasures possessions & enjoyments and considering the high value we usually set upon Earthly objects, the eagerness with which they are pursued, the large share of our affections they most commonly engross, it is not much to be wondered at that the thoughts of leaving them forever should wrack & disturb us, especially when we have nothing before us but the dreadful solitude of the Grave the awakening prospect of an approaching dissolution, & the dismal attendants of it weakness both of body & mind.

[p. 188] Nor indeed would a total indifference about parting with the things of this World, be in itself laudable or commendable. The principles of our Nature direct us to have some affection for them, they are present & always before our eyes, they are the means by which much rational pleasure & satisfaction are conveyed unto us, & therefore when all these are instantly to be removed, when Death is taking us away from these objects of our love & solicitude, when we reflect that a few moments more, & we shall be carried away from the midst of our fortunes our honours our pleasures, & what to a generous mind is more than fortune honours or pleasure, our friends & Dearest Relations it is impossible but Nature should feel some shock & *humanity recoil* <Man start> back at the thought.

But was our Faith & confidence in the [p. 189] Resurrection of our Lord & Saviour, strong & stedfast. Religion would get the better of Nature, & Reason *lessen the throbs of Humanity* <soften it's panes & throbbings>, They would if not totally suppress, at least prevent the continuance of these impressions of horror to the disturbance of the peace & serenity of our last hours; For with a thorough perswasion that Christ is truly risen from the Dead, we are enabled to discover in that Eternity whose truth & certainty it so unquestionably confirms, blessings far exceeding those which we leave behind, far more satisfactory than *these* <any> which the present Oeconomy can possibly afford.

Do the treasures we are *in* <to yield> possession of, *the Earthly wealth we are blessed with, the Goods of pleasure we are now to give up* occasion our uneasiness & trouble? The Resurrection of Christ fixes our thoughts [p. 191] upon Heavenly & Lasting treasures, It presents us with the fullest enjoyment of the most solid & real good, freedom from all Corruption & sin, the contintual feast of a clear & serene Conscience, Deliverance from misery trouble & danger, the daily incessant improvement of our Moral faculties & power, the accession of new knowledge, of new matter to exercise our understanding & intellectual capacities.

Do we Lament & bewail the Pomp and Grandeur of this World, *the loss of* those flattering distinctions with which we are honoured, *the passing away of that* <and all that> glittering shew which attended our condition here? The Resurrection of Christ offers to our view whatever is in reality most flattering, most worthy of ambition & desire, *An admittance into the presence of him,* For can any thing be more so <flattering>,[367] than to be admitted into the Immediate Presence of that Infinite [p. 192] Supreme Being, unto whom thousands minister[368] & before whom ten thousand times ten thousand stand[369] & worship, to be particularly chosen to dwell forever in the Splendor of this Divine Court, to be Inhabitants & Members of that State which was perculiarly designed to be the highest reward of God's faithfull & best beloved Servants, to contemplate fully that Celestial Glory & radiancy, in comparison of which all the Pomp & Greatness of this World are of no value no significance.

Do the Friendships we are parting with, fill us with anxiety & anguish, Friendships fleeting, inconstant, frequently treacherous friendships, at best uncertain as our continuance here? The Resurrection of Christ promises unto us the only desirable the only alluring the only satisfactory friendships, a Communication with those whose interest whose virtue whose love is the [p. 193 blank, p. 194] same, who dwell continually together linked by the closest bonds, inspired with the same affections, concurring to the advancement of the same end, whom no jarring Interests divide, no boisterous Passions vent, no tumultuous Appetites toss & tear, A Communication with an innumerable Company of Angels, with the general assembly of the first born which are written in Heaven, with God the Judge of all, with the Spirits of just Men made perfect, & with Jesus the Mediator of the new Covenant,[370] whom we are *now* to see face to face, *whose glory we are to behold* & into whose presence we are to inhabit forever.

Do our families the Dearest part of ourselves engross our affection, & the thoughts of their <future> desolate condition cause anguish in our breasts? The [p. 195] Resurrection of Christ sweetens, mitigates softens these distracting reflections, It shews us that we are not to be deprived of them for ever, that they who are to be the Heirs of our fortune here, are to partake of our happiness here-after, that like Provident Guardians we are going before them *only* to prepare them a Mansion in our Common Father's house, that yet a little while & we shall all meet together, & see each other happy beyond our present wishes and expectations, when liable to no change & free from all disaster, we shall be eternally happy, & together with the Children whom God has Given us, shall *abide for ever* <for ever live> with him in Glory.

Finally. Does the Gloomy prospect of the Grave *awaken our fears*, the weakness of a perishing body, the Decays of Nature the thoughts of a mouldring corruptible [p. 196] body, soon to be reduced into powder, & <to> become the sport & prey of the vilest & most offensive Creatures, *pursue us with their wracking* ... <present themselves to us>? The Resurrection of Christ brightens even this dark, this dispiriting view. It assures us that as he triumphed over Death, so shall we in like manner triumph over it, that what is sown in Corruption, shall be raised in Incorruption, that what is sown in dishonour shall be raised in Glory, that what is sown in weakness shall be raised in power, that what is sown a Corruptible body shall be raised Incorruptible, that as we have born the Image of the Earthy, we shall also bear the Image of the Heavenly, that our vile body shall be fashioned like unto Christs glorious body, *that* <when> Death itself shall be, when Death itself shall be swallowed up in Victory, & *that therefore at our departure out of thus World we may* [p. 198] *join with the Apostle in this axclamination* <every sincere Christian made to triumph over it in the words of the Text> O Death where is thy sting. O Grave where is thy Victory? The Sting of Death is sin & the strength of sin is the law, but thanks be to God which giveth us the Victory, through our Lord Jesus Christ[371]

Such then <These> are the powerful weapons with which the Resurrection of Christ enables us to defeat the attacks of Death & <to> disarm it of it's sting; but as effectual as they may prove they are only so to those *the uprightness & integrity of whose conversion give them the right to consider them with confidence & Assurance* <whose Consciences bear them witness, that in simplicity & godly sincerity they have had their conversation in time past>,[372] *The* <Such> Virtuous & faithfull Sons of obedience are the only Persons to whom the Resurrection of Christ can afford either comfort of support. To all others it becomes matter for the highest anxiety & anguish. The Certainty of the truths which it confirms *only* serves to fill their minds with dread & terror, & the dismaying prospect it opens to them, rots & deprives their [p. 199] Soul of every quieting consideration, Their existence here-after, the horrors for which they are reserved, the thoughts of an Angry & *provoked* <offended> God, *provoked* <offended> at their numberless & repeated transgressions, the Testimony of their Conscience approving the Dictates of Religion assault them by turns & leave their condition desperate & irremediable.

Therefore my Beloved Brethren To *secure these* prevent <therefore> this most real evil & <to> secure to ourselves the invaluable comforts I have been mentioning <Let us> follow the Apostle's advice in the Conclusion of this whole matter, Be stedfast immovable always abounding in the work of the Lord, *since* <for as much as> we know that labour is not in vain in the Lord,[373] Let us *settle the grounds of our confidence* <build our hope & confidence where above it is to be built> upon the firm & steady foundation of [p. 200] a good & virtuous life, dye unto sin & rise again unto righteousness, depart from inequity & perfect holiness in the fear of the Lord, that by thus living the life of the righteous we may dye his Death, & make our *latter* <last> end be like unto his, so that when we are called upon to walk thro' the Valley of the shadow of Death, God may lead us with his right hand, sustain us with his rod & staff, & thro' the Grave & Gate of Death admitt us to a joyful & Glorious Resurrection for his merits, who dyed, & was buried, & rose again for us <even> his son Jesus Christ our Lord.

To whom with the Father & the Holy Ghost & etc.

Sermon XVIII

Volume 5 (50)

[p. 232]

Belfast May the 7th 1749
Ditto December the 8th 1751
Ditto October the 13th 1754
Ditto August the 14th 1757
Ditto September the 16th 1759
Ditto November the 7th 1764
Ditto September the 11th 1768
Anacloan February 4 1821[374]
Ardmore 20 April 1822

[p. 233] In the Fourth Chapter of Saint Paul's first Epistle to the Thessalonians at the Sixth Verse.

That no Man go beyond & defraud his Brother in any matter, because that the Lord is the avenger of all such.

The Command in the Text not to go beyond & defraud our Brother in any matter, seems to contain & forbid all possible ways *whereby we may injure or do* <of doing> wrong one to another, whether we openly attack our Neighbour's Person by attempting upon his life, raising up quarrels & contentions to the endangering of his safety, or otherwise maiming [p. 234] and wounding those with whom we are at variance, Or whether we injure his reputation & character by false & scandalous reports, inventing what we know to be untrue & even spreading about what is true with no other view than to lessen his Influence, *& credit* & satisfy an ill-natured & bitter spleen, Or whether we aim at his property & fortune, coveting what he possesses, & endeavouring to wrest it out of his hands, *which we have no right to demand nor title to claim* <without any right or title>.

I shall for the present wave the consideration of the two former ways of *whereby we may* go<ing> beyond & defrauding our Brother, and <shall>

confine myself to that kind of injustice which regards the property and goods of our neighbour [p. 236], and this I shall endeavour to speak to, 1st By shewing the particular ways that Injustice suggests of injuring & spoiling the possessions of others *which are proved by the precept* <or as they are expressed> in the Text of go<ing> beyond & defraud<ing> our Brother *in his fortune and effects* & 2nd By laying before you the hatefulness, baseness & dangerous tendency of them included under these words, Because the Lord is the Avenger of all such.[375]

1st Part.

First. I am to endeavour to shew the particular ways that Injustice suggests of injuring & spoiling the possessions of others, or as they are expressed in the Text of going beyond & defrauding our Brother.

These indeed are many & various, as many & complicated as the Passions of Men who model & frame them according [p. 237] to their own desires, & which to be narrowly enquired into, would far exceed the *compass* <limit's> of one Discourse, I shall therefore comprehend them in general under the following heads, 1st. That of Acquiring by indirect & unlawful means what belongs to our neighbour, & 2nd. With-holding from him what we justly owe to him, and know to be his.

1st. Acquiring by indirect & unlawful means what belongs to him. I say by indirect & unlawful means; For it is allowable to endeavour to *encrease* <enlarge> our fortune whenever *it comes unto our way to do so* <we can do so> consistently with conscience & duty, to consult the interest of ourselves & families, & by our own labour & industry to promote the encrease of their wellfare & happiness; And to do this Honesty & fair dealing [p. 238] are the surest & safest means, But as these methods appear too slow & tedious to those whose hearts are set upon wealth & impatient of any delay *or restraint*, other arts & stratagems have been found out to attain the same end tho' *by* <in> a different & quite contrary *method* manner.

I do not here mean that open violence & force, with which some seize upon the goods & fortunes of others, attacking them *as it were* with an armed force, & directly & barefacedly appropriating to themselves what belongs to others; Acts of this kind are generally condemned by every Person, they become the objects of the Civil Magistrate's resentment, & the unhappy offenders are cheerfully given up to the severity of the Law, each finding his security in their punishment & detection.

[p. 239] *There are other secret & sudden* <But what I principally intend to condemn are those secret & hidden> methods of acquiring, which tho' not so daringly wicked, are no less criminal, & by being concealed from the publick notice become more dangerous & ensnaring, <& what is more attended with a sort of sanction>, capable of gaining upon those who would shudder at the former, & be violently incensed at the bare suspicion of it.

Among these must be reckoned all dissimulation & insinserity in enhancing the value of what we sell, hiding the<ir> real defects under a deceitful gloss, *&* <or> extolling the<ir> perfections beyond what they deserve, imposing in this manner upon the judgment of those we deal with, & putting it out of their power to find out the deceit till it be too late, for if in Solomon' opinion it be unjust in the buyer to say, it is naught, it is naught whilst he boasteth [p. 240] in his heart of his purchase,[376] sure it must be equally so in the Seller to attempt to represent things to the buyer in a different light from what they really are *to raise* <in order to excite in him> a desire which *he cannot gratify* <is not to be gratified> but at his own visible expence & loss.

Much of the same nature is Cunning in improving the weakness & ignorance of those we deal with to our own ends, *when conscious of* <turning & directing> their inability *we leave it* to our own advantage, & *pursue* <pursuing> our private interest at the same time that we loudly profess to have nothing in view but their's, & this frequently in cases where a visible confidence is reposed in us, & much dependence laid upon our judgment & honesty.

Such again is Cruelty in making a handle of the wants & necessities [p. 241] of others whether they be of a Publick or of a private nature, whether in times of dearth & scarcity we monopolize necessary and useful Commodities, & raise their price at pleasure to the ruin & destruction of the poor & needy, or whether knowing the extremity of those we deal with, we beat them down to a low & *unreasonable* <pitiful> price & *force them to come to our own unjust & cruel* <force them thro' poverty & necessity to comply with & unreasonable> terms, A Species of injustice this particularly observed by Solomon in these strong & emphatical words, He that withholdeth corn, the people shall curse him, but blessing shall be upon the head of him that selleth it.[377]

No way inferior to this piece of Barbarity is exacting to the utmost of our power, what was really our own, but by several [p. 243] concurring circumstances ceases to be so, when we consider not & make no allowance for the real incapacity of those who without any fault or crime of their own but thro' the common & unavoidable misfortunes of life are disabled from doing what their own Conscience would willingly prompt them to, had they it in their power, whom therefore we should make the objects of our Compassion & Charity, not the Subjects of our Cruelty & severity, & rather help & assist ourselves than add a load to their affliction, by our ill timed & improper demands.[378]

Liable to the same Charge of injustice is he who breaks thro' the Laws of the Land he lives in, & by a prohibited & forbidden trade frustrates those who rule over [p. 244] him of what is necessarily due to them for the support of their authority & power, not only violating the most solemn engagements, but also offering a manifest injury to the fair & honest Trader, whose goods he is hereby enabled to undersell, the growth and extent of whose Trade he hereby greatly checks, & rob of the reward so justly due to his integrity & uprightness.

To all which methods of unlawfully acquiring what belongs to our neighbour, I shall add but this one, the artfulness of those who living in idleness & sloth abuse the charity & beneficence of good & well meaning Persons, & who counterfeiting misery & poverty deprive real objects of the bounty of their Fellow Creatures, and apply to the encouraging of their idleness, what was intended for the relief of the [p. 245] honest poor and the Comfort of sickness and old-age.

2nd. We not only go beyond and defraud our Brother, in acquiring by indirect and unlawful means what belongs to him, but also by with-holding from him, what we justly owe to him & know to be his.

And this is particularly the case of three sorts of Persons.

The 1st. are they who being entrusted with the management and administration of other People's fortunes abuse this trust either by neglecting their interests, or what is worse by applying to their own use what belongs to those, who have committed them to their care and custody.

For where ever so much confidence is placed in a Person as to leave to him the [p. 246] care of what is most valuable *to us*, how highly unjust must he be deemed, if by a Criminal carelessness <he suffers> those interests to be disregarded & lets those opportunities of improving them pass unnoticed, which he would eagerly catch at, were they his own interest he managed, if he brings not the same exactness & attention to the settling of other Peoples affairs that he does to his own, especially if he converts to his own use what he has no right to claim, spoiling the Orphan & fatherless of their due & building his own fortune upon the ruin of the Widow and the friendless.

The second sort of Persons who defraud their Brother by with-holding from him what they know to be his, are they that use their neighbour's service without wages, & give him not for his work,[379] who [p. 247] are so cruelly unjust as to require their labour & service, & yet with-hold from them their poor pittance, & refuse to allow them what their tedious toil deserves, & their own tacit agreement obliges them to.

Men of this turn & disposition of mind generally add one act of injustice to another, & as they exact their labour without hire, so do they often require more from them than is reasonable, adding work to work, & like the task Masters of Egypt, demanding the tale of Bricks where no straw was given,[380] for when once violence is so far offered to our Nature as to stifle generous & equitable sentiments, t'is hard to tell how far we may *be carried* <go>, the evil insensibly & by degrees grows upon us, and from being hard & unjust to the poor & defenceless hire-ling we may easyly become so to those of our own family [p. 248] and house-hold, who being part of ourselves & more peculiarly recommended to our care *should* <ought to> be the most intimate & constant objects of our justice & Compassion.

The Last Class of People I shall mention who come under the heavy charge of going beyond & defrauding their Brother by keeping back what is his, are they that live above their circumstances, & the station of Life God has placed them in, & thence bring themselves under a necessity of contracting unnecessary debt, & so failing in the*ir* engagements & *breaking the contracts* <obligations> they have entred into.

A Species of injustice so much the more to be insisted upon, as it is but too often practised & prevails but too much to the utter ruin & destruction of several honest & industrious families; T'is highly [p. 249] probable that Many who have been guilty of *this gross* <such glaring> injustice never intended to be so. Had the *consequences* <dreadful effects> of *such a* <their> conduct been laid before them, they would have trembled at the very mention of them, but love of pleasure, a desire of conforming to the manners of those above us, & chiefly a degree of Pride & vanity carry us these great lengths, till the Danger is too near to be avoided, & the prospect too gloomy to be dwelt upon.

But whence so ever the injustice proceeds the consequence is the same, It is purchasing our pleasures & extravagancies at the expence of our neighbour, It is cloathing ourselves with the spoils of the poor, It is using our influence & directing our outward pompous appearance to the ensnaring of the ignorant & credulous, It is deliberate fraud & determined [p. 250] injustice, as it's foundation is laid upon falsehood & deceit, so does it always end in misery disgrace & infamy.

Which leads me *to* in the 2nd place to lay before you the hatefulness, baseness & dangerous tendency of such unjust & unrighteous practices.

2nd Part.

And Little need be said to shew the hatefulness & meanness of injustice & dishonesty, The thing sufficiently speaks itself. Where is the Man hardened & obdurate enough to avow himself guilty of it, Where is the Man that would openly & publicly acknowledge himself griping, covetous, lying, cruel, rapacious, & oppressive? For in reality each of these form the unjust Man's Character, each of these is the spring & [p. 251] motive that sets him to act; To what purpose would he so often break thro' the strict and sacred rules of truth & sincerity, unless he preferred some present Worldly gain & lucre to the inviolable regard he has for veracity & candor, To what purpose would he maintain the most constant attachment to his interest & profit at the expence of virtue & honesty, unless he considered these as inferior & subordinate considerations, no further to be minded than as the others are served & attended to, To what purpose would he so frequently commit oppression <&> extortion, violence *oppression* and injustice, unless he found more pleasure & satisfaction in his own depraved & corrupt sense of advantage & gain, than in all the solid quiet & lasting delights inseparable from the practice of universal [p. 252] justice and equity.

Is there then a real baseness in lying, deceit, fraud, insincerity & dissimulation? How base & dishonourable must he appear who is alternately swayed & moved by these, whose actions are ever directed by such vile & unworthy motives, who takes counsil from, & continually listens to the suggestions of them.

But 2nd. The Evil of Injustice extends further, & affects Society in General.

All Society is founded upon a mutual compact & agreement, a reciprocal trust & confidence in each other, which is the true & only cement that *can* keeps us together, No entercourse can be carried on among Men but upon such a supposition, If we treat with others, we must understand that they carry on the same design with [p. 253] ourselves, & as we mean to act fairly with them in discharging our just obligations to them, that they in like manner intend to keep up exactly & rigorously to the terms in consideration of which we enter into such engagements.

But Injustice & dishonesty at once dissolves this compact, It means the very reverse of what we do, It breaks thro' the sacredness of bonds & obligations, It is restrained by no terms or conditions, It offers a manifest violence to us, It encroaches upon our natural rights, it invades all property & dominion, It overturns the sence of law & equity; Hence must Society sink & be destroyed, Men are kept together by no link or bond, An end is put to trust, confidence, & faith in each other, Nothing but rapine & violence [p. 255] ensues, Every Man's hand is against his Brothers Suspicions take place of reliance & good opinion, & Communication and entercourse with others for ever cease & vanish.

3d. Injustice & dishonesty removes the Blessing of God from our endeavours
3d. And as Injustice is thus prejudicial to Society in general, it proves equally so to our private interest & concerns, in as much as it necessarily tends to remove the Blessing of God from us & our endeavours.[381]

Except the Lord build the house, their labour is but lost that build it, It is but lost labour, that we haste to rise up early & so late take rest & eat the bread of care-fulness,[382] unless the Blessing of God furthers our labour, prospers our endeavours & accompanies our toil with his favour and protection.

But Can they expect this that build their fortunes upon extortion & oppression, Can the unjust Man promise to himself [p. 256] the assistance of the most just & upright God? Can he flatter himself that he will look down with complacency & satisfaction upon his unrighteous doings, that he will further his unjust designs, that he <will> send down his choicest blessings upon his uncharitableness, his oppression, his Cruelty, his extortion?

Whence it holds often true, that fortunes raised upon such rotten foundations soon come to the ground, & crush the vain Possessor under their ruins, a secret curse attends them which wants & consumes them, they unaccountably dwindle away, & leave nothing but shame & disgrace behind them, Whilst the more silent & less pompous acquisitions of the honest & upright wear & thrive [p. 257] well, generally gather new strength, make continual & incessant advances, & from low beginnings often rise to a great & surprising height. And upon this is founded that vulgar but very rational observation; Honesty is the best Policy. It is the highest wisdom because it is the probablest means of attaining what we aim at, It is the truest advantage because the most durable & lasting the best security against the changes & vicissitudes of life; for which reason are all the unjust Man's pursuits & actions represented through-out the Sacred Scripture as fruitless & ineffectual, tending to no end, answering no purpose, but productive only of disappointment and vexation. He hath swallowed down riches saith the Spirit of God by the mouth of Job, He hath swallowed down riches & he shall vomit them up <again>, God shall cast them out of his Belly, [p. 259][383] Because he hath oppressed & forsaken the poor, Because he hath violently taken a house which he builded not, surely he shall not feel quietness in his belly, he shall not save of that which he desired,[384] Tho' he heaps up silver as the dust, & prepare raiment as the clay. He may prepare it, but the just shall put it on, & the innocent shall divide the silver.[385] He that by usury saith Solomon, & unjust gain encreaseth his substance, he shall gather it for him that will pity the poor,[386] As the Partridge sitteth on eggs & hatchet them not, so he that getteth riches & not by right shall leave them in the midst of his days & at his end shall be a fool,[387] he shall appear to have laboured to no [p. 260] purpose to have toiled in vain, to be deceived in his most pleasing expectations.

Lastly to deter us for ever from the practice of injustice and dishonesty, Let us consider the dreadful reflections they occasion in the mind at the approach of Death & the terrible judgments reserved to them in a future State.

Death that formidable Period of our present existence to which we all must come, places objects in their true & proper light, Every accidental adventitious circumstance is then removed. Partiality, prejudice, affection no longer take place or biass our judgments, we view our actions as they are in themselves, we hardly err or mistake in the opinion we conceive of them, the Judgment we pass upon them, is a fore-runner [p. 261] of that which God shall pass upon us here-after, and the Sentence of our own hearts generally confirmed and ratified at the last & final day of retribution.

But <with> what hopes can he *conceive* <support himself> who has lived in unrighteousness & deceit, what desponding thoughts must that life occasion, which has been spent & consumed in perverting equity & justice; The Unjust Man laid upon the bed of sickness, surrounded with the Messengers of Death, finds himself <equally> surrounded *and in care passed with his numerous* <with the rememberance of his former> oppressions & iniquities; If he looks back upon his past life, he hears the Cries of the Orphan, the destitute & the friendless, bespeaking, solliciting, requiring his condemnation, If he looks forward into Eternity, he considers himself as *just*, summoned to [p. 262] appear before the Tribunal of a Just and equitable God clad as he is with the spoils of the poor, & loaded with the gains of injustice & oppression, If he ventures to carry his view beyond the Grave, & to dwell upon his last & final State, the Voice of just judgments sounds in his ears, & these Denunciations of Divine Wrath are ever present to his mind, Go to now ye Rich men, weep & howl for your miseries, that shall come upon you, your riches are corrupted, & your garments moth-eaten, your gold & silver is cankered, & the rust of them shall be witness against you, and shall at your flesh as it were fire, ye leave heaped treasure together for the last day, Behold the fire of the Labourers which have reaped down your fields, [p. 263] which is of you kept back by fraud, crieth; & the Cries of them which have reaped, are entred into the ears of the Lord of Sabaoth.[388]

Applic[ation].

Such is the Nature & such the tendency of injustice and dishonesty, It's own original deformity, it's manifest injury to Society, it's unprofitableness, & above all it's unavoidable fatal consequence shew the folly and extravagance of it, Let us then abstain from *& beware* <the practice> of so dangerous a sin, Let all our actions, our schemes, our pursuits be founded upon honesty & justice, Let uprightness & integrity rule & direct them and if any among us have been so unhappy as to fall into the snares of unrighteousness, & <to> build their chambers by wrong[389] let them with Zaccheus restore four-fold refund,[390] [p. 264] if it is still in their power, their ill-gotten wealth, & by compensating for their injustice remove the accused from their senses.

Let such as are yet untainted *& free them* innocent *of* <from> this great offence, guard against the very first principles of it & root out the most distant tendency to it, The first steps to it are imperceptible & hardly to be discerned, A little Art or Deceit departing from inviolable truth, may insensibly ripen into open acts of fraud & injustice; this should be more particularly attended to by those, who either from Nature or Profession are entrusted with the weighty & important care of Youth. Youth is the time to inspire cander & truth, & raise a detestation for lying & insincerity, And Yet it is to be feared the foundation [p. 265] of injustice is often laid then, Children are frequently taught to think a lye a less evil, than any little indiscretion they may be guilty of, they fly to this for refuge or shelter from reproof or correction, & the mistaken parent lays himself the foundation of his Offspring's future misery.

When on the Contrary frankness and open-ness of Conversation free from any subterfuge or hidden & secret arts, should be cherished & encouraged,

Any Lye or deceit however trivial, any cunning or distant appearance of craft, ought to be represented to them as the highest Crime, & the properest object of resentment, confession of a fault, always obtain for them a release from the punishment *it ought*< it should otherwise> be attended with.

[p. 266] This will by degrees *raise* <produce> in them a love for truth & sincerity, They will admire it's beauty & lustre, They will maintain an inviolable regard for it in their whole conversation & entercourse, they will grow up Men of integrity & honesty, They will by this benefit Society, adorn the World, tender it a Scene of much comfort & delight, Mercy & truth shall <then> meet together righteousness & peace shall kiss each other, truth shall then flourish out of the Earth & righteousness shall look down from Heaven, Yea the Lord shall shew loving kindness, & our Land shall give her increase, Righteousness shall go before him, and he shall direct his going in the way.[391]

Now to God the …

Sermon XIX

Volume 6 (54)

[p.1] Belfast July ye 29th 1750
Ditto April ye 29th 1753
Ditto March ye 16th 1755
Ditto September ye 11th 1757
Ditto September ye 23rd 1759
Ditto April ye 16th 1769
Ditto March ye 29th 1772
St. Dolough's July ye 11th 1784[392]
Ditto April ye 30th 1786
Ditto June ye 3rd 1788
Ditto December 19th 1790
Ditto March 13 – 1791
Ditto October 20 – 1793
Ditto November 30 – 1794
Ditto June 30 – 1799
Rosenallis July 24 1803
M[oun]t Melich Same Day
M[oun]t Melich June 9 185
Rosenallis June 22 1806
M[oun]t Melich September 27 1807
Clonaslee March 13 1808
[p. 2] Rosenallis July 17 1808
Donoghmore September 11 1808
Rosenallis August 19 1810
M[oun]t Melich September 15 1811
Dunnaghmore August 20 1815
Anaclone February 24 1822
Ardmore 25 May 1823
[Lough]Brickland 24 April 1825
Ditto 26 May 1826

[p. 3] In the Fifth Chapter of St Paul's first Epistle to the Thessalonians at the Seventeenth Verse

Pray without ceasing.

The Precept in the Text to pray without ceasing, may appear at first of an extraordinary nature, & considering the circumstances of Mankind, to be in some sort impracticable, I shall therefore begin by stating the true notion of it, that from thence we may be better prepared to *appreciate* <understand> the grounds & reasons upon which it is founded.

1st Part:

And *by this* <Here it>t is not *meant* <certainly intended>, that we [p. 4] should be employed in long prayers & petitions, rather made up of far fetched tedious expressions than of sentiment or affection, using vain repetitions,[393] & imagining like the *Pharisees* Heathens, that we shall be heard by our much speaking, for the whole use & efficacy of our prayers depend upon the fervency & heartiness with which we offer them up to God, & when this begins to cool, as it necessarily must, if they be carried to too great lengths, they become of no value in his sight, & can be of no avail to ourselves, whence the Royal Preacher gives us this caution, God is in Heaven, & thou Upon Earth, therefore let thy words be few,[394] & O[ur] B[lessed] S[aviour] has left us the model of a Prayer so concise & with all so full, that as <it includes> every material blessing *is included in it*, so every one's attention may carry him thro' it with <an> equal <degree of> zeal and earnestness.

[p.5] Much less would the command before us have us engage in those superstitious practices, for which the Church of Rome is remarkable, where under pretence of constantly attending the Great duties of prayer, Men separate themselves from the World, retire in to desarts & Monasteries; & lead a life of useless contemplation & supine indolence. Religion & piety are not to be *dressed* <painted> in such gloomy colours, they tend to improve, but not to banish the social affections, they recommend a friendly entercourse with each other, they forbid idleness & sloth, as the fruitfull Parent of all that is bad, & tho' O[ur] S[aviour] upon some occasions went up into a mountain to pray, & was there alone, yet *in general* was his time <mostly> laid out upon concerns of a publick nature, & the powers he had to do good instead of being cloistered [p. 6] & confined within himself, were all exerted for the benefit & advantage of Mankind. But there is no great occasion to insist upon this, we seem <in general> to be in no danger from a mistake of this sort, & need rather to be convinced of the extent of this duty, than to be cautioned against any excess in the performance of it.

And to this purpose we may observe that by praying without ceasing, we are required 1st To attend the Publick Worship of God, & offer <up> to him our prayers in his house, whenever it is in our power to do so; I say when-ever it is in our power, because the different callings of Men are <often> such, as *require daily* <demand a close> & constant attendance, so as not to allow them to be daily present in the Publick service of the Church, this is more particularly incumbent upon those who freed from the necessary cares of life & [p. 7] blessed with a more easie & affluent *way of living* <fortune> have more leisure *as well as abilities to* <for the frequent & repeated> discharge <of> this duty.

But whatever be the circumstances of Men, it is *at least* incumbent upon them all, to appear before God in his house & service at least upon the particular day set apart for that purpose, & nothing but absolute necessity can excuse them from the constant observance of it, this being the most solemn way of worshipping him, a way *founded on Reason as well as Revelation* <which Reason dictates & Revelation enjoins>.

For as we <all> receive the gifts of God in common, as we <all> are preserved by *the same* <his> hand, guided by *the same* <his> light, redeemed by *the same* <his blood>, entitled to *the same* <his> promises, it is highly reasonable that we should unite together in publick & common acknowledgements of his [p. 9] goodness, that we should have stated times to celebrate with one voice his mercy & to make our Gratitude *as publick & conspicious as his favours & benefits* <known to all around us>, hence have men *from the first* <in all> ages of the World agreed to have some kind of publick worship, & whatever differences there may have been <among them> about the mode & manner of *worship* <performing it> there have been none that we *hear* <read> of, concerning the <general> times & propriety of offering publick homage & honour to God.

Assemblies *were* <have been> universally held to this end, Rites & Ceremonies of various kinds appointed, Different expressions of Gratitude & acknowledgement used in proportion to the knowledge & opportunities Men had, till an immediate Revelation from God set this duty upon a right foundation, prescribed the manner in which it was to be discharged, instituted a fixed Ministry for the due performance of it, & pressed the obligation of it upon the Conscience of Men by strong and weighty motives.[395]

To absent ourselves then from these <Religious> Assemblies <thus recommended & appointed> is to renounce our fellowship with *and relation to Gods love* God, to declare that we look not upon ourselves as the objects of that power & goodness which are there celebrated <to disclaim all obligation to a dependence upon him>, to reject the properest means we have to warm our Devotion *with a true fervent spirit*, & I may add to give a proper consistency to our virtue [p. 10] and Morality, for he *that* <who> is never seen in the house of God, & <who> makes his boast of not appearing in it, may well be deemed little solicitous for to maintain & preserve his virtue, & whatever *he may pretend* <his pretensions are>, to be as little concerned for the one as he *is* <appears to be> for the other.

And yet to the eternal reproach of many Christians this reasonable this natural duty of Publick Worship is shamefully and basely neglected, how many are there *even among us who are never present at these exercises* <who totally withdraw themselves from the Religious assemblie of the faithfull>; how many who upon every *little* trifling occasion *stay from* <leave & make> them, how many who when they do come, seem to do it more to conform to custom than out of any sense of the importance of the duty, who tho' present in body are about in spirit, & by *rambling roving* <slumbring> eyes <or roving> & unattentive looks, <to speak the language of scripture> truly give the sacrifice of fools, not considering that they do evil.[396]

[p. 11] To pray without ceasing implies 2nd that to the publick acts of worship we add those acts of Devotion *that* <which> are to be performed daily in each family, the Parents & the Children, the Masters & the Servants meeting together to *pay their worship* < worship & adore> their Common Father & Lord.

And this *how indispensible soever*, (it is to <be> feared) is still more neglected, than the Publick, worship of God *yet it ... it ... feel the obligation of it to be the same* <tho' of equal *consequence* usefulness & importance>, For the <private> blessings of a family can never be so properly acknowledged in a publick & mixed Assembly, as in one entirely made up of those, *that* <who> are immediately favoured with them, the form of prayer <which> we use *in such a case* <when we pray in common> is composed in general terms, it can not take in each particular mercy, or each particular want, & this must be supplied by the wise & virtuous Parent & Master, who like a Priest in his [p. 12] own house is to offer daily incense to God, & minister to him in holy things, he is to consider himself as one, to whom the eternal as well as temporal interests of his Children & Servants are committed, & as he would blush to have it said, that he with-held from them what was necessary for their bodily sustenance, so ought he to be equally ashamed to with-hold from them what is absolutely necessary for their spiritual improvement.

And indeed the very circumstances of a family shew the propriety of this duty, some of the members of it thro' their tender age & the levity inseparable from youth, need to have their attention fixed, & to be reminded of their duty by stated and periodical times of devotion, from which they dare not be absent, Others rather thro' the misfortune of their circumstances than their own wilful neglect require instruction & assistance & have no other [p. 13] way of obtaining them but what these oportunities give them. All want the blessing of *their* God upon their endeavours, the Servant upon his labour, Master upon his affluence & wealth, and this is the probable & the only means of drawing it down upon *them* both.

For it makes Servants honest & industrious, faithfull to the trust committed to them, hearty & zealous in their ministry, It disposes Masters to be humane & gentle in their treatment, checks pride haughtiness & presumption, teaches them that they have one Common Master, engages them to use their Inferiors & dependants as Creatures of the same Heavenly Father with themselves, & by producing these happy effects, it frees them from the dreadful charge of sharing in a Guilt which others run themselves in thro' their neglect or bad example, if Children & Servants see no [p. 14] appearance of Religion in a family, if examples of impiety & *debauchery* <infidelity> come recommended to them by those who were appointed to instruct & direct them, if they are so loaded & burdened with cares as to have no time left to attend upon higher duties, they indeed shall die in their iniquity, but their souls shall be required of those unjust Parents & Masters who laid temptations in their way which they had not courage to conquer, & who omitted to teach them, when they had it in their power to do so, very different from Abraham to whom God himself gives this glorious commendation, I know him that he will command his Children & his household after him to do justice & judgment,[397] or from Joshua who makes this declaration that as for him & his house they would serve the Lord.[398]

[p. 15] *By praying without ceasing we are … to … and* <Nor is this precept confined to these two kinds of publick worship. It also takes in 3dly> that private entercourse which every Man <ought> to keep up with God in his closet, without any witness but his own heart.

We have all temptations peculiar to ourselves, temptations arising from the frame & constitution of our bodies, from the profession of life we follow, from the company we keep, from the circumstances we are in, every morning we rise, we are going to be exposed to these, every night we lye down we are uncertain what the morrow will bring forth, whether we shall live another day or whether we shall awake, only to appear in judgment. It is then every man's most serious concern to begin the day, & close the evening with exercises of Religious prayer & reflection, tending to preserve *them* <him> against the dangers *they are* <he is> in, or to secure <to him> a retreat with God, let what will [p. 17] happen, *Here it is* <and it is in such devout Exercises only> that the soul can freely & truly unbosom itself, *here it is* that it can expose it's *most secret* infirmities, weaknesses *foibles* and defects …[399] <that it can commune with itself & by so doing obtain that perfect knowledge of itself without which no progress can be made in virtue, no proficiency in moral rectitude & goodness>.

4th This Duty recommends to us no less strongly, perseverance in our prayers or as O[ur] S[aviour] expresses it, that we pray always & faint not,[400] that tho' we do not *attain* <receive in every case> what we so earnestly pray for, we be not discouraged, but as assiduously & diligently apply to God, as if each petition we sent up, had an immediate return because as prayer is the publick acknowledgement [p. 19] of his power & wisdom both of which are infinite & beyond our comprehension to fathom, we are to suppose them equally exerted in our favour, whether we have our requests granted or denied unto us *we are not able to determine often what & for our advantage & tho' we boldly presume to dictate to God … too often of his mercy vouchsafe to refuse us our desire & to save us from ourselves by being deaf to our unreason[able] demands, if therefore we be the … of the wisdom & power of God, we must … continue … in prayer … we … for any discouragement we meet with … our faith were shaken, or our … of God impaire but with holy Job we find ourselves ready to make this declaration Tho' he slay me, yet had I trust in him*, <and to presume that since we are not able to determine what is for our real advantage, God by turning a deaf ear to our most hardy prayers, only means to save us from ourselves, & to deliver us from those great Evils, into which we should have fallen, had the foolish desires of our hearts been attended to & therefore it is our duty to continue constant in prayer, fully satisfied of the wisdom & power of God; not suffering our faith to be shaken, or our sense of him impaired, but with Holy Job to trust in him, even tho' he slay us,[401] as he emphatically expresses it>.[402]

And this brings me to the last sense in which the words of the Text [p. 20] may be taken that by praying without ceasing, we are required to carry about us those dispositions of heart & mind, *that* <which> always accompany the actual practice of prayer, when we are heartily & sincerely engaged in it.

For at this time we have an inward conviction of our own indigence & unworthiness, we feel our helplessness & dependence, we are conscious how much we stand in need of God's assistance to help our infirmity & of his mercy to blot out our transgressions, we are under the most awful sense of his infinite presence, Majesty & power, we humble ourselves before him, & offer and present *unto him* ourselves, our souls & bodies to be a reasonable holy & lively sacrifice unto him.

And sure these dispositions inseparable from the due performance of prayer may equally attend us in the ordinary course [p. 21] of our lives, they may season our respective actions employments & callings, they may manifest & shew themselves in all our undertakings, they may sanctify the most common & indifferent actions & render them as pleasing to God & as salutary to ourselves, as the immediate & particular acts we perform in his honour & service.

And thus much may suffice to explain & illustrate the precept in the Text, I now proceed to offer the grounds & reasons upon which the frequency of it is founded.

2d Part

And first There ought to be some proportion between the frequency of God's benefits to us & the frequency of our grateful returns to him, between our [p. 23][403] necessities & our asking for relief.

The mercies we receive from Heaven as they are without measure, so are they without number. Every blessing we enjoy, every breath of life we possess, every comfort we have, every pleasing hope we entertain, comes down from above, & is the gratuitous & undeserved gift of God, Of his own will begat he us[404] at first, by his Providence does he continually preserve us into being, & by his gracious Redemption does he give us the reviving expectation of another & a better State; whatever wants we have, he alone can supply them, whatever infirmities we labour under, he alone can remove them, whatever difficulties we are reduced to, he alone *can* <is able to> rescue us out of.

Can then a Being from whom we [p. 24] receive such a portion of good now, and expect so great a one here-after, of whom we stand in such continual need, & to whom we are so constantly beholden, Can such a Being I say, be too often adored & celebrated by us, Can we too often praise him for his goodness, & declare the wonders that he doth for the Children of Men?[405] Had *he* <God> in return for such repeated benefits required us to do some great thing, would he not have thought it just, how much more when he vouchsafes to accept the lively expressions of our gratitude & is satisfied with the oblation of our hearts & minds & when this is the case, is it not Incumbent upon us to pay him this tribute, not once, slightly or cursorily, but constantly, frequently, in each day, & always with zeal, earnestness & pleasure.

[p. 25] 2nd. What he refuses once, he may grant our more earnest petitions, for he not only denies us our requests, because they are unreasonable in themselves or would be detrimental to us, but also deffers returning them an answer, that we may have an opportunity of shewing ourselves truly sensible to the value of what we ask for, by persisting in our application to him & proportioning our earnestness to *their ... of ... pledge they are of to us* <their usefulness and importance>

This more particularly regards spiritual blessings which we can never be too zealous in using, nor too importunate in applying for, there is no danger of mistaking or misapprehending them, we may safely pray for the forgiveness of our sins, for the assistances of God's Grace, for the meriting intercession of our Blessed Redeemer, we are assured that in asking for such [p. 26] things, we ask what is for our good, what God will undoubtedly grant us if we labour to deserve them; <And> if we do not find our prayers heard, if God appears for some time deaf to our petitions, it is in order to engage us to seek till we find, & to knock with opportunity till finally the door be opened. St. Paul besought God thrice to remove the Messenger of Satan that buffeted him, before he received an assurance that God's Grace was sufficient for him[406] & O[ur] S[aviour] under the similitude of a Judge, who thro' the importunity of a Widow at length granted her that justice which she had so vainly sought for, recommends unto us the same importunity with God & draws from it this just inference, Shall not God avenge his elect which cry unto him day & night, tho' he bear long with [p. 28] them, if an unjust Judge had so much regard for the solicitations of a poor widow, Shall not God the just & upright God attend the prayers of his faithful people & *delight himself to grant to grant them their favour & equitable petitions* <grant them their heart's desire & fulfil all their petitions>.[407]

3rd. The more of our time we spend upon the Religious exercises we have been considering, & the more time we take off from the World & the temptations of it.

When we have been seriously intent upon prayer, & regularly & frequently practised it in each day, we not only have gained so much time in each day, which we might have unprofitably spent in the allurements & enticements of the World, but we also lay up a sure support & security against all the temptations we may be exposed to, in the remaining part of the day [p. 29], the impressions which the sense of God's *providence & mercy* <Prudence & Goodness> make upon our minds, whilst we are engaged in prayer, remain with us long after the <action itself is over> & the oftener they are renewed, the stronger must their power & influence be, if sin offers itself to us, they at once present us with the odiousness & deformity of it, if Sinners entice us, they prevent our consenting to them, if our own hearts solicit us to sin, they are stronger than our hearts, & enable us to stifle & smother their evil tendencies & motions, whence O[ur] B[lessed] S[aviour] in the most trying circumstance of his life & the most capable of staggering the courage & resolution of his Disciples, advises them if they would not fall into temptation, to watch & pray,[408] & St Paul makes frequent prayer part of that Armour with which ever Christian is to repell the fiery darts of the wicked [p. 31], Take unto yourselves the helmet of salvation, the sword of the spirit, praying always with all prayer & supplication in the spirit, & watching there-unto with all perseverance.[409]

I need hardly add any other consideration to what has been said to induce us to the frequent practice of this Duty, we have seen it incumbent upon us in point of Gratitude, in point of interest, in point of security, I shall therefore *only* conclude with observing that it is equally so in point of regard to the Dignity of our nature.[410]

For it is by the <repeated> practice of such spiritual & intellectual Duties that we can raise & advance it to some degree of perfection, it is this *that* <which> distinguishes Men from the beasts that perish, This *that* <which> establishes [p. 32] a converse between the Creature & his *Maker* Creator, This *that* <which> unites us with him, *that* <which> enables us to enter into close Communion with the Saints & the Blessed spirits above, *that* <which> anticipates upon & gives us a fore-taste of that happy State where we are to employ our thoughts, our time, our faculties in a due contemplation of God's power & goodness, in lively & strong acknowledgements of his bounty, in loud seraphic expressions of gratitude & thankfulness.

To him therefore Let us often address our vows & prayers, Let us be frequent & earnest in his service & worship, Let us accustom our hearts & voices to praise & adore his holy name, that our prayers & petitions may come up as a memorial before him, & after having made us plentiful & abundant returns by improving [p. 33] our virtue & exalting our nature, they may length open unto us the gate of everlasting life & procure unto us the fruition & enjoyment of God to all Eternity.

Which God of his infinite mercy grant, to whom etc. etc.

Sermon XX

Volume 6 (57)

[p. 88] Belfast April ye 14th 1751
Ditto October ye 8th 1752 N[ew] S[tyle]
Ditto October ye 6th 1754
Ditto September ye 19th 1756
Ditto November ye 27th 1757
Ditto March the 11th 1759
Ditto January the 18th 1761
Ditto August the 1st 1762
Ditto August the 26th 1764
Ditto October the 11th 1767
Ditto October the 8th 1769
Rosenallis March 31 1805[411]
Mt. Melich September 29 1805
Rosenallis July 12 1807 SC
Mt. Melich October 25 1807
Rosenallis August 20 1809
Mt. Melich August 26 1810
Rosenallis December 8 1811

[p. 89] In the Fourteenth Chapter of the Proverb of Solomon at the Twelfth Verse.

There is a way which seemeth right unto the Man, but the end thereof are the ways of Death.

There is hardly any <one> thing in which the evil of self love is more fatally apparent, than in the various *devices by which it lures us into a deceitful* <arts it employs, to deceive us into an> opinion of our own sanctity and *holiness* <goodness>, One would imagine nothing could be more simply expressed than the true way to eternal life, & yet how many & intricate are the paths which the Passions of Mankind draw out to themselves, with what seeming confidence do they persist in them, what strong hopes do they *conceive* <entertain> that then will bring them to salvation, answer the purpose of their present Being & procure to them the happiness of [p. 90] another here after, (There is a way which seemeth right unto a Man but the end there-of are the ways of Death).

And if this was true in Solomon's time it holds equally so in our's, One single road leads to heaven, & yet we daily seek out many inventions, we embrace Systems, adopt maxims, follow courses as opposite to this one road, as light is to darkness, or sweet <is> to bitter, till by continual ramblings we find ourselves deceived & *our* <the> ways <we walk in> to be the ways of Death.

I propose in this Discourse to consider what those different ways are, which seem right unto a man, & to apply them more to the circumstances of the World, & the State of Religion at present, than to those which Solomon might *perhaps* <have> had in *his thoughts* <view> when thes<e> *was* <words were> wrote, And in order to treat this Subject with all the conciseness possible, I shall reduce them to the five following 1st Trusting solely to the [p. 91] profession of a true faith, & placing our dependance upon the purity of the Religion we have embraced, 2nd Pretending to Moral Honesty separate from Religion, 3rd Expecting favour with God from a partial & not an universal obedience, 4th Deeming cessation from evil sufficient <to entitle unto ye acceptance of God>, without *doing* the <practice of> any real good, Lastly Relying upon mistaken notions of mercy in the Divine Being.

1st Consid[eration].

To trust upon the profession of a true faith, <only> & to place our dependence upon the purity of the Religion, we have embraced <with looking any further> is one of those ways which seem right unto a Man, but the end where-of are the ways of Death.

I have so often had occasion to enlarge upon this mistake *which indeed is one of the most general & fatal & have* so frequently shewn the danger of separating faith from [p. 92] practice, & of making our zeal for the one attone for the omission of the other, that I shall not at this time add any more upon it, but observe in general that he who thus glories in the profession of truth only without making this truth a lamp unto his feet & a light unto his paths,[412] shall woefully experience when it is too late, that his knowledge will prove his condemnation *& his sentence is in proportion* *to the greater … & opportunities he had* <enhance the bitterness of his sentence & punishment>, I therefore proceed to consider another Delusion namely Pretending to Moral Honesty separate from Religion which I mention as the second way that seemeth right unto a Man, but the end whereof are the ways of Death.

2nd Consid[eration].

This is <indeed> the very opposite & reverse of the former, They ascribed too much, these give too little to Religion. They made the observance of it a sufficient compensation for every offence, these allow it no worthier value, they pretend [p. 93] to virtue exclusive of Religion & provided Men are honest just & upright in their dealings, they maintain it to be of very little significance what Religion they profess or whether they conform to any of *the established forms* <Religious ordinances> or not, A Delusion which at present is very common, which Writers of late have industriously spread to wound Religion the better, & which being so soothing & flattering to the passions & lustful appetites of Men, & withal gilt over in this specious manner, meets with a very ready & easie *an admittance* <reception>; Virtue it must be confessed, is the very end & substance of Religion. Without this all pretences to it are vain & idle, but the matter is, whether Virtue can subsist upon any other foundation than that of Religion, or be preserved where this is totally lost *or* <and> neglected *at this* <of an absurdity there is in supposing that> I hope we shall be convinced, if we consider these two things, 1st The palpable imperfection of these <Men's> system of Mortality, & 2nd The Insufficiency of the motives they use to the practice of it.

1st. I say their System of Morality is [p. 94] extremely defective, for View these Moral Men these loud Talkers in behalf of Moral Honesty, View them in their private life, & you will find them fall far short of the noble Character they assume to themselves, Some thinking it consistent with this honesty, to <3> indulge their pride and vanity at the expence of other people's labour & industry, to live above their circumstances & fortunes, to <2> contract debts which they can never pay, & <4>what is a natural consequence to grind & oppress those who are under their influence & authority, Others not scrupling to invade the most precious & valuable rights, when their passions require it, & the Meaner circumstances of their neighbour allow them to do it with impunity, triumphing in their cruelty & at the same time that they commit the grossest outrages, vaunting themselves out for Men of honour & honesty, Whilst by many Virtue is allied to an almost incessant course of Drunkenness, revelling, revenge, and resentment.

[p. 95] Nor is this much to be wondered at, if we consider 2nd. The insufficiency of the motives upon which their System of Morality is founded, for as they put Religion out of the Question, & consequently the Great rewards of another State, at least so far as they are confirmed, established & improved by Christianity, t'is plain they must derive their obligation to Virtue entirely from the native beauty of it, or from an inward principle teaching them to distinguish between right & wrong.

If from the native beauty of it, Are there not many cases in which Passion is so far prevalent as to hide this natural & original beauty from their eyes, in which they find more real & solid contentment by yielding to their appetites than they possibly can by adhering to this empty & airy notion of original beauty & conformity to Nature, words that <which> may indeed sound big in the mouth of a Philosopher, or give a System of [p. 96] Morality an air of greatness & disinterestedness, but which I fear in practice will prove too weak a prop against the corruption & depravity of Mens' hearts.

Or If they *cede* <join> to this the inward sense they have of right & wrong, as an additional motive *support* to the <practice> of Morality, not to mention what was said above, that this *doth not* <by no means> prevents their cherishing many great & <heinous> vices. What is a principle of this sort without the culture of Religion, without that nourishment of Devotion & piety, which are necessary to give it substance & consistency? How often is it lost amidst the boisterous storms of appetites, How still is it's voice compared to the loud clamours of unruly lusts, above all how does it require a constant sense of God's infinite presence, power justice & goodness to preserve it in full vigour, & where can this be had but in the true Doctrines of Christianity & in the outward ordinances of that Religion. This [p. 97] it is alone *that* <which> supplies us with motives strong enough to overcome passion, to fortify us against the delusions of sin to confirm & settle us in virtue & he who departs from this & builds the grounds of what is laid by Christ & his Apostles, how specious so ever his conduct may be, or however high his pretences to virtue, does in reality deprive it of it's chief support & expose himself to the greatest dangers, This is a way that seemeth right unto a Man, but the end there-of are the ways of Death.

3rd Consid[eration].

Those who expect favour & acceptance with God from a partial obedience to his laws equally stand upon as false & deceitful a ground as the former.

There are many, who flatter themselves that provided they rigidly observe the commands [p. 98] of God in some cases, they may plead exemption from them in others, that if they be Charitable ready to relieve the wants, & minister to the necessities of the indignent, God will readily excuse any act of Intemperance they may be guilty of, that if on the other hand they be temperate & sober, they are from thence more at liberty to pursue their schemes of ambition & covetousness by all the means in their power, or if they be neither covetous nor Worldly-minded that they may reserve to themselves some darling & favourite passion without fear of check or rebuke.

But against this mistake it is proper to observe, that a Man's right to the character of a Good Man, does not so much arise from the number of virtues he is possessed of, as from the principle upon which he is really virtuous, Want of health may make a Man extremely temperate, A Natural indolence & heaviness [p. 99] of spirits less anxious about the World, An innate softness of nature merciful & compassionate but if he is not so from a sense that he is doing his duty to God, & bound by the consideration of his authority constantly to do so, he can no more call this virtue, or boast of the merit of it, than an Engine wrought by hands or water can boast of it's ability & willingness to benefit Mankind.

To denominate a Man virtuous & good, a sense of God must be the ruling principle of his actions, & where it is so, it will be uniform & influence *the* <his> whole *mean* life, it will bridle & restrain him in passions the most pleasing & delightfull to him, it will in all cases bring to his mind the authority of the Great Law-giver whom every disobedience in the smallest matters tends to infringe, whence is it the perfection of the Christian Religion that under this oeconomy whoso-ever keepeth [p. 100] the whole law & yet offendeth in one point, is deemed guilty of all,[413] that is not equally guilty with him that offendeth in every point, for that would be a manifest absurdity, but as much derogates from the authority of God as he that offendeth in every point, *tho'not in a equal degree* for as the Apostle argues, he that said, Do not commit adultery, said also, Do not kill, now if thou commit no adultery, yet if thou kill, thou art become a Transgressor of the Law,[414] if the authority of God does not restrain thee in the one instance, t'is ardent it doth not in any other, because the same regard to it would produce the like effect in all.

Besides such a partial observance of God's laws carries with it this unavoidable consequence that it tends to give a sanction to all vices however heinous, for if one Man may transgress one law so he keeps strictly to another, it must [p. 101] necessarily come to pass, that every Man will chuse the vice he cherishes most, hence will God be obliged according to the present supposition to over-look sensuality in one Man, uncharitableness in another, fraud in a third, violence in a fourth & so on till every one pleases his own fancy best & violates which of his Great Creator's laws he pleases, A Supposition so very absurd, so very contra*dictory*<ry> to the sanctity & holiness of God, that I need not add any thing to expose it further.

Here then is a broad but common way, that seemeth right unto a Man but the end where-of are the ways of Death, and yet how often are the best of us deluded by this vain pretence, how often in our most secret moments when we grow serious & review our own life calmly & sedately, do we lull ourselves into quiet & security with the delusive hopes [p. 102] of pardon because we find our hearts bear witness to us in some instances tho' at the same time we see no becoming harm for those evil practices in which we continue, As if the all seeing eye of our Maker took not every object within it's all comprehending view, *could* <did> not penetrate into the bottom of our hearts, saw not every latent & lurking evil & formed his judgment of us <not> from a general *not* <but> a partial & superficial knowledge.

4th Consid[eration].

Another Delusion by which we are often lost under the specious pretence that all is well & right, is to Deem cessation from evil sufficient to entitle us to the favour of God without the practice of any real good.

And under this Class may a large number of Men be ranked, especially of those whose [p. 103] circumstances <in life> are the most easie, These live a constant round of uninterrupted pleasure, trifle away their time in idle <tho'> not in vitious pursuits, & seem from their conduct to imagine yet they were sent into the world like the Leviathan in the water,[415] to take their pastime in it. Upbraid them with the kind of life they lead, their answer is ready, that t'is true they seek amusement & pleasure but still they do no harm, they are guilty of no excess, they transgress not the bounds of right & wrong, & if they do no good, they are sure at least they do no evil.

But supposing this to be true & it <is> very hard it should, considering the natural tendency of a life of pleasure to slacken & relax all the *powers of* rational powers of the Soul, Is there no evil in wasting away time idly & unprofitably? Is there no evil in not improving the talents which God has given us to the good of Mankind & the advantage of the [p. 104] World? Is there no evil in letting our faculties lye waste & useless for want of culture and improvement? Is there no evil in stifling all useful reflection & disgracing our rational part by low & unworthy occupations? What account will such be able to give of themselves when God shall call them to judgment, How poor a plea will it be barely to say they have done no evil when the Righteous Judge of the World shall ask them, What poor *& wretched* has their wealth relived, what <oppression> has their authority removed, what ignorance *& neglect* has their <superior> understanding enlightened *& instructed*, To no purpose will it be to alledge, they have done no evil, when it shall appear that their Being was given them to ...[416] <do real good, to discharge positive precepts, to fulfil great & important duties>, for which reason it is that in the Parable of the Talents the unprofitable Servant is represented as cast into outer darkness not for having abused the Talents he had [p. 105] received or for misapplying them contrary to the design of his Master but for having hid them letting them lye unimproved & being a slothful <unactive> Servant, A very just Emblem it is of these Person's conduct, & very proper to strike a serious & considerate mind![417]

5th Consid.

I come now to the last of the ways I have mentioned that seem right unto a Man, but in *the* <whole> end *thereof* are the ways of Death namely, relying upon mistaken notions of mercy in the Divine Being.

We are apt to perswade ourselves that a kind & merciful Creator will overlook the faults we may be guilty of, What pleasure say we should God take in punishing his Creatures for taking vengeance on them for their transgressions. Would he have created them had he meant to make them miserable, & are not mercy & [p. 106] compassion the most *dazzling* <darling> & favourite attributes for Perfect Being.

But here may we not say as Rabshakeh to the people of Judah, Beware lest any perswade you saying the Lord will deliver you,[418] No doubt God is merciful, no doubt he is delighted with the exercise of mercy & compassion, no doubt he willeth not the death of a Sinner, but rather that he should repent & live,[419] this is evident from his very nature, from the continual acts of his Providence & from the declarations of his word, the point is not whether God be merciful but whether his mercy has bounds & limits to it, whether where mercy ends, justice does not take place, & whether the gracious promises of pardon & mercy are applicable to our own particular case.

That God's mercy has certain bounds fixed to it, & that in many instances Justice becomes an essential attribute of God can be denied [p.

107] by none who consider him as the Legislator of the World, since laws without a proper sanction of punishment attending the breach of them would be such an imperfection in the Moral Governor of the World as would destroy the very end of his government, *where* <accordingly> in <Holy> Scripture does God represent himself not only as a merciful but also as a Jealous God, Jealous of his own honour & ready to vindicate it from the abuse of evil men.

If then there be a time in which mercy must give place to justice, which of us that *must* live in the known practice of sin can be sure that mercy is still within his reach, which of us can say that by his transgressions he has not filled up the measure of his iniquity[420] & tired out the patience & long-suffering of God, which of us can know how far he may depend upon mercy, or how far he must look for justice.

[p. 108] Pardon is indeed promised to Sinners, but it is only to the repenting & contrite Sinner, to him who forsakes his iniquity, who acknowledges his faults, & whose sin is ever before him,[421] who not only abandons his former course but who endeavours to attone for his transgressions by a new life & who persists to the end in a steady & uniform obedience to God.

But is this the case of those we have now under consideration, they purposely continue in sin that grace may abound,[422] they persevere in their ill practices, & in the midst of their unrepented guilt, they daringly lay claim to God's promises, & presumptuously depend upon his mercy, Is such a dependence reasonable, Can such ill grounded hopes of mercy be cherished, or made a fit subject for support & reliance, There is a way that seemeth right unto a Man, but the end there of are the ways of death.

[p. 109] Applic[ation].

I have *now* thus considered some of the most visible ways by which we are unhappily deceived into false notions of ourselves, many more might be added to these since, they are as various as our passions, peculiar to our age, to our profession to our Station in life, but the time will not allow us to speak particularly to each, I shall only conclude with the observation with which I began, One Single road leads to Heaven What that is our own Conscience can tell us, To do good, to eschew evil, to love mercy, to walk humbly with our God, to add to Morality the practice of Religion, to use the one & the other as the best means to advance both, & to *claim* <acquire> to ourselves the happiness we aim at, is our duty & at the same time our security, he that walketh in this way, walketh surely, His confidence can never fail nor forsake him, no accidents can lessen nor no changes affect it, it raises him above the chances of this World, It comforts him in [p. 110] affliction, it attends him in prosperity, & when something else yields him no support, it alone lends his friend, & becomes his stay, for altho' the fig tree should not blossom, neither should fruit be in the Vine, Altho' the labour of the olive should fail, & the fields should yield no meat, Altho' the flock should be cut off from the fold, & there should be no herd in the stalls, yet does it still make him to rejoice in the Lord, & to joy in the God of his salvation.[423]

To which happy state of mind that we may all arrive, God of his infinite mercy grant, To whom etc. etc.

Sermon XXI

Volume 6 (62)

[p. 218] Belfast July ye 22nd 1753
Dublin St. Ann's November ye 18th 1753
Ditto St. Peter's March ye 30th 1754
Belfast August ye 29th 1756
Ditto December ye 5th 1757
Ditto January ye 4th 1761
Ditto August ye 15th 1762
Ditto May ye 5th 1765
Ditto October ye 1st 1769[424]
St. Doloughs June ye 27th 1784
St Peters April ye 10th 1785 at Slieran
St. Doloughs July 16th 1786
Harrogate September 3rd 1786
Christ Church June 1789
St. Doloughs June 1789
Ditto October 23rd 1791
Ditto June 9th 1793
Ditto June 14 1795
Ditto July 1798 S.C.
Ditto August 11 1800
Rosenallis July 18 1802
[p. 219] M[oun]t Melich June 1804
Ditto February 2 1807
Ditto February 4 1810
Rosenallis February 25 1810

[p.220] In the Fifth Chapter of St Paul's Epistle to the Ephesians at the fourth Verse.

Nor jesting which are not convenient.

It is the singular advantage of the Religion, which we profess, that it extends itself to all the actions of Men, of what Nature so-ever, & thereby enlarges the scheme of Duty, beyond what was ever known before; To this purpose it regulates our thoughts, & our [p. 221] words, it descends to the minutest particulars, & is as extensive in it's degree, as it is perfect & compleat in it's nature.

A signal instance of this we have, in that variety of direction which are occasionally given to us, to render conversation improving to ourselves, & inoffensive to others. One of these I have chosen for the subject of our present meditation, It alludes to that part of Conversation, which chiefly regards the hours & seasons of recreation & amusement, & cautions us against one common abuse at that [p. 222] time, namely against jestings, which are not convenient. In the prosecution of which subject, I shall endeavour to expose the nature of these jestings which are not convenient, & then shew some of the great & real evils, which they often give occasion to.

1st Part.

This very expression jestings which are not convenient, is plainly intended to shew us, that it never was <the> Apostle's design to forbid all jesting & mirth, & to introduce a sullen moroseness [p, 223] & austerity, void of that frankness & openness which is the very soul of all friendly entercourse & conversation; The Nature of Man doubtless requires some relaxation, some release from intense care & application, without which it would soon grow barbarous & savage, unfit in great measure to discharge the social duties of human life. It requires to unbend itself it's freedom & ease, & to range at will in the ample field of imagination & fancy; But the misfortune is, that under pretence of using the liberty, which is allowed unto us [p. 224] we act in this *occassion* <case> or we do in many others, we turn it into licentiousness, & abuse it to our own detriment & loss. It is the prevalency & frequency of this practice, which makes it necessary for us to be told, when we do so.

And 1st. when we jest upon things sacred, we jest in a manner, which is not convenient. There is such natural weight & solemnity in things of this sort, as utterly exclude our treating them in a loose & ludicrous manner. The infinite concern they are of to us, the extraordinary manner in which they have been revealed, [p. 225] the Great Being about whom they are chiefly conversant, & the high importances they are of to the World in general are so many reasons, why a Person who is really affected with a true sense of their dignity & consequence, will always be serious, when he talks of them, grave & composed, when he makes them the subject of his conversation & discourse, His piety will season his words, & the Religious abundance of his heart[425] will guide them with discretion,[426] so as to prevent all irregularity & disorder, whence it follows, that who-ever allows himself [p. 226] to make Religion & the awful truths of it, the subject of his raillery & mirth, gives the most signal instance in his power of the little attachment he bears to it, & justly becomes answerable for all the evil consequences, which may arise from his profane & Irreligious conduct, for by this he not only himself wantonly sports with what is too sacred to be thus used, & in this respect acts the most absurd & irrational part, but he impairs as much as in him lies, the reverence & veneration, which all Persons ought to have for things of this sort, he represents [p. 227] them to others in the lowest light, he prejudices perhaps young & tender minds against them, he teaches them to consider that as light & trivial, which it is their interest & duty to form the most solemn & awful conceptions of, he lessens the ties of Religion, he unhinges the great sanctions of God's laws, he endeavours to get the better of the natural hopes & fears of Men, he derides & ridicules under the name of Superstition, what is in truth real piety & devotion, he makes way for the introduction of the most dangerous & most destructive Tenets, & tho' his [p. 228] pretence be the innocent pretence of contributing to the mirth & entertainment of others, yet the real effect of his Discourse tends to the decay of piety, & to the advancement of Vice & licentiousness; So very big with evil is the practice of profane & Irreligious jesting, which like a two edged weapon, peirces the hand that indiscreetly & unwarily uses it, to the advancement of Vice & licentiousness; Whom does it reproach & blaspheme, Against whom does it exalt it's voice, & lift up it's eyes on high, Is it not against the Lord of Hosts, the Holy one of Israel.

[p. 229] 2nd: All those jestings are not convenient, which are contrary to Decency & are in themselves of a loose & licentious nature. Discourses of this kind are indeed strong indications of great corruption & degeneracy in the heart for as a Good Man out of the <good treasure> of his heart, bringeth forth that which is good, so an evil Man out of the evil treasure of his heart, bringeth forth that which is evil,[427] Where this is full of foul & impure thoughts, where we delight in harbouring & indulging vitious desires, where no care is [p. 230] taken to preserve that fountain of life, the heart free from all poysonous & infectious streams, it naturally must be expected, that the mouth will be tainted with the venom, & the fruit of our lips savour of the rankness of the soil, in which it rec[eive]d it's growth.

And as such Conversation betrays our inward corruption & degeneracy, so is it of the very worst consequence to others, it tends to no other end, that to vitiate the Imagination of Men, to accustom them to think of vice, with less reluctance, & from speaking of it with pleasure, to lead them to the [p. 231] actual practice & committal of it. It is more particularly injurious to those, who are themselves pure & virtuous, & when uttered in sober discreat company, carry with them this offensive insinuation, that we take others to be as corrupt as ourselves, & as well pleased as we can be, with such loose & idle Discourses, & thence it is, that as often as we transgress in this point, we not only violate the laws of politeness & good-breeding, those rules & restrictions, which the higher rank of Men have set to themselves, & by the observance of which those in a lower station entitle themselves to respect & [p. 232] regard, but what is a consideration of much higher moment, we violate the great & unchangeable laws of Religion which absolutely forbid all corrupt communication to proceed out of our mouth, all uncleanness, filthiness & foolish talking,[428] to be even once named amongst us, as becometh Saints, but which require us to be holy in all manner of conversation, as he that hath called us, is holy,[429] holy in our words, as well as in our actions, in our Discourse as well as in our more secret thoughts.

[p. 233] 3rd. The next sort of jesting which falls under the character of jestings which are not convenient, is the indiscreet raillery of Superiors over their Inferiors, or of Men in station over Persons beneath them in rank or fortune.

It is not to be questioned, but that many who are guilty of this, have never attended to the mischievous consequence of it, & only mean the entertainment of their idle hours, without any design to injure or give offence to others. Did they allow themselves time to consider it coolly, their own good sense would soon convince them, how ungenerous [p. 234] their behaviour is, how unbecoming their superior state & condition, for what can be meaner, than to insult by pungent & peircing jests, when they are conscious, that their behaviour how-ever improper, is not be resented, what can be more so, then to make those the objects of their laughter, who they well know, dare not make them the objects of their revenge & resentment, than to single out a Person, & set him up as a butt, for the mirth of others to play upon, with no power left either of attack or defence. There is an inhumanity in this, which every good natured [p. 235] Man must be shocked at, a Cruelty which destroys the merit of any good office that may be done us, for how-ever valuable the favour which is conferred upon us may be, it is never great enough to conquer the aversion we must have at the manner in which it is done, & act the dear price we pay for it, no less a price than the sacrifice of our own honour, of our own peace, & of our own ease & satisfaction.

And this kind of jesting naturally introduces a 4th which savours much of the preceeding one, & that is, when [p. 236] we jest upon those, who tho' they are equal to us in point of rank are yet below us in understanding, & thro' a natural weakness, or perhaps modesty of temper are not capable of jesting upon us in their turn.

I know it is pretended by some, that such jestings are perfectly innocent, because the Person jested upon has not sharpness & penetration enough to perceive it, but not to mention, that there are very few, who are so thoroughly void of sense, as not to see that they are ridiculed & laughed at, tho' their own bashfulness prevents their expressing any resentment at it [p. 237], not even in this case. Is not this to express the weakness of a Man, probably to many who might otherwise have remained ignorant of it? Is not the slight we thus publickly put upon him, an injury <which> we offer to his family & connections? Is the short & transient pleasure of shewing our witt, any excuse for lessening a Person in the opinion of others, who for virtue, sincerity, truth, uprightness of heart & intention, is truly valuable, & deserving of our utmost regard & esteem? Indeed Raillery to be agreeable & innocent, is only allowable among those, who are able to retort [p. 238] as well as to minister matter for a jest, for where it is only the triumph of a Superior over an Inferior, or of the sprightly & confident over the humble & diffident, there is little honour to be had in the combat, little credit to be gained by the conquest.

5th. All those jestings are not convenient, which give others pain, whatever the rank, the parts, or the abilities of Men may be. And this is one of those general rules, which ought to be observed in all conversations, & which it carefully attended to, would remove from the midst of company [p. 239] what-ever is in any degree offensive & injurious, for tho' the subject we jest upon, be in itself innocent & harmless, & the little indiscretion we charge our brother with, be so small & trifling, as to deserve no consideration, yet when we see him rattled & disconcerted at it, when we perceive any emotions of discontent & displeasure rise within him, when we do not find him more ready to make free with himself, than we can possibly be to make free with him, we surely ought to forbear our jesting, to repress at once the sallies of our imagination, & to restore him [p. 240] to his former peace & quiet, chusing rather to part with our present entertainment, than to enjoy it at the expence of another Man's ease & happiness, because the sole end of all conversation is to unite us together in closer bonds of friendship & love, to *refresh* relax the mind by an innocent & inoffensive mirth & joy, to minister to the pleasure of others, at the same time that we minister to our own, & therefore when raillery interrupts these great & noble purposes, & breaks thro' these great & sacred laws, it is justly to be looked upon as the [p. 241] bane & pest of Society, & to be shunned & avoided with the nicest care, & the utmost circumspection.

6th. & Lastly. All those jestings are not convenient, which are ill-timed & at unseasonable hours. They are ill-timed in presence of a Superior, before whom the Subject of our Discourse ought to be such, as best suits with the respect & reverence, which is due to him, & seasoned with that modesty & humility, which the distance between him & us always requires, They are ill-timed in presence of those, who [p. 242] are under affliction & trouble, whose minds are ill-disposed for jocularity & mirth, & who may indeed be relieved & receive comfort from a serious rational Discourse, & a grave & sober conversation, but whom such an unbounded merriment justly disgust, & in their present circumstances violently hurt & offend, lastly They are ill-timed, when we ourselves are immediately under the hand of God, visited by some sore judgment, threatened with misfortune & the approach of Death; At this time indeed a sense of Religion, if added to a good Conscience [p. 243] may dispose us to be resigned, & even cheerful, under our severest trials, to support them with dignity, & to avoid all that anxiety & uneasiness, which weak minds are too apt to feel in such cases for want of proper knowledge & virtue to ballast the storms of adversity, yet still a degree of seriousness & consideration is ever to be preserved, the hand of God is ever to be respected, the Dispensations of Providence are ever to be regarded, & the foundation of our confidence & hope to be laid upon the Being & mercy of God, not upon the irregular sallies of a lively [p. 244] Imagination, which may blaze & support us for a while, but which in the end yields no true nor solid comfort; whence we may venture to affirm, that those Men are justly blameable who have left the Stage of this World in a jocose jocular manner, & who under pretence of establishing their imaginary strength of mind, by ill-judged & unseemly jests, have given us too much reason to suspect, that want of faith or at least an unaccountable levity of mind & temper have been the only cause of the courage & seeming resolution they then expressed [p. 245] But enough has been said to shew the nature of those jestings, which are not convenient, Let us now in the 2nd place briefly consider some of the great & sore evils which they often give occasion to.

2d Part.

And 1st They are a visible abuse of the noble faculty of speech, with which it has pleased God to endure us. It is the Glorious privilege of our Nature, to be distinguished from the rest of the Creation, by a power of communicating our thoughts to one another, & of conversing together, in a manner unknown [p. 246] to the Beings, which surround us; It is thro' this, that we are enabled to form friendships & relations in life, to enlarge our scene of happiness, to enter into various connections & combinations, & to taste much social joy & satisfaction; Now what return do we make to God for such undeserved mercies, when we open our lips, & exercise our tongues, to profane his sacred name, or the sacred Ordinances of Religion, to dishonour the cause of virtue, to lessen the sanctions of every Divine & Moral law, when we make Conversation a channel to convey foul & impure [p. 247] streams to the infecting of those who were before pure, to the poysoning the minds & Morals of others, to the spreading of a Contagion, which ever carries ruin & destruction in it's train, when in a word, we so far forget the ends of conversation & Society, as to destroy the pleasure, which others have a right to expect from it, by our indiscretion & folly, by our inconsiderate babbling, by our gross & offensive jests & raillery, Is this to shew ourselves truly sensible of the greatness of the blessing, with which God has vouchsafed to favour us? Is this to make a suitable [p. 248] return to him for it, or rather, Is not this to turn the bounty & mercy of God against himself, & to make his own grossness recoil back upon him*self* in the most outrageous & insulting manner.

2nd. Such jestings are very hurtful & prejudicial to ourselves. They render our company disagreeable & distasteful to others, every Person fearing the lash of our tongue, flying from it as they would from the pestilence that walketh in darkness, or from the sickness that destroyeth in the noon day.[430] They raise up Enemies to us, They involve us [p. 249] into various broils & quarrels, which besides disturbing our inward peace & quiet, often endanger our life & safety, & how badly does experience confirm this truth, how often has an unguarded & improper jest turned the dearest & tenderest friend & benefactor into the most bitter & implacable Enemy, how often has it unsheathed the sword, & thrown the seemingly best disposed company into a lamentable state of confusion, blood shed & disorder, nay how often has it embroiled even States of Nations, & made the most insignificant accidents produce the most dreadful & lasting evils.

Or if thro' the [p. 250] superior understanding of others, & a incurrence of happy circumstances, our conduct in this respect does not bring upon us such fatal evils as these, yet at least does it never fail to expose us to the scorn & contempt of others it disposes them to think slightly of us, it inclines them to embrace every opportunity which offers of jesting & railing upon us, & of making us feel in our*selves* <turn> the smart of the ill usage, which we so lavishly bestow upon others.

Lastly such jestings are contrary to Christianity, because they spring from principles quite opposite to, & [p. 251] inconsistent with it. They generally arise from pride, self-sufficiency, & presumption, there is some thing in this disposition of mind, which is the very reverse of what Religion requires from us; For Christianity would have us be full of compassion & indulgence for the faults & infirmities of our neighbour, but the Indiscreet Jester makes them the subject of his mirth, & of his ill-natured sport & diversion, he catches at them with a cruel pleasure, he places them in the most glaring light, he uses the keen-ness & poignancy of his wit to display them the more, [p. 252] & to render their deformity the more visible & striking, Christianity would have us upon all occasions, minister to the comfort & pleasure of our fellow creatures, but the Indiscreet Jester delights in embittering & poysoning, what is intended to procure them recreation & amusement, now see him rejoicing in the pain he puts others in, greedyly feeding upon the ill-natured satisfaction of having established his own title to wit & humour, tho' upon the ruin of another Person's peace & quiet, testyfying by his looks & countenance, by his gesture & department, by his language & air [p. 253], the joy he has in so cruel & inhuman an entertainment. Finally Christianity would have us be ever humble & modest void of pride & presumption, furnished with the Divine Graces of meekness, charity, & love, but the Indiscreet jester is presumptuous, vain & arrogant, he exalts in his own perfections, & despises those of others, he raises himself up above the rest of Mankind, his vanity & arrogance seldom leave or forsake him, till his own tongue makes him fall,[431] insomuch that whoso seeth him, laughs him to scorn.[432]

[p. 254] Applic[ation]:

Thus have I endeavoured to shew the nature & evil tendency of those jestings, which the Apostle tells us, are not convenient. And Let no one think a Subject of this sort improper for this place, The Government of our tongue & the right ordering of our speech, is a matter of the highest importance to us, tending to our welfare here, & to our happiness hereafter; when this is attended to, when a proper Dominion is preserved over all it's irregular motions, when we endeavour to keep & restrain them within due [p. 255] bounds, we strike at the very root of several great & flagrant vices, we avoid many crying & heinous sins, we remove many great obstructions to our spiritual welfare & improvement, but where this is neglected, where no watch is let to the door of our lips,[433] & no pains taken to keep our mouth, as it were with a bridle,[434] while such grievous temptations lye in the way, we inevitably lay ourselves open to a multitude of wills, we are in danger of becoming guilty of slander, detraction, calumny or profane-ness, we run ourselves into all the guilt attending practices of this sort, nay we even debar ourselves [p. 257] of the benefit of those other virtues & graces, which we may happily possess, or if any Man among you, saith the Apostle St. James, seemeth to be Religious bridleth not his tongue, that Man's Religion is vain.[435]

The only effectual method to preserve a constant rule & government over our lips, is always[436] to remember, that we are accountable to God for the words of our mouth <as well> as for the actions of our life, or the thoughts of our heart, that a day is at hand, in which we shall appear before his awful Tribunal, called upon to answer for the blasphemies, which [p. 258] we have uttered. The oaths which we have rashly taken, the slanders, which we have spread, or the censures, which we have passed, that by our words we shall be justified, & that by our words we shall be condemned.[437]

Such thoughts often cherished & indulged, would secure us against the common, but no less dangerous defects in our speech & conversation, They would season our words with true preserving salt, cause Religion, charity, & purity to breath thro' every thing we say, and what should be [p. 258a] our constant aim & desire, They would make the words of our mouths, as well as the meditations of our hearts, to be at all times, acceptable in the sight of God our strength & our Redeemer:[438]

Sermon XXII

Volume 6 (63)

[p. 260] Belfast October the 27th 1754
Ditto September ye 12th 1756
Ditto July ye 30th 1758
Ditto January ye 13th 1760
Ditto May ye 23rd 1762
Ditto September ye 2nd 1762
Ditto November ye 22nd 1767
Ditto May ye 6th 1770

[p. 261] In the Sixteenth Chapter of the Gospel by St Matthew at the Eighteenth & nineteenth Verses.

And I say also unto thee that thou art Peter, & upon this rock I will build my Church, & the Gates of Hell shall not prevail against it.
And I will give unto thee the Keys of the Kingdom of Heaven, & whatsoever thou shalt bind on earth, shall be bound in Heaven & whatsoever thou shalt loose on earth, shall be loosed in Heaven.

The Passage I have now read unto you is one of the most remarkable in the New Testament, not indeed so much from the nature of the truth it contains, as from the strange & monstrous conclusions *that* <which> have been drawn from it; for on the promise here made to St. Peter the Doctors of the Church of Rome lay the foundation of that Supremacy, which for so many ages the Bishop of that See has usurped over the whole Christian World. To this he ascribes the extraordinary & [p. 262] unlimited power he claims of deposing & excommunicating Kings, of absolving Subjects from the allegiance they owe to their Prince, of issuing bulls & decrees *of* to the most distant parts of the Earth, of determining finally & without appeal all controversies relating to faith & practice, of granting plenary indulgences to unrepenting Sinners, & in a word of erecting such an entire & universal Dominion over the Consciences of

Men, as must lead them captive to his will & render all resistance to it sacrilegious & impious.

In order therefore to know what foundation there is for such pretensions, I shall in the following Discourse endeavour to give you the true meaning of the words of the Text, that from thence we may the better see the nature of the promise here made to St Peter, & the insufficiency of the reasons *that* <which> are generally alledged in support of the above strange & surprising Doctine.

1st Part

The meaning of the words will best appear by attending to the particular occasion *that* <which> [p. 263] introduced them;[439] O[ur B[lessed] S[aviour] being come to the coasts of Cesarea Philippe, & conversing with his Disciples in that free & improving manner with which he was wont, puts this Question to them, Whom do Men say that I the son of Man am, he probably did it not with a view to inform himself of the reports *that* <which> were current concerning him, but *rather* to give his followers an opportunity of displaying their faith, & of receiving in return from him fresh assurances of his tenderest love & protection, They said, some say that thou art John the Baptist, some Elias, & others Jeremias, or one of the Prophets, the Generality of people concluded from the miraculous works which he wrought, that he was either a fore runner of the Messiah, or one of the antient Prophets, who now anew made his appearance among them, for the notions they entertained of the Temporal Grandeur of the Messiah would not allow them to take Jesus for him in his low estate, but only to acknowledge him for a Person of high worth & dignity, & this naturally gave him occasion to carry his inquiry nearer home, & to ask his Disciples what their particular opinion about him was, He saith unto them, But whom say ye that I am? [p. 264] Upon which Simon Peter, whose zeal for his Master had ever been of the warmest kind readily answered Thou art Christ the Son of the Living God, Thou art the Messiah the Son of God of the same nature & substance with his father, who was the desire of all Nations,[440] & to whom every former dispensation bore a constant reference, for which frank & open confession he receives from his Lord this Glorious commendation, Blessed art thou Simon Barjona, for flesh & blood hath not revealed it unto thee, but my father which is in Heaven, Blessed art thou Simon Son of Jonas, because the knowledge thou hast of me is not the result of Human wisdom nor the suggestion of Human Rulers & Teachers, but the immediate Revelation of the Spirit of God, Wherefore I say unto thee, as a reward of this thy Confession that thou art Peter, that thou shalt hence-forth be called Peter in allusion to the meaning of the word which signifies a Rock, & that upon this Rock, upon thee as upon a rock I will build my Church, & the Gates of hell shall not prevail against it.

[p. 265] Some have thought that the Rock upon which Christ promises to build his Church is not, as I have explained it, the Person of St Peter, but the Confession he had just now made that Jesus was the Christ the Son of the Living God, & that it was upon this truth as upon a strong and immoveable foundation that Christ's future Church was to be erected, & it must be owned that this opinion if it could be warranted, would sap at once all the pretensions of the Church of Rome, & by excluding the Person of St. Peter from having any share in the promise *that* <which> is here made, would leave no room for his Pretended Successors to pride themselves upon it, but whatever advantage we might draw from this explanation, as the words of O[ur] B[lessed] S[aviour] are immediately addressed to St. Peter in this determinate manner, I say also unto thee that thou art Peter, As his name is upon this account changed to that of Peter or Cephas, which in the language of Syria signifies a Rock, to make the application to him still more striking, As the General Current [p. 266] of Interpreters both of the Romish & Protestant Communions agree in acknowledging something peculiar to the Person of St Peter, and above all, as the principles of our faith are too well established to stand in need of any evasion or subterfuge to elude the force of truth, we readyly agree with those of the Church of Rome that whatever *in* the nature of this promise is, it is in a particular manner addressed to St Peter, & that he is that Rock upon which Christ was to build his Church, & against which the Gates of Hell were not to prevail.

By the Gates of Hell we may understand either the power of death, which is often in Scripture expressed by Hell & the Grave, or else the power & policy of the Rulers of the Infernal Regions, which are well prefigured by the expression of Gates, as it was chiefly at the Gates of Cities, that Judges & magistrates assembled in antient times to determine controversies, or to *determine* <deliberate> upon matters of security [p. 267] & defence, & in either of these senses it denotes to us the permanency & stability of that Church which was now to be established, & which was to be too firmly built for time to destroy, or for the cunning of it's Enemies to over-throw.

And Thus far in our explanation of these words do we fall in with the Professors of the Romish Religion, Happy had it been if their adherence to truth had left it in our power to close with them in what follows, I will give unto thee says O[ur] S[aviour] the keys of the Kingdom of Heaven, The Kingdom of Heaven *here* <in this place> as in many other parts of the H[oly] G[ospels] signifies the Gospel Dispensation, & as the use of a Key is to open & disclose what *was* before <was> kept shut & secret to give to St. Peter the keys of this Kingdom is to grant unto him a power of first publishing & preaching the Gospel to Jews & Gentiles, & of thus being the first to make known the glad tidings of the Religion of <Jesus> Christ; And in this alone consists what is peculiarly promised to St. Peter by O[ur] B[lessed] S[aviour] for as *to* <to what is contained in the following words [p. 268] whatsoever thou shalt bind on earth shall be bound in Heaven, & whatsoever thou shalt loose on earth, shall be loosed in Heaven, <or> whatever the power they confer may be, it is indifferently bestowed upon all the Apostles in the 18th Ch[apter]: of St Matthew, & again renewed to them by O[ur] B[lessed] S[aviour] after his resurrection in words still more explicite, Whosoever sins ye remit they are remitted *unto them*, & whoso-ever sins ye retain, they are retained.[441] Remitting or retaining sins being the same with binding & loosing in the Text & both <being> the consequence <& effect> of that Divine Spirit of Discernment <with which the Apostles were endued & by> which they *allowed the Apostles to* were judge<d so> infallibly of the inward dispositions of the heart, *& therefore* as <to> pronounce pardon or condemnation, *abdication or punishment* <to Sinners> without *the* <any> possibility of error or mistake, *but which* <& this Grace> St Peter shared in common <& in equal degree> with the rest of his Brethren, the only difference between him & them consisting in the <single> promise that he should be the first who should preach the Gospel to the World.

[p. 269] And accordingly was this promise <to him> most remarkably fulfilled *in him*, for on the day of Pentecost he had the singular privilege of preaching the word with such efficacy as to bring three thousand to the faith he some days after added five thousand <more> to the Church,[442] & at last did in the Person of Cornelius open the door of knowledge & salvation to the Gentile World, as we have it mentioned at large in the 10th Ch[apter] of the Acts of the Apostles, thereby giving the fullest illustration to O[ur] S[aviour]'s promise that he was to be the Rock upon which his Church was to be first founded, & to whom the Keys of his Kingdom were to be first delivered.

Yet *plain* <easie> & simple as this explanation is, the Doctors of the Church of Rome are not satisfied with it, They extend the power given to St. Peter much beyond these bounds, They not only give him the keys of the Kingdom to the Messiah here, but even the keys of the kingdom of *the* Glory here-after, so that when [p. 270] he shuts, none can open, when he opens, none can shut,[443] his pre-eminence *according to them* was <in their opinion> pre-eminence of superiority & dominion, not resident in his particular Person, but transmitted by him to all those who in after ages became his Successors in the See of Rome, by which investiture they like him are infallible in matters of faith, they like him ride triumphant over all the powers of the World, they like him exclude from or admit into Heaven whom they please, & are like him the sole & unerring Vice Gerents of God, accountable to none for their actions, sitting as Gods upon the Earth, & requiring a blind & servile submission from all the Members of their Church, but how absurd such daring pretensions are will I hope appear from the following plain & simple considerations.

2nd Part.

1st. We do not see any traces of such a superiority in St. Peter over the rest of the Apostles [p. 271] as is here contended for, & this *I offer as* <is>a strong presumption that none like it ever existed, because if it had been of Divine Institution, St. Peter no doubt would have asserted it, & maintained upon proper occasions his supremacy & pre-eminence,which we have not had would *we never find that* <the opportunities of doing so were many, & yet it is never once mentioned in Scriptures that he did, nay the evidence to the contrary is full & conclusive>.

For When the Apostate Judas had fallen & a Successor was to be appointed in his stead, the Apostles neither refer to him for a proper choice, nor does he claim the least authority upon this solemn occasion, They jointly appointed two of whose integrity & zeal they had the highest opinion, Justus sirnamed Barsabas & Matthias, & then left the decision to the casting of lots, by which Matthias was numbred among the eleven Apostles;[444] When Deacons were to be elected to attend upon the service of the poor, St. Peter is not distinguished from the other Apostles in the approbation which [p. 272] they gave to those seven whom the multitudes had chosen for this high office;[445] When a Council is to be held at Jerusalem to determine the Question concerning the obligation of Circumcision, St. Peter neither convenes the assembly, neither presides in it as chief, nor decides the Question by his authority, after much disputation he delivers his opinion[446] & St. James's judgement of this matter is preferred before his, & When again St. Paul withstood him to his face, because he was to be blamed,[447] he assumed no authority to himself, he alledged no pretended commission with which his Lord had invested him, he neither complains of the injury *that is given* <which was offered> him, nor does he remind St. Paul of the respect & submission *that* <which> he owed him, A very plain proof that he himself was an entire stranger to this groundless notion of pre-eminence & superiority; Now if he had not any himself [p. 273] as it appears from these instances that he had not, it surely follows that he could not transmit any to his Successors, & that therefore the authority which the Bishops of Rome ... <claim> over the rest of the Christian Bishops cannot be owing to or derived from him.

And it is very observable that after the promise in the Text, the Disciples had a contest among themselves, Who should be the greatest in the Kingdom[448] of the Messiah, not apprehending doubtless, that this honour had as yet been conferred upon any, which have occasion to O[ur] S[aviour] to rebuke them for their pride & ambition, & to assure them that unless they became as little Children in innocence meekness & simplicity they should *never be exclaimed great in his kingdom, nay they could not expect to get any admittance into it at all* <of manners they should not enter into his Kingdom nor be esteemed great in its light, true greatness there consisting not in pomp & power but in humility & humbleness of mind>.

2nd. The Promise here made to St Peter in the sense in which I have explained it, [p. 274] and as the words of the Text lead us to understand it, was not of a nature to be transmitted down to his Successors.

For it consisted merely in his being the first who was chosen by God to preach the Gospel to the Gentiles,[449] when he had discharged his commission in this respect & laid the foundation of the Church of Christ by the conversion of Cornelius to the faith,[450] he then received what had been peculiarly promised to him by O[ur] S[aviour] & those who in after ages succeeded him in the Ministry of the word, may indeed be said to have improved upon the foundation which he had first laid, but can never be said to be the first *that* <who> laid it, the nature of the thing limits it to one, & nothing less than the utmost prejudice can make a Person swallow down the manifold absurdities with which the contrary opinion is attended.

But even supposing the promise to be of such a nature as to regard St Peter's [p. 275] Successors, it does not appear 3rd. that the Bishops of Rome are these immediate Successors.

For whatever pains the Doctors of that Church have *been at* <taken>, they have never been able to prove to any degree of satisfaction that St Peter was ever at Rome, much less that he was Bishop of it. It is certain he was not there during the two whole years that St Paul[451] dwelt in it, nor when he wrote his Epistle to Rome or his other letters from that City to the Churches of Ephesus Galalia & Philipp, since they make no mention of St Peter nor contain any salutations to him or from him. It is then probable that if he was there at all, it was not for any considerable time, & never in so conspicuous & exalted a way as to make the future Bishops of it the Channel & the only Channel thro' which God is pleased to convey his gifts & graces to Men.

And indeed such a fixed residence for so many years as it is pretended he spent [p. 276] at Rome seems inconsistent with his Duty and character as an Apostle, to whom it properly belonged to have the overseeing & inspection of all the Churches, to appoint Ministers & Teachers in the different Churches which they founded, to exercise a fit Discipline, & to advise instruct & correct, according as there was occasion, & who therefore were to remove from one place to another, as the nature of their office & the exigencies of the people required.

What then should distinguish the city of Rome from any other place where St Peter either dwelt or founded Churches, we know from the Sacred Scripture that he was at Antioch[452] & founded a Church in that city, It is more than probable that he appointed one to succeed him in the Government of it when his duty called him away, If there was such a right of pre-eminence in him as is pretended, Is it not more natural that it should have descended to the Bishops of Antioch rather than to those of Rome, or [p. 277] can any tolerable reason be assigned why it should have been entailed upon these last to the exclusion of the former or of those of any other City.

Whence *it is* <is it> (and it is the 4th & last observation I shall offer) that in the early ages of the Christian Church the Bishops of Rome know of & assumed to themselves no such power, They affected no empire or dominion, They considered the other Pastors & Governors of the Church as their brethren & fellow-workers in the Lord, They allowed their own opinions to be contradicted, & their rules & decrees to be reversed, They rejected all pompous & invidious marks of distinction, They behaved with respect & reverence to Secular & Civil powers, They confined their jurisdiction within proper limits, They did not wrest the sword of justice out of the hands of those with whom it was lodged, much less did they daringly use it to support [p. 278] their usurpation & tyranny, till rising by imperceptible degree to power & wealth, Political reasons concurred to give them height. Temporal Princes found it their interest to court their favour, Times of ignorance & confusion paved the way to their arbitrary & despotic dominion, & the ambition of some of the Bishops of Rome improved these favourable circumstances to the setting up of such an Universal & absolute Monarchy in the Church, as was plainly subversive of the rights of

Mankind, and ended in the total corruption of Doctrine with, faith, worship & Morality.

I have now briefly shewn the little foundation the words of the Text afford for the strange Doctrine they are generally sought to support, I shall *now* proceed to take some application of what has been said to ourselves.

[p. 279] Applic[ation]:

And from the promise made to St. Peter that the Gates of Hell should not prevail against the Church of Christ, we may reasonably *depend upon* <hope for> the kind protection of God *for its defence and preservation* <to improve the Piety of it's faith & worship form the overflowing of ungodliness & to secure it against all the power & cunning of its Adversaries.>

Not indeed that he hereby engages to maintain it pure & perfect in one particular place preferably to any other but only to preserve the purity of its faith & perhaps in some part of the World from the overflowings of ungodliness & corruption & still to reserve to himself a peculiar number of true & faithful worshipers. We <My Brethren> have long since been singled out by God as his chosen people, profess a genuine incorrupt faith, to offer a rational & spiritual worship, to *be blessed with* <receive> the highest means of Improvement & instruction that we *can* <could> desire, We have experienced in a singular manner the Providential mercies of our God, rescued early from Superstition & error, [p. 280] matched as firebrands out of the midst of the fire of persecution, & surprisingly carried by a series of wonderful events to that pitch of divine knowledge to which we are now arrived, and so far we find the truth of O[ur] S[aviour]'s Promise fulfilled in our particular case, but Let us not infer from hence that this Happy State is too firmly fixed to be ever changed, or the Tenure we hold it by, too strong to be ever *shaken* <taken from us>.

If we disgrace the Church we are members of, by bad lives & dissolute manners, we turn the Grace of God into lasciviousness, Infidelity in principle & unbounded by licentiousness in practice, If an open contempt of God & a daring perseverance in impiety & wickedness, if uncharitable animosities, ungoverned passions & unrestrained appetites, If profaneness & blasphemy, drunkenness & intemperance, violence & injustice reign among us uncurbed & uncontrolled, We have just reason to fear that God will be induced to *remove* <withdraw> his [p. 282] protection from us, & to transfer the advantages we enjoy to other Nations, more sensible of their worth than we are, more deserving of them than we prove ourselves to be, The

Glorious light of the Gospel is *now* extinguished in those places where it first shone in it's active splendour & purity, & how long it may be suffered to shine among us, the bounds of God's patience & long-suffering can only determine. *Let then our endeavours be to each of us in our respective duties to take the profession of it to ourselves by a strict & active obedience to it.* His arm is now lifted up, the Cups of his anger is poured out, Discord & Dissention shake the land & the enormous load of National sins & vices adds weight to the impending evil. Let then our endeavours be, each of us in our respective stations, to prevent the Danger we have so just cause to fear, by a timely & active repentance,[453] Let us vow all holy obedience unto Christ our head let us study to adorn his Church with the great virtues of piety, charity justice and temperance, & as we justly boast to be Members of the Reformed Church of God, & to excel others in the purity of our faith & worship, let us equally strive to excel them by the superior purity & holiness of our life, that so we may make this Church, a Glory and a Praise upon Earth.

[p. 283] This is the way to defeat the stratagems of it's Enemies, to secure to it the favour & protection of God, to preserve it against the corruptions of error & vice, to add Lustre & splendour to it, and what is a most engaging motive, this is the way, to make every Individual professor of it happy in the enjoyment of his own mind here, & unspeakably more so in the enjoyment of God here-after. I shall conclude all with an excellent Collect of our Church.

Keep we beseech thee O Lord thy Church with thy perpetual mercy, And because the frailty of Man without thee cannot but fall, keep us ever by thy help from all things hurtful, lead us to all things profitable to our salvation thro' Jesus Christ our Lord,[454] To whom with the Father & the Holy Ghost be ascribed all honour power & Glory now & for ever.

Sermon XXIII

Volume 6 (64)

[Note: The cover and probably the first page of this sermon is missing so the beginning of the text and dates of preaching are not known]

[p. 284] ...World, whilst the Virtuous & Righteous are often oppressed, tormented and afflicted, has been matter of Speculation in all ages, & has even sometimes shaken the faith, & staggered the resolution of Good & well meaning Persons. Many have taken this opportunity to call in Question God's Providence, to arraign his wisdom, to doubt whether he interfered in or concerned himself with the administration of things below, & to draw this hasty Conclusion that since the Ungodly so manifestly prospered in the World, since their undertakings were thus blessed, & their designs thus successful, there was either no knowledge in the most High, or no Divine Providence [p. 285] to dispense good & evil, no advantage accruing form the practice of virtue, no temporal benefit to be reaped from innocency & integrity, but that all things were probably left to chance, or determined by a blind & undiscerning fate.

I shall in the following Discourse consider more particularly the unequal distribution of the Good things of Life, & endeavour to reconcile it with the wisdom of God, & the knowledge of the most High, that our faith & trust in his Providence may be strengthened & confirmed, & our reliance upon his equity & justice may be more firmly settled & established.

And this I shall endeavour to do by shewing 1st. That the unequal [p. 286] distribution of the Good things of Life, or the prosperity of the wicked & the troubles of the righteous can never be made an Argument against God's Providence, & 2nd That far from that *that* it is founded upon several Reasons, all equally worthy of his wisdom & equity, after which I shall conclude with some practical Improvement of the whole.

1st Part

That the unequal distribution of the Good things of life, or the prosperity of the wicked, & the troubles of the righteous can never be made an Argument against God's Providence.

And Here Let us examine, how far this inequality takes place [p. 287], & how true it is in fact, & by this we shall perceive that it is not as Great & universal as we may imagine, nor the number of prosperous wicked & unfortunate righteous so large, as we in our murmuring & impatience may conceive.

There are many virtuous, who reap the fruits of their virtue, even in this Life, many wicked who receive the just wages of their iniquity, many Good Men who are visibly blessed for their integrity, & as many bad who deservedly feel the weight of their unrighteousness.

In the Nature & original constitution of things Virtue is of itself conducive to make Man happy in this Life, & to supply him with [p. 288] the Good things of it. It makes him industrious, & thereby helps to make him wealthy, honest & thereby it enlarges his Credit, frugal & prudent, & thereby it *enlar[ges]* encreases & preserves his Store, just as Vice & licentiousness tend to poverty & misery, to cloath a Man with rags, & to consume the largest & best established fortune; This is the natural consequence of Virtue & Vice, & where-ever that does not take place, there must be some external Cause, counter-acting this General Rule, & disturbing the primary & first Disposition of things.

And what brings the number of afflicted virtuous, & prosperous wicked still lower is, the uncertainty we are in of judging & determining, who are [p. 289] truly virtuous, & who are not so, & consequently of knowing whether they are justly or unjustly dealt with; For our knowledge is extremely narrow & short-sighted, we only judge from appearances, & know but little of the real & inward sentiments of a Person.

How often may an outward shew of sanctity & purity conceal many secret & hidden vices? How hard is it to judge so perfectly of any particular Person, as to charge the Providence of God with being too severe, when we cannot tell, what such a Person's private thoughts are, what his Conduct what the principle from whence his Actions spring.

And the same holds true [p. 290] with respect to many whose Characters are branded & stigmatised without Reason, whose Actions were they thoroughly displayed & laid open, would appear in a quite different light, from what they do now, & manifest abundantly the justice & wisdom of God's proceedings towards them.

I would not by this be thought to insinuate that Virtuous Men under affliction & trouble are Counterfeits & Hypocrites, or the Wicked in prosperity virtuous and Good Men, tho' at present hid & concealed from our view. Far am I from intending this, The troubles of one & the prosperity of the other are often undeserved, & their Characters exactly conformable to [p. 291] what they appear; All I would infer from hence is, that this Inequality which without all doubt obtains in many instances is not near so General, as we at first may think, & thence to make Room for a 2nd Observation to shew, that nothing can be inferred to the disadvantage of God's Providence, & that is the absurdity there is in concluding from some few instances of apparent irregularity & seeming inconsistency to the overthrow of a Doctrine, which is founded upon a multitude of positive proofs, & a number of strong & undeniable arguments.

2nd: For is there any object in Nature, that doth not bespeak God's Providence, any Created Being, in which [p. 292] we do not discover the visible footsteps of it.

What Regularity, what harmony, what just Contrivance in the disposition of their parts? With what order & Decency does every Part of the Creation answer it's particular purpose, & the end intended by it's Great Author? With what wisdom & Constancy do the different Seasons of the Year succeed one another, & promote our conveniency & pleasure? With what profusion & yet with what uniformity does the Earth pour out it's Riches, & in it's own appointed time open & display it's treasure? With what seeming Dread & awe does the Sea observe it's bounds, & in the midst of it's most boisterous fury respect the hand, who has ordered it to come hither & no further?

[p. 293] Can these & such like things which we daily observe, & with which we are almost always conversant, Can these be the effect of Chance or the product of blind & irregular motion? And are they not rather to be resolved into the immediate Agency of God, & to be entirely ascribed to his Providence & Direction?

And if this be the case, How unfair is it from the appearance of Irregularity in the distribution of the Good things of life to deduce an Inference, which tends to the utter subversion of so plain & obvious a Consequence? Suppose we knew none of the reason of this apparent inconsistency, which how-ever is not the Case, we are certain & convinced of the times & propriety of the Works of Nature to demonstrate the Certainty of God's [p. 294] Providence, & shall our ignorance in this & some other particular instances, be thought sufficient to destroy that wisdom & Guidance, which all the works of God, all his other actions so strongly manifest & set forth.

But 3rd. Let us proceed one step further, & consider more particularly the nature of those advantages of which the Virtuous are deprived, & with which the wicked seem to be blessed and rewarded, & see what real benefit arises to the one, or what real damage to the other from the want of them.

And this our own Experience often teaches us, Adversity & Affliction, a narrow fortune, an infirm body, a Life of trouble & anxiety how ever irksome [p. 295] & unpleasant, are yet the happy means of making Men considerate & serious, of convincing them of the vanity & emptiness of this World's enjoyments, & of the folly & weakness of laying too great a dependence upon them; They dispose them to be Religious & Devout, to place their full confidence in God, to expect help & deliverance from him, & to build their hopes & expectations upon him, They help to fitt & prepare them for Death, to make the thoughts of it less terrifying to them, & to wean them from the World, & it's respective enjoyments.

Whilst the prosperity of the wicked in Solomon's words doth slay them,[455] Their Affluence & many opportunities of satisfying their craving appetites [p. 296], only create new one's as loud & pressing as the others, They kindle within them violent passions, They fill their hearts with pride & vain-glory, They divert their eyes from the consideration of themselves, to that of their abundance & wealth, & in the end produce disappointment, remorse, trouble & anxiety, when the Virtuous & faithfull enjoy that peace & serenity of mind, that inward calm & quiet, which no mean-ness of Circumstances can possibly alter, nor no enjoyments ever so great compensate the want of, & to which of these two the Providence of God appears kinder, or where the Great Irregularity in the distribution of things below, Every Impartial Man may judge.

[p. 297] And tho' God indeed pleased to conceal himself from us on several occasions, yet does he in the 4th place frequently justifie his Providence even in this Life by sudden strokes & unforeseen events, either blasting the prosperity of the wicked, or rewarding the virtuous & obedient.

How many Vitious Persons can attest the truth of this? How many have been tossed down from the height of power to receive the Contempt and punishment they laid themselves open to; How many fortunes, built upon oppression & injustice, that moulder away by God's Appointment, that carry with them evident marks of God's anger & displeasure, & after having [p. 298] for some time glutted the vanity of the Possessor, ministered to his Passions, & thereby raised the astonishment of Good Men, vanish *away* & disappear, dwindle away into nothing & leave behind them but an empty & unsatisfactory a rememberance, I have seen the wicked in Great power, & spreading himself like a Green bay tree, yet he passed away, & lo! he was not, yea I sought him, but he could not be found.[456]

As on the other hand, How many Virtuous are there, whose misery & trouble have at length a fortunate & happy issue, whose honest Labours are crowned with success, whom their [p. 299] Discretion & Integrity, their Submission & resignation to the will of God has led to the enjoyment of happiness, & the attainment of many temporal advantages.

But what-ever may be the Case, whether the Righteous be recompensed in this World, or the wicked punished, nothing can be inferred from this to the disadvantage of God's Providence by us, who thro' the profession of Christianity, & the suggestions of our own Reason upon this very Inequality, confirmed & supported by Revelation, are enabled to look forwards into another World, to expect another & a better State, to see a day drawing nigh, in which such seeming Irregularities are to be set right [p. 300], in which the secret & hidden mysteries of Providence shall be explained and justyfyed, in which by a signal and universal judgment God shall render to every one according to his work, when his Justice & Equity shall be manifested to the full conviction & satisfaction of Men, when they who at present cavil at the measures he takes in the administration of the World, will adore & admire them & when the pretended defects we conceit to be in them, shall turn out to the clearer illustration of his wisdom, & far from being reflexions upon his Providence, shall abundantly appear to be founded upon Reasons all equally worthy of his Justice [p. 301] and Equity; What these may be now remain to be considered in the 2nd & last place.

2d: Part

And 1st. This Inequality in the Distribution of the Good things of Life, is perfectly agreeable to the Design of God & the purpose for which he sent us into the world.

We are here only upon trial & probation, to manifest the sincerity of our obedience, & some temporal rubs & difficulties must be in our way to enable us the better to shew our Resolution & stedfastness.

[p. 302] Was Virtue ever happy, the practice of it would become too selfish, it would lose it's Lustre, degenerate into a mean & sordid interest, and might indeed illustrate the prudence but never the real & inward integrity of the Man; Was Vice on the other hand ever prosperous & successful, the

Virtuous would be discouraged, they would by degrees be disgusted with a Course of Life, that always tended to make them miserable, & by degrees would become careless & indifferent about it.

But as things are now established, the views of God are answered & the choice & Liberty of his Creatures [p. 303] preserved & maintained; Our Virtue is some times tried, & sometimes rewarded, Vice is permitted to triumph for a short while, & by this to enhance the worth & add to the Glory of the Virtuous.

2nd. This Inequality convinces us, what little value God sets upon the Good things of this World, since he thus promiscuously dispenses them, & often showers them down upon those, who are the least objects of his love & concern.

He suffers them to be seized upon, & possessed by Persons, for whom he bears no affection or regard, whose wishes he gratyfies, & whose [p. 304] ambitious views he satiates in this manner, tho' they are the Greatest obstacles to the promoting of his honour, & are themselves reserved for the severest & most afflicting judgments.

Whilst to the Virtuous he often chuses to deal out the bread of affliction & sorrow, He thinks such a portion fitter for those, whom he particularly & remarkably loves & cherishes, He considers such a Condition in a far different light from what we do, & how contrary so-ever this may be to our notions & opinions he plainly declares it to be the most eligible State, the strongest indication of his true concern & regard.

[p. 305] Lastly. This Inequality is of use to shew us, how Great & beyond Conception so, must that happiness be, which is laid up for us in a future State, since all the enjoyments here on Earth, all the felicity this World can afford, are still too frail and imperfect, to fill up that plan of Happiness, which God has formed for his faithfull & obedient Children.

Let all the different Enjoyments of Life be supposed to center in one Person, Let his Condition be as prosperous, as we can possibly conceive it, his Riches & Wealth immense, his Character & Reputation firmly [p. 306] established & universally spread, Let all the Honours of this World, the most pompous & flattering distinctions be heaped upon him, God who loves his Virtuous Servants, who desires their happiness, who labours to promote it, might have but them in possession of all these, he might have made the fruition of these eternal & never failing, & secured to them the enjoyment of such blessings for ever.

And yet he has not done it, Such a prosperity does not answer his purpose, nor sufficiently come up to his Scheme, He has provided for them other kinds of [p. 307] joys, He has laid up for them advantages highly transcending these, which are more, than eye hath seen, or ear heard, or the Heart of Man ever conceived.[457]

And there-fore How Compleat must they be? What warm & affectionate desire of enjoying them should they raise in us? With what zeal should they kindle & excite our endeavours, fill us with a noble & Generous Emulation, & engage us to put forth our whole activity & strength to enter into the possession of them.

And this brings me to the [p. 308] Last thing proposed, to make some practical Improvement of the whole.

3d. Part.

And Hence we may Learn not to be envious & impatient at the Prosperity of the wicked; Their Affluence & fortitude is frequently a punishment from God, & their Desires gratyfyed only to add to their Guilt, & encrease their misery; And could we but see the trouble & vexation of Spirit, the anguish & remorse that attend their enjoyments, the uneasie reflexions, the stings of Conscience, that continually wrack & torment them, Would we but consider the severe account they are to give of their ill Gotten or ill spent fortune, & the fatal miseries to which their [p. 309] present circumstances shall infallibly lead them, we should think their enjoyments too dearly bought to covet the purchase, we should prefer our obscure & low condition to all their Glittering appearance, & secure in the approbation of our own hearts, & the reflexions of our own minds, we should soon find Reason to bless God, for refusing to us, what he grants to others upon such dangerous & dreadful terms.

2nd. The Consideration of God's Providence being perfectly reconcilable with the unequal distribution of the Good things of life, furnishes abundant comfort & consolation to the true & virtuous, who are now struggling against adversity, & exposed to infinite [p. 310] sorrow & anguish.

They hereby see themselves under the Direction of a kind & Gracious God, whose favour & protection their virtue has engaged to them, They are in the hands of a Compassionate & just Father, who dispenses all things for their advantage & benefit, whose wisdom is best able to chuse for them & without whose leave & appointment no evil or misfortune can befall them.

And if they submitt to their condition with a firm reliance upon his justice & goodness, if they endeavour to fix in their minds a due and proper sense of his Providence, if content *with* <under> & satisfied with his [p. 311] present dispensations they leave the end & issue of them to his own disposing, They may securely rest upon the hopes of seeing their troubles done away, & their sorrows rewarded, They may look upon themselves, as entitled to those Great & Glorious promises, which Virtue in Distress can only claim, They may expect that joy & happiness, those high & inconceivable rewards, which are reserved for those, who like them endure chastning, suffering will-fully,[458] & who commit their Souls to God, as to a faithfull Creator,[459] thoroughly able to change their low condition, & to exalt them to Honour peace & Immortality.

[p. 312] As for the Virtuous & Upright who enjoy a plentiful share of this World's Goods, & visibly prosper upon account of their Integrity, Let them Learn to esteem the Gift of God, to set a true value upon his favour, & to be truly thankful to him for thus exempting them from those temporal evils, to which others are often exposed.

But Let them above all things take care by their own conduct & behaviour, not to bring a reflexion upon God's Providence, & by a fatal abuse of his Bounty give occasion to Infidels & Libertines to accuse God's wisdom or Justice.

[p. 313] They are entrusted with weighty & valuable Talents, but no further valuable to them, than as they apply them to the purposes, for which they were given them,[460] Let their wealth minister to the wants of others, supply their necessities, be spent in acts of Charity & beneficence, Their interest & authority be exercised to the support of Innocence against Lawless power, the advancement of Religion, & the promoting of virtue, Their time & leisure to the Improvement of Society, & the furtherance of the welfare & happiness of the Country in which they dwell, & Every Temporal advantage which God [p. 314] in his mercy has been pleased to give them, be used with that Temper & moderation, that Prudence & Caution, which so highly becomes those, who are accountable to the Lord of all things, for every thing they enjoy & strictly answerable for the use, they make of it.

This will sanctify & secure our wealth, engage God to encrease & continue it unto us, This will make us reap the sweets & real comforts of it, & so strict an adherence to virtue & integrity, shall enable us whether we be Rich or poor, to lay up for ourselves treasures in Heaven,[461] that never moulder [p. 315] or decay, to make every trial and circumstance of our lives turn out to our benefit & advantage, & in the end & final issue of all things to receive in exchange for our Wealth, Heavenly & Lasting Riches, & instead of our present wretched & afflicted Condition, to be admitted into that State of Happiness & Glory, which admits of no interruption, but remains the same, yesterday & today, & forever.

Sermon XXIV

Volume 7 (71)

[p. 209]

Belfast 27 August 1749
Ditto June the 9th 1754
Ditto February ye 4th 1759
Ditto August ye 23rd 1761
Ditto March ye 11th 1764

Copied Ep[ist]le to Collo[ssions][462]

[p. 210] In the Fourth Chapter of St Paul's Epistle to the Colossians at the sixth Verse.

Let your speech be always with grace seasoned with salt.

There is *no* <hardly any one> thing which <which gives us > we <take> so much *delight in* <pleasure> as in Conversation, & a*n* <Social> entercourse *of Society* with each other, *It is* <This that becomes> the <proper> bond of friendship, the tie that keeps us together, the release of the mind after fatigue, & the <chief> joy & *pleasure* <delight> of every humane, & *generous, social* <benevolent> heart, Nature leads & inclines us to it, & [p. 211] Religion far from condemning, allows of & recommends it to us.

But to enjoy this pleasure in it's *height* <perfection & purity>, certain rules & Directions are to be observed, which reason as well as Religion lays down for the right ordering of our speech, & which the Apostle seems to comprehend in the words now read unto you, Let your speech be always with grace, seasoned with salt, where by a plain allusion to the nature of salt, which at once renders our meat savoury, & preserves it from Corruption, he intimates to us that some qualifications must necessarily attend our Discourse, like proper seasoning to render it both palatable & free from Corruption.

[p. 212] I propose at this time to consider what these are & to lay before you the seasoning with which we are to accompany our words & Discourses, and this I shall reduce to the three following, 1st. A seasoning of Piety 2nd *A seasoning* of Charity, & 3rd. *A seasoning* of Discretion <Decency> and *moderate* Discretion.

1st Part.

1st. Our Speech should be seasoned with piety, or with *such* <so strong> a sense of God & Religion as *tends* remove every thing from it that *tends to express a respect & regard for it and this in general is the deepest of that seasoning of piety which I should now reccomend* <savours in any shape either of Infidelity or Impiety>.

[p. 213] *It stands opened to that Conversation which consists of Blasphemy & profaneness directly levelled against the majesty of God.* <Directly contrary to this rule is that Conversation which consist of blasphemy & profaneness>, *a* Crimes of so daring & *audacous a nature* <hideous *in itself* a nature>, that I may with confidence presume *that* none here present *are* <to be> guilty of them, A sett of *offences* <transgressions> these, *which* <what> ought to be rooted out of Society as the bane & pest of it, Men who open their mouths purposely to revile the God that made them, who judge it their Glory, *to offer insults to his infinite purity & holiness, who* < to> launch out their venom against the King of Heaven and Earth, & by their blasphemous profane scoffs *challenge him to reveal & exercise his* <to defy and set at nought his authority and> power, Men in a word whom every one <ought to> look upon with horror, [p. 214] to dread & detest their entercourse, and <who> as they are *them* condemned by others, & condemned by their own hearts, so are they justly exposed to the severest *judgements* <strokes> of Divine wrath & indignation.

But as generally as we may agree in this, there is another *species* <branch> of this Religious seasoning <we are now speaking of> which our Conversation often wants, *& that is* a seasoning of reverence & awe for the sacred name of God in opposition to rash & vain swearing upon every light and trivial occasion.

This is a Vice which is of most universal extent, which the corrupt fashion of the World has almost rendered reputable, which the character *of those that practice it* < of the offender>, too often [p. 215] recommends, & which by being so general & common, passes often unnoticed & unobserved, since there are but few conversations where the infection is not more or less prevalent, The serious & jocose, the great & the small, the old & the young, nay the stammering lips of the Infant sound<ing> oaths and imprecations in our Streets.

And yet consider this vice in itself, examine it's nature & consequences, & you'll find that if blasphemy be more daring, this is very near as injurious to God, & as fatal to the World.

I say as injurious to God, for can it be supposed that if we had a due & proper regard for him, if we believed [p. 216] him to be that powerful just & awful Being we profess *to* <we> do, we would use his tremendous name upon every occasion we would by a most solemn appeal call upon his infinite wisdom power and knowledge to bear witness to *every* our idle insignificant talk, or if we really thought the judgments denounced against *us* <Sinners> were true, that we could in cold blood out of <meer> mirth & festivity invoke them down *upon us*, & desire of God to inflict them upon us in full measure.

Whence *it is* <the> unavoidable consequence of rash & vain swearing <is> that we impair by degrees the sense we ought <always> to have of the Majesty & power [p. 217] of God, we accustom ourselves to make mention of his Nature & Essence without *much* thought *&* <or> reflection, & what is most hurtful to Society we lessen the sacredness of that bond, which is the only security we can have between Man & Man, & the only method to *determine* <put an end to> strife & contention, we open a door to perjury, we think less of the solemnity of this act of Religious <swearing> & by our example *may* <often> betray others into the same dangerous opinion with ourselves.

And these evils we voluntarily run ourselves in without the least temptation <without passion> to <blind> us, without any plea to offer in our behalf, No end is [p. 218] attained, no desire gratified, no appetite indulged by it, but the vain swearer hazards his Immortal Soul, barters his birthright, loses it for ever upon a smaller consideration than a Mess of Lentils,[463] *wherefore Let the Apostle St James his advice be always in our mind* Above all things <therefore> my Brethren swear not, neither by Heaven, neither by the Earth, neither by any other oath, but let your yea be yea, & your nay nay, lest ye fall into condemnation.[464]

And Equally void of this seasoning of piety is that Conversation which tends to turn the mysteries & truths of Religion into ridicule, another most [p. 219] conspicuous defect in our Discourse.

For there are many who boast and *glory* <triumph> in their disbelief of the truths of Christianity, *who to raise themselves in the world pretend not to believe what others do &* who imagine they give a great proof of the superiority of their understanding by rejecting the evidence *they go upon, hence do they* <which others yield to, & who> upon all occasions vent their sentiments in speech & conversation, *hence do they* <who> cast<ing> a ridicule upon the Professors of Religion *& piety* deriding the true worshippers of God, & representing them *as weak & credulous Persons* <to others in a most contemptible light>.

And as they do this with an air of confidence & assurance, generally [p. 220] when no one present can answer them, in a mixed company of young and unguarded people, so is the bad effect of their Discourse very visible, The restraints of Religion are *made little of* <slackened>, the ties of piety & devotion< slighted> the Character of pious & good Men treated with contempt.

And is this desirable or to be wished for? *Is it* <Would it be> for the advantage of *the World* <*Mankind* Society> that virtue & a sense of God *be* <was> banished out of it, let *there* <Religion> be policy superstition or what they *will* <please to suppose it> *is it not highly advantageous* <must be universally allowed, to believe it is> highly conducive to the happiness & prosperity of Mankind?

What service <then> do they *then* mean the World, who with their mouths [p. 221] endeavour to represent *these* <it> as absurd & unreasonable, & who turn against Religion the most rational & natural method of improving in it, an easy friendly & affectionate Conversation.

For tho' matters of Religion are not to be made the constant subject of our Discourse as being of a solemn serious nature, that an ordinary coversation can well bear Yet etc.[465] it is certain that much good may be done in that way & virtue and piety be much promoted did we more frequent[ly] than we now do take occasion from the Common occurrence of life to press & inculcate in those we converse with the great and weighty truths of religion.[466]

For <Yet> it is certain *this would* <we should> much promote our virtue & piety did we more frequently *make these the subject of our discourse* < than we do talk a discourse about them>, did we take occasion from the common occurrences of life, the return of solemn festivals the deaths of our friends or other such causes, to press & inculcate the important truths of God's *mercy & Providence* <Prudence judgments & mercies> for them the great objection that is made against Discourses *of this sort* <upon these matters & which considerably lessen their worth>[467] that they are the trade & profession of those *that* <who are appointed to> speak or write them <would> fall to the Ground, we <would> render [p. 222] them particularly applicable to those to whom we speak, & from the friendship *that* <which already> subsists between us <& the disinterested manner in which we convey our instruction, we may expect> *we may expect* to make the greater impression, & as they think well of us, that they *will* <would> also do so, of what we deliver to them for their good & advantage, for which reason it is, that David invites all those that fear God, to come & hear, & he would declare what he hath done unto his soul,[468] & that the P[rophet] Malachy mentions it as the distinguishing characteristic of those that feared God, that they spake often one to another, & turned their Discourse upon their mutual improvement in Religion, which was so agreeable to him that he [p. 223] hearkened & heard it, & a book of rememberance was written before him for them that feared the Lord & that thought upon his name.[469]

2d Part.

The next seasoning of our Speech that I mentioned is a seasoning of Charity & good nature, which is indeed a principal & necessary ingredient in all Conversation.

But do they act according to the laws of Charity, whose Discourse chiefly consists of slander & calumny, who are themselves the Coiners of the false & injurious stories they repeat to the prejudice of their neighbour's reputation, [p. 224] & who delight in *stigmatising* <charging> & loading Men with imputations <which> they have not deserved *& wherein lies to create fear trouble & uneasiness the baseness of* <& with crimes which they are then sensible they have never been guilty of, the hellish villainy> of such a disposition <of mind> is too apparent to be dwelt upon, it springs from principles too odious not to be perceived, as Cruelty <malice, envy, jealousy> lying, ill-nature & uncharitableness, and the repeated judgments denounced against it in Sacred Scripture *are sufficient to disuade us from it & to expose the* <sufficiently shew the odiousness of it in the sight of God & the great & extreme> danger we lay ourselves open to by so vile & detestable a practice, Whoso privily slandereth his neighbour, him will I cutt off, he that telleth lies shall not tarry in my sight,[470] The lip of truth shall be established for ever, whilst [p. 225] the lying lip is but for a moment,[471] may possibly for a short time deceive *both ourselves &* <and impose upon> others but must soon end in *our* <it's> own *ruin* <infamy> & disgrace.

Near a akin to this, tho' of a less dye is the common fault of Detraction & evil-speaking, which differs from the former, in that the facts we relate, are true not feigned, but uttered & published without reason or necessity, to every body alike with[ou]t choice or discernment, for there are some cases in which speaking evil of our neighbour cannot be called Detraction, when *it* <the fault> is so publick, that it cannot be concealed, when we are called upon by legal authority to deliver our testimony [p. 226] against him, or even when friends thoroughly conscious of each other's secrecy and discretion speak & converse together with[ou]t *the least* reserve or restraint.

But the evil speaking I now discourse upon, regards those who no sooner hear an injurious whisper of their neighbour than they go from house to house, carry it from one to another, add, exaggerate blacken matters, represent them in the most hateful light, put upon them the worst & most ill-natured constructions.

And what excuse can be offered to justifie so black yet so general a practice. It cannot be concern for the welfare of those upon whose conduct [p. 227] we thus animadvert, for is this promoted by lessening them in the opinion of others, & where we truly love, we industriously conceal, hide palliate defects, it cannot be regard for those before whom we speak, for <ye reserve good or advantage from it> often-times the offence Men give would *be* <have been> buried in oblivion *were it not* <had it not been> for *such infamous* <our babbling> tales *& tale bearers* <and reports>, *It* <neither it> can *not* it be out of a sense of honour for God, since the divulging of another's faults is really casting a slut upon his workmanship, and vilifying his Creatures.

But from whatever principle it proceeds, the consequence of it are most fatal & prejudicial, fatal to our neighbour whose character it [p. 228] blasts, whose influence it lessens, whose peace & happiness it interrupts, & most prejudicial to *us whom* <ourselves as> it deprives us of the regard of all good Men, *when* <as> it exposes <us> to infinite inconveniencies, *& when* above all as it *excludes* <has a natural tendency to exclude> for ever from the presence of God, & *dependence on* <to from ye enjoyment> his most precious & lasting blessings, Lord who shall abide in thy Tabernacles, who shall dwell in thy Holy Hill? He that back-biteth not with his tongue nor doth evil to his neighbour, nor taketh up a reproach against his neighbour,[472] What Man is he that desireth life & loveth many days, that he may see good, Let him keep his tongue [p. 230] from evil, & his lips that they speak no guile.[473]

And it is Discourses of this sort which O[ur] S[aviour] Comprehends under ye general expression of idle words that we are to give and act of in the Day of judgement, not strictly idle & useless, trifling and insignificant, but such as are really injurious hurtful & pernicious.[474]

From the same *desire of evil speaking* <want of Charity> proceeds another defect in our Discourse, <contrary to ye Grace & salt mentioned in ye text>, namely Censoriousness, the Character of those morose & sullen Men, who spread gloominess & austerity over every Company they go to, who convert into a Crime every unguarded word, every ill-managed gesture, every unmeaning look, who censure the most innocent amusements & customs of the World, who reprove contradict & rebuke with bitterness, who seem if they would make others bear the punishment of their own peevish<ness> *& disagreeable temper* & ill humour, who upon all [p. 231] occasions set themselves up for Judges, & erect in every Society Tribunals to condemn the views, designs and action of *others* their Brethren.

What right have they to do this, what right have *we* <they> to wrest a power out of the hands of God, which belongs to him alone, Can *we* <they> like him *judge* look into the heart, or judge of the secret springs by which others are wrought, May not deceitful appearances be still consistent with the most upright intentions, Do some little improprieties in a Man's behaviour some-thing arising from his circumstances in life, the education he has had, the company he has kept, [p. 232] justifie *us* <them> in the severe sentence they pass *on* <upon> him, Are there not subjects enough for censure in *our* <their> own behaviour to engage *us* <them> to spare others, *& by this censorious malocious disposition do we not deserve to rouse the censure of others & to set the tongues of the … in array against us* <& ought they not to fear that by censuring they may bring down, censure upon themselves, & open a field for the malice & ill nature of others to work upon>.

To *all which* <these> different branches of uncharitableness in our Speech, I shall add but this one, railing and scoffing at others before their face out of mirth & for entertainment sake.

There is indeed less baseness in this than in slander & detraction, & it may be done with[ou]t any of those [p. 233] infamous vices which occasion the former, but still it is cruel to delight in that which must inevitably give another pain, for no one bears to be made the object of contempt, & tho' we should mean & intend no hurt by it, yet it often throws a ridicule upon a Person which he never can thoroughly get the better of, it weakens his authority in Society, & may possibly impair the good effect of is influence & example.

Raillery to be agreeable & entertaining ought to be under some restraint, & should upon this account prevail mostly among those, who are nearly upon an equality both in rank & [p. 234] understanding, & who are able to retort as well as minister occasion for a joke, for where it is only the triumph of a Superior over and Inferior, or of the *strong & understanding* <mighty and confident> over the *weak & ignorant* <humble and diffident>, there is little honour to be got in the combat, little credit to be gained by the conquest.

But when Conversation is cleared from those different corruptions of uncharitableness, when instead of making it a Channel to convey & disperse the faults & defects of others, we endeav[ou]r by our Discourse to lessen & diminish them, when thro' this we rescue *the* <fair & honourable> Characters *of others* from the censure unjustly thrown out [p. 235] upon them, when we take every occasion which this affords of saying obliging & encouraging things to the good & virtuous, when we only offer wholesome & charitable advice with a Spirit of concern for our neighbour, void of all sharpness & acrimony, when an honest innocent mirth & joy, harmless & inoffensive, glows in our words & Speech, when conversation becomes the means of uniting us together by closer bonds, of raising & increasing our love & friendship for each other, when *we send dismiss persons from us as well pleased with us as they properly can be with themselves, then do* <at the end of it we are convinced that we dismiss others from us equally well pleased both with themselves & us>, we *truly* <properly> make conversation useful & pleasant, we season it with true preserving salt, [p. 236] we accompany it with that Grace which the Apostle recommends in the Text, we render it at once savoury to others, <equally> improving & entertaining *both* to them & us.

And this will be still more perfectly attained, if we consider the third & Last seasoning, which ought to attend our Speech a seasoning of <Decency> & Discretion.

3^{d} Part.

And by this rule are excluded all positiveness & peremptoriness in Conversation, all obstinacy in persisting in an argument, whether it be right [p. 238] or wrong, all disputing with acrimony & bitterness, all roughness & rudeness, all talkativeness & immoderate unbounded flow of words, according to the observation of Solomon, In the multitude of words there wanteth sin, but he that refraineth his lips is wise,[475] all neglect &[476] all neglect & disregard for those we speak to, how superior soever we may be to them, all treatment of Persons in our words & discourse, as is not suited to their age their rank, their circumstances & character with several others of the like nature, but the time not allowing me to speak to each of these in particular, I shall for the present confine myself to *two* <one> of the principal offences against decency & discretion.

The 1st is talkativeness & an immoderate unbounded flow of words.

It may perhaps appear strange to reckon this among the Moral defects of speech, but when we consider it's [p. 239] *origin & effect, the wonder will cease, since there is nothing more unjust, more presumptuous, more disagreeable nor more dangerous than this.*

It is unjust as it encroaches upon & invades the right which every Man in Society has to speak & to contribute to the entertainment of others, It is presumptuous & vain, as it necessarily arises from a fond conceit, that we have a superior strength of understanding to what others possess, & are better able than any one present to keep up, enliven & improve Conversation, It is disagreeable to those that are by, as it mortifies their pride & vanity, & attacks their self love, and more than all this It is highly dangerous [p. 240] *as it deprives us of the guard of our reason & exposes us to all the different dangers of slander detraction censoriousness & the like, for where there is so vast a flow of words, it is hardly to be avoided but some of these furnish us with materials, & the common scandal & report of the World be brought in to supply so constant & plentiful a consumption according to Solomon's observation, that in the multitude of words there wanteth not sin, but that he that refraineth his lips is wise.*[477]

But what above all things is directly contrary to decency & discretion are 2d All loose & licentious Discourses, which as much offend good breeding [p. 241] & good manners, as they do purity and Religion, for which reason St. Paul commands us to let no corrupt communication proceed out of our mouth, but such as is good for the use of edifying that it may minister grace unto the Hearer.[478]

And indeed Discourses of this sort are strong indications of corruption & depravity in the heart, for as a good Man out of the good treasure of his heart bringeth forth that which is good, so an evil Man out of the evil treasure of his heart bringeth forth *evil things* that which is evil,[479] [p. 242] They shew a mind strangely perverted that can take delight in what is most notoriously & confessedly base & dishonourable, They tend to no other end, but to corrupt & vitiate the imagination of the young & innocent, to use them to think of vice & licentiousness with less reluctance, & by degrees to grow familiar & acquainted with the committal of it, They are more particularly injurious to those that are themselves pure & holy, & when uttered with them this offensive insinuation, that we fancy others are as corrupt as ourselves, & as well pleased as we can be, with such impure & loose Discourses.

[p. 243] So corrupt & depraved a taste must necessarily arise from the disorderly Company we have kept, or from the licentious Books we have read, which have poisoned our hearts, vitiated our palates & given us a relish for filthiness & impurity; And in how shocking a light do they appear, who not content with destroying the virtue *of those which they conversed with by their foul speech* <of their companions by their foul speech & conversation> have spread the same infection over their writings & *after their deaths*, transmitted down to their posterity the <deadly> venom which their lips were hourly spitting out.

Of what importance is it then to [p. 244] us to avoid whatever tends to so bad & dangerous an end, How ought we to fill our minds with a hearty sense of Religion & Charity, to have as constant regard for holiness & purity in our words *as well as in our actions* <and Discourses>, to be <suffer> according to the Apostle's exhortation no uncleanness, filthiness, foolish talking nor jesting be once named amongst us as becometh Saints,[480] but to be holy in all manner of Conversation, as he that hath called us is holy.[481]

Above all. How ought we to remember that we are accountable to God for our words as well as for our works, that we are one day to appear at his awful Tribunal [p. 245] called upon to answer for the blasphemies we have uttered, the oaths we have lightly taken, the slanders we have spread, the censures we have passed?

How ought we to anticipate this Great Day, & by examining our words at the Bar of reason & Conscience, judge whether they entitle us to pardon or condemnation, whether they bespeak our absolution or *sentence* <our punishment>, for by our words we shall be justified, and by our words we shall be condemned.[482]

Then shall we truly avoid the common & dreadful defects of speech, Then shall the virtuous [p. 246] abundance of our heart[483] dictate & inspire our words, Then shall Religion charity, Purity breath thro' every thing we say, and Then and Then only shall the words of our mouth as well as the meditation of our heart be always acceptable in the light of God, our Strength & our Redeemer.[484]

NOTES TO THE TEXT

1 Allusion to Matt. 3.15.
2 Original text illegible.
3 Rom. 6.3,5.
4 I Pet. 3.21–2.
5 A page has been removed here and pp 156 and 157 thus represent a redraft of this section of the sermon by Saurin with approximately five lines added to the original text.
6 Allusion to Heb. 10.1.
7 This is the end of the revision and the 'etc' indicates that he returns to his original text here.
8 Gal. 3.16.
9 Acts 16.14–15; I Cor. 1.16.
10 Allusion to Exod. 6.8 or Ps. 135.12; Ps. 136.21–2.
11 A page has been cut out here so p. 165 must represent a redraft of the original text.
12 A page has been removed here suggesting p. 166 is a redraft.
13 Eccles. 8.11.
14 Mark 10.14; Luke 8.16; Matt. 19.14. 'Now to God the Father etc and the Grace of our Lord J[esus] C[hrist] the love of God & the fellowship of the Holy Ghost be with us all evermore' added in a later hand.
15 Saurin's son, James, was curate in St Doulagh's, Co. Dublin, from 1783 to 1801, see J.B. Leslie & W.J.R. Wallace, *Clergy of Dublin and Glendalough* (Belfast, 2001), p. 281.
16 This entry and subsequent dates of preaching for this sermon are in later hands.
17 Saurin's son, James, was vicar of Rosenallis and Oregan (Mountmellick), Co. Kildare, from 1804 to 1812; see J.B. Leslie, *Clergy of Meath and Kildare* (Dublin, 2009), p. 281.
18 Mountmellick was in the parish of Oregan and Rosenallis where Saurin's son was vicar.
19 II Tim. 3.1–4.
20 A page has been removed here leading to a lacuna in the text.
21 A page has been cut away here leading to a lacuna in the deleted text.
22 Jas. 2.19.
23 I Cor. 13.1–2.
24 Matt. 23.23, 25.
25 At this point Saurin redrafted the remainer of this section of the sermon on a later occasion. This alternative is printed as an appendix to the sermon below. The result of this is that much of the original of this second section of sermon has been deleted. The details of the deletions have not been given for the sake of simplicity.
26 Ezek. 33.30–1.
27 Rev. 3.16.
28 Allusion to Luke 9.55.
29 Deleted passage replaced with text on p. 322: 'like the wisdom from above, be first pure; then peaceable, gentle, easie to be entreated, full of mercy & good fruits, without partiality, & without bitterness'.

30 Allusion to Gal. 4.18.
31 Deleted passage replaced with text on p. 322: 'Which are generally the most powerful arguments & the likeliest, if any can, to overcome the torment of prejudice and passion'.
32 See Exod. 28.36; 39.30; Zech. 14.20–21.
33 Deleted passage replaced with text on p. 327: 'And as he at present notes our deceit, so will he most assuredly in a subsequent Oeconomy remove all false & deluding colurs, manifest our folly to the eyes of the whole World, & render our consessions glaring & conspicuous'.
34 Job 27.8.
35 Allusion to Job. 8.14
36 Matt. 6.22; Luke 11.34.
37 Probably an allusion to Ps. 139.23.
38 Rev. 2.23.
39 From the post communion prayer in the *Book of Common Prayer.*
40 Jer. 7.5–6.
41 This entry and subsequent ones are in later hands.
42 James's son was archeacon of Dublin 1813–18 and this use of the sermon may relate to an archdiaconal visitation, Leslie & Wallace, *Clergy of Dublin and Glendalough*, p. 16.
43 Saurin's son was rector of Donoughmore in Ossory from 1808 until 1818, see J.B. Leslie, *Ossory clergy and parishes* (Enniskillen, 1933), p. 238.
44 Isa. 5.20.
45 Rev. 3.17.
46 Rom. 12.3.
47 Pages 13–14 are a later insert in a different, later hand with further material on this text. This is printed in the appendix to this sermon.
48 Dan. 4.30.
49 Job 4.19.
50 Job 13.25.
51 Allusion to Ps. 37.2.
52 Prov. 23.5.
53 A later insertion to the sermon is indicated at this point with the text opposite on p. 28: 'when it seeks for esteem, it merits with contempt, when it aims at regard & admiration, it only excites laughter & pity, a mans Pride (says the wise man,) shall bring him low, but Honour shall uphold the humble in spirit; and what else can be expected from it'. This is in the same hand as the insertion on pp 13–14.
54 Prov. 29.23.
55 Prov. 16.5.
56 As related in the Book of Esther
57 Acts 12.21–3.
58 Job 40.15.
59 Dan. 4.15, 25, 36.
60 Jer. 49.16.
61 Prov. 11.21.
62 Isa. 2.12, 17.
63 Three lines of original text deleted and illegible.
64 Jas. 4.6
65 Allusion to Philem. 2.7.
66 A number of words in this passage are unreadable due to the tight binding.
67 Isa. 57.15.
68 Matt. 5.3.
69 This entry and subsequent ones are in later hands.
70 The deleted passages here are transcribed on p. 43 in the hand of Saurin's son.
71 Ps. 119.97.
72 'if moreover ... importance of it' transcribed on p. 47 opposite in Saurin's hand.
73 'they look upon it ... their labours' transcribed on p. 49 opposite.
74 Matt. 13.3; Mark 4.3; Luke 8.5.
75 Matt. 22.29; Mark 12.24, 27.

76 Eph. 4.14, 16.
77 The influence of *The whole duty of man*, a frequently reprinted work on religion in early eighteenth-century Ireland, is clear here.
78 Prov. 2.10.
79 Ps. 119.11.
80 'we content ourselves ... advantage of the' transcribed on p. 62 opposite by Saurin's son.
81 Isa. 29.12.
82 A later insertion in a different hand is indicated here. The text from p. 65 is 'and which makes the attainment of it necessary to Persons of all ages & conditions, is the want of a ...'
83 John 16.33.
84 John 14.1.
85 'the thoughts ... in Solomon's words' is marked in Saurin's hand as an insert here from p. 69.
86 Prov. 6.22.
87 This sermon would appear to have had two versions. The text as printed here seems to represent the sermons as originally preached and in the manuscript p. 75 follows after p. 70. The alternative ending recorded in pp 71–4 is reproduced as an appendix to this sermon.
88 John 7.17.
89 The deleted passage is replaced by text on p. 83 in Saurin's hand: 'Hence that warmth and zeal in some for matters of Religious Speculation only, Hence that contention & acrimony in others to load with reproaches those who differ from them in opinions, & Hence that Superstitious concern in many to keep up the term of Religion whilst they deny the whole power, neglect the true & real substance of it'.
90 Luke 1.78.
91 Allusion to Rev. 2.5.
92 This entry and subsequent ones are in later hands.
93 Parish of Annaclone, diocese of Dromore.
94 Possibly parish of Ardmore, diocese of Dromore, where Saurin's grandson was vicar 1822–3, see H.B. Swanzy, *Succession lists of the diocese of Dromore*, ed. J.B. Leslie (Belfast, 1933) p. 99
95 Probably in the parish of Seagoe, diocese of Dromore, where Saurin's grandson was incumbent 1827–70, see Swanzy, *Succession lists of the diocese of Dromore*, pp 46, 242.
96 Exod. 32.1–15.
97 Allusion to Matt. 198 or Mark 10.5.
98 Eph. 4.26.
99 Matt. 5.22.
100 Prov. 24.17.
101 'that he never suffers ... reason it is etc' appears facing p. 101 to be inserted to replace deletion.
102 Eph. 4.26.
103 'whenever it is encouraged' in a later hand. On p. 104 facing this passage is the insertion 'which demonstrates its folly'.
104 Isa. 57.20.
105 Prov. 25.28.
106 Prov. 17.14.
107 Eph. 4.31–2.
108 Prov. 22.23–5.
109 Prov. 26.20.
110 Matt. 5.5.
111 The sermon is unfinished and was presumably so in the late eighteenth century since 'thus fit us .... J[esus]X[rist] O[ur] L[ord]' is in a later hand, probably that of Saurin's son.

112 Presumably Anahilt, Co. Down since New Church is described in Sermon XVI (47) as in Co. Down. Saurin preached in Anahilt on 11 Aug. 1754 and in 'New Church' on five occasions. The church at Anahilt had been built in 1741, hence the name, see E.D. Atkinson, *Dromore: an Ulster diocese* (Dundalk, 1925), p. 181.
113 Acts 17.18.
114 Acts 17.22–4.
115 Acts 17.23.
116 Ps. 19.1–4.
117 Rom. 1.20.
118 Acts 17.27.
119 Allusion to I Kings 20.28.
120 Rom. 1.23.
121 Lev. 18.21; II Kings 23.10; Jer. 32.35.
122 Ps. 115.4–6.
123 Exod. 15.11.
124 I Chr. 16.27.
125 I Chr. 29.11.
126 Ps. 90.2.
127 Ps. 8.1.
128 John 4.24.
129 'But is not ... one man etc.' appears on facing p. 185 to be inserted to replace deletion.
130 I Sam. 15.23.
131 'Let us not then ... Let us maintain' appears on facing p. 187a marked to replace deletion.
132 Allusion to Deut. 32. 18.
133 Ps. 73.25.
134 Ps. 97.7–9, 12.
135 Presumably a reference to Sermon V above first preached on 16 July 1749 with this one a fortnight later.
136 Acts 17.18; Acts 18.25.
137 Gen 5.15.
138 Gen. 3.10.
139 Gen. 2.5.
140 I Cor. 15.45.
141 Matt. 19.3; Mark 10.2.
142 Gen. 2.24.
143 Exod. 1.5–7; 13.57.
144 'born with the same ... and all these' appears on facing p. 233a marked for insertion here.
145 Job 31.15.
146 I Kings 16.2.
147 I Tim. 5.8.
148 Gal. 6.10.
149 Gen. 2.23.
150 Lev. 19.34.
151 Eph. 2.12.
152 'they considered them ... & even &' appears on facing p. 239a marked for insertion here.
153 Parable in Luke 10. No sermon on this parable survives in the collection.
154 Acts 14.17.
155 Matt. 25.24.
156 Allusion to Acts 10.35.
157 Isa. 60.14.
158 Ps. 72.10–11.
159 Phil. 3.16.
160 Dan. 12.3.
161 This entry and subsequent ones are in later hands.
162 Parish of Aghaderg, diocese of Dromore, where Saurin's grandson was vicar 1823–6, see Swanzy, *Succession lists of the diocese of Dromore*, p. 78.
163 The copy of the sermon (no. 30) adds '& at the Event of performing affecting this most solemn Act of our Christian Worship' for insertion here. On p. 256 opposite is the comment 'more particularly at this time when we are going to join in' that is neither in Saurin's hand nor that of his son.
164 The copy of the sermon (no. 30) has 'pious' instead of 'sacred'.

165 Rom. 10.10.
166 II Cor. 1.3.
167 Luke 22.19.
168 II Cor. 11.25.
169 The copy of the sermon (no. 30 in appendix 1) has 'advantage' instead of 'consolation'.
170 Ps. 26.6.
171 Allusion to Matt. 22.11–12.
172 Matt. 26.36.
173 Hos. 6.4.
174 I Cor. 10.17.
175 I Cor. 11.30.
176 'the unhappy consequences ... set forth' the copy of the sermon (no. 30) has 'the dreadful judgments reserved unto it here-after'.
177 Eph. 5.2.
178 Copy of the sermon (no. 30) adds 'thee O Holy Ghost who liveth & reigneth ever one God world without end.'
179 Acts 22.3–5.
180 Acts 9.1.
181 The remainder of this sermon, while in Saurin's hand, is in a different ink and with a different pen suggesting that pp 38–42, which have fewer corrections, are a later redraft of the start of the sermon.
182 Acts 16.1.
183 I Cor. 15.6.
184 I Tim. 1.3.
185 Acts 19.26–8, 34–5.
186 Acts 19.17, 20.
187 Luke 24.21.
188 Allusion to Rom. 1.4.
189 I Cor. 15.14.
190 Acts 1.3.
191 Allusion to Rom. 1.4.
192 I Cor. 15.14.
193 I Pet. 1.3.
194 I John 4.10.
195 Rom. 4.25.
196 Rom. 8.33.
197 I Cor. 7.31.
198 Rev. 21.1.
199 Heb. 12.22.
200 'those suffering ... recompence' from p. 62 opposite marked for insertion here.
201 I Cor. 15.42.
202 I Cor. 15.49.
203 Phil 3.21.
204 I Cor. 15.55.
205 Allusion to I Cor. 15.58 and Col. 1.10.
206 Gal. 5.24.
207 II Cor. 7.1.
208 Allusion to Ps. 118.24.
209 This entry and subsequent ones are in later hands.
210 The Dublin Foundling Hospital was established in 1730 as part of the Workhouse on St James's Street.
211 Rom. 13.4.
212 This appears to echo Sermon V above. This sermon is clearly the older of the two, being first preached in April 1748 with Sermon V on 4 June 1749 but in 1750 they were preached within a fortnight of each other suggesting they were seen as a pair on that occasion and may relate to specific local circumstances in Belfast in that year.
213 Rom. 12.19–21.
214 Allusion to Gen. 50.28.
215 Prov. 24.17–18.
216 Exod. 23.4.
217 Matt. 5.44.
218 Prov. 19.11.
219 I Pet. 2.23.
220 Acts 17.18.
221 Hos. 11.4.
222 Gen. 22.23.
223 Matt. 7.2; Mark 4.24.
224 Matt. 18.35.
225 Ecclesiasticus 28.1.
226 This entry and subsequent ones are in later hands.

227 The Dublin Magdalene Asylum for penitent prostitutes was established in Leeson Street by Lady Arabella Denny in 1766. It became one of Dublin's most fashionable charities. The chapel, opened in January 1768, was a popular place of worship for the gentry and a fund raiser for the asylum through charity sermons, see Ada Peter, *A brief account of the Magdalene chapel* (Dublin, 1907).

228 The Hibernian Marine School was founded in 1766 at Ringsend for the orphans of seamen in the Royal and merchant marine. In 1770 it moved to Rogerson's Quay. In 1788 there were 150 boys enrolled there. See Michael Quayne, 'The Hibenian Marine School', *Dublin Historical Record*, 21 (1966–7), pp 67–78.

229 Eccles. 3.16.
230 Eccles. 4.1.
231 Eccles. 3.17.
232 Acts 17.31.
233 I Cor. 4.5.
234 Possibly an allusion to Zeph. 1.14.
235 John 5.22.
236 Ps. 139.4.
237 Heb. 4.15.
238 Acts 10.34.
239 Rev. 20.13.
240 Allusion to Matt. 25.32.
241 II Tim. 4.1.
242 I Thess. 4.17.
243 II Cor. 5.10.
244 Matt. 25.24.
245 Rom 2.12.
246 Allusion to Rev. 6.16.
247 Rev. 6. 12–17.
248 Rom. 2.16.
249 Allusion to Isa. 3.10.
250 John 9.4.
251 Matt. 25.21, 23.
252 In a later hand, probably that of Saurin's son.
253 Isa. 53.2.
254 Luke 1.35.
255 Allusion to Rom. 1.4.
256 Rom. 8.17, Heb. 1.2.
257 John 1.1.
258 Rev. 22.13.
259 Isa. 44.6.
260 Rev. 1.8.
261 John 1.3.
262 Col. 1.16. Two pages have been removed here with four lines on one of them.
263 John 2.25.
264 Matt. 18.20.
265 John 5.23.
266 Matt. 17.2–5; Mark 9.2–6; Luke 9.29–34.
267 Acts 10.43.
268 Luke 2.25.
269 Hag. 2.7.
270 Heb. 1.3.
271 Matt. 3.1–12.
272 Matt. 2.1–2.
273 Luke 2.14.
274 Matt. 3.17.
275 Luke 22.42.
276 Acts 10.34.
277 I Cor. 1.27.
278 II Cor. 4.7.
279 I Cor. 1.23–4.
280 Rev. 6.16–17.
281 This would appear to have been left from an earlier draft of the sermon.
282 Ps. 73.24.
283 Ps. 2.1–4.
284 Eph. 4.1.
285 I Cor. 13.12.
286 John 1.9.
287 Luke 2.32.

288 A proclamation of 27 March appointed a general thanksgiving to be held on 25 April 1749 for the peace of Aix-La-Chapelle, signed on 18 October 1748, that ended the War of the Austrian Succession. See James Kelly with Mary Ann Lyons (eds), *The proclamations of Ireland, 1660–1820* (5 vols, Dublin, 2014), iii, no. 217. For the sermon preached on the same occasion in Second

Belfast Presbyterian church see Gilbert Kennedy, *The great blessing of peace and truth in our days: a sermon preached at Belfast on Tuesday, April 25th 1749* (Belfast, 1749).

289 The discussion here would appear to be about the 1745 Jacobite rising.

290 William Augustus, first duke of Cumberland and second son of George II, was captain general of the British army during the 1745 rising.

291 Culloden in April 1746.

292 Allusion to Deut. 32.30.

293 Lev. 26.8.

294 Isa. 38.29.

295 A variation on the passage 'us till ... whereby' appears on p. 308 opposite in a later hand, possibly that of Saurin's son: 'us, till that ever memorable God himself appeared on our side & stretched out his powerful arm to our assistance, When Rebellion was crushed in the midst of it's highest expectations, which restored ease and tranquillity to our troubled & affrighted hearts, which furnished us with means, to finish & compleat the work we now commemorate, whereby'.

296 'which restored ... the means to' is written in Saurin's hand on p. 308 opposite the text and seems to have been meant to be inserted here.

297 This deleted section appears to belong to an earlier version of the sermon that was rewritten.

298 George II personally commanded the British forces at the Battle of Dettingen in the Low Countries as part of the war in 1743.

299 Ps. 33.16–17

300 Gen. 49.23–4.

301 Mic. 4.3.

302 It is not clear what Saurin is referring to here. The Belfast militia was not called out in 1745 but it was called out for the Jacobite scare in 1715 and this may be what is intended.

303 The experience of the reign of James II in Ireland, 1685–90.

304 I Sam. 9.20.

305 Isa. 58.5.

306 Ps. 72.1.

307 Ps. 72.6–7.

308 Allusion to I Cor. 9.25.

309 Amos 4.11.

310 Based on Ps. 78.35.

311 This paragraph in Saurin's hand is copied and then deleted on p. 331 opposite.

312 Based on Ps. 118.14–15.

313 Ps. 46.9.

314 Ps. 118.28.

315 I Chr. 16.34.

316 This entry and subsequent ones are in later hands.

317 Jer. 31.29.

318 'to endeavour ... and by' from p. 308 opposite marked for insertion here.

319 Ezek. 18.20.

320 Ezek. 18.21–2.

321 Exod. 20.5.

322 Jer. 2.13.

323 'that portion ... of misery' from facing p. 321 marked for insertion here.

324 Allusion to Prov. 22.6.

325 I Cor. 15.58.

326 Allusion to Isa. 46.8.

327 Possible allusion to Deut. 5.10.

328 'and is of ... in particular' from facing p. 101 marked for insertion here.

329 Presumably on the previous Sunday which, if this was the first occasion on which this was preached, would be 8 January 1748. That would be sermon 45 in the catalogue in appendix 1. That sermon is not included in this selection.

330 On p. 104 opposite is the phrase 'if we confirm their use to the purpose of this world', which might be intended here.

331 Phil. 2.12.
332 'generality of ... people live' from facing p. 108 to be inserted here.
333 Matt. 6.33. 334 Titus 2.12–13.
335 Luke 10.41–2.
336 On p. 112 is an alternative opening for this sermon in a later hand, probably that of Saurin's son, which allows for a shorter version of this sermon to be preached: 'In the Fifth Chapter of St. Pauls Epistle to the Ephesians & at the 16th Verse.
Redeeming the Time. The Subject I am now to Discourse upon from the words just read unto you, is of a very important & interesting nature. It regards the use we are to make of our time, & the manner of redeeming it, when we have been so unfortunate as to lose & misspend it, & tho' it was at first addressed to men under Persecution & tryal, from whom greater degrees of prudence & Circumspection were required, yet is the usefulness &, propriety of it, the Same, in all the circumstances of Life. For if any Fault may be deemed universal & General, Surely this of Squandering away time idly & to no purpose may be justly called so ...'
337 Gal. 3.13.
338 'lost and mispent' from p. 114 opposite marked for insertion here.
339 I Cor. 10.7. 340 Rom. 13.12–14.
341 Ps. 90 but from the Book of Common Prayer psalter.
342 Rom. 2.5.
343 From a prayer by John Tillotson, archbishop of Canterbury, see John Tillotson, *The works of the Rt Rev. Dr John Tillotson* (10 vols, Edinburgh, 1772), i, pp 247, 253.
344 This entry and subsequent ones are in later hands.
345 Job 28.12.
346 p. 135 has an alternative beginning to this sermon in a later hand, possibly that of Saurin's son: 'In the 28th Chap[te]r of the Book of Job at the 28th verse Behold the fear of the Lord that is wisdom. These words were originally designed to answer a very important question where shall wisdom be found & where is the place of understanding & they tend to lead us to this conclusion, that they who fear ...'.
347 Ps. 19.7. 348 Deut. 4.6.
349 Prov. 18.14. 350 Prov. 3.13–24.
351 This entry and subsequent ones are in later hands.
352 Heb. 2.15. 'But the misfortune ... slavery and bondage' from facing p. 169 marked to be inserted to replace deletion.
353 I Cor. 15.6.
354 'And in order ... of confidence & joy' from facing p. 173 marked for insertion here to replace deletion.
355 Heb. 6.19. 356 Three lines of original text illegible here.
357 John 14.3. 358 I Cor. 15.35.
359 Allusion to Ezek. 37.3. 360 Allusion to I Cor. 6.15.
361 Rom. 6.5. 362 I Cor. 15.22.
363 Acts 7.55; Job 19.26–7. 364 Rom. 2.8.
365 I Pet. 1.3 366 Rom. 9.33–4.
367 'flattering' from facing page p. 190 marked for insertion here.

368 Possible allusion to Dan. 7.10.
369 Rev. 5.1.
370 Heb. 12.22–4.
371 I Cor. 15.42–58. 'the sting of death ... Jesus Christ' from facing p. 197 marked for insertion here.
372 II Cor. 2.12.
373 I Cor. 16.58.
374 This entry and subsequent ones are in later hands.
375 'included … of all such' from facing p. 235 marked to be inserted here.
376 Prov. 20.14.
377 Prov. 11.26.
378 'whom therefore … improper demands' from facing p. 242 to replace seven lines deleted and illegible here.
379 Jer. 22.13.
380 Exod. 7.16.
381 'And as Injustice … our endeavours' from facing p. 254 marked for insertion here.
382 Ps. 127.1; Ezek. 12.19.
383 A page has been removed here and p. 259 begins with the last three lines from p. 257 that have been deleted suggesting that the sermon was reorganised at some point between preachings.
384 Job 20.15, 19–20.
385 Job 27.16–17. 'Tho' he heap up ... divide the silver' is from facing p. 258 marked for insertion here.
386 Prov. 28.8.
387 Jer. 17.11.
388 Jas. 4.1–4.
389 Jer. 22.13.
390 Luke 19.1–10.
391 Ps. 85.10–13.
392 This entry and subsequent ones are in later hands.
393 Matt. 6.7.
394 Eccl. 5.2.
395 'Assemblies were ... weighty motives' is from facing p. 8 marked for insertion here.
396 Eccles. 5.1
397 Gen. 18.19.
398 Josh. 24.15.
399 Seven lines deleted and illegible.
400 Luke 18.1.
401 Allusion to Job 13.15.
402 'and to presume ... expresses it' in Saurin's hand from facing p. 18 marked for insertion here.
403 Page 22 contains notes by Saurin's grandson, James. These have been omitted.
404 Jas. 1.18.
405 Allusion to Ps. 107.8, 15.
406 II Cor. 12.8–9.
407 Luke 18.1–7.
408 Matt. 26.41; Mark 13.3; Mark 14.38; Col. 4.2.
409 Eph. 6.17–18.
410 On p. 30 opposite is a note in hand of Saurin's son: 'and it is equally <more especially incumbent on us in> point of regard to the dignity of out nature.'
411 This entry and subsequent ones are in later hands.
412 Allusion to Ps. 19.105.
413 Jas. 2.10.
414 Jas. 2.11.
415 In the Old Testament Leviathan was described as a water dragon, see Ps. 74.13–14, Isa. 27.1, Job 41.
416 One line deleted and illegible.
417 Matt. 25.14–30.
418 Isa. 37.18.
419 Ezek. 18.23.
420 Allusion to Gen. 15.16
421 Allusion to Ps. 51.2.
422 Rom. 6.1.

423 Hab. 3.17–18.
424 This entry and subsequent ones are in later hands.
425 Matt. 12.34; Luke 6.45. 426 Possibly an allusion to Ps. 112.5.
427 Matt. 12.35; Luke 6.45. 428 Eph. 5.4.
429 I Pet. 1.15. 430 Allusion to Ps. 91.6.
431 Possibly a reference to Ps. 64.8.
432 Matt. 9.24; Mark 5.40; Luke 8.53.
433 Allusion to Ps. 141.3. 434 Ps. 39.1.
435 Jas. 1.26.
436 Opposite this point Saurin's son has written 'the best Rule we can lay down to preserve a proper Government over our lips is always to'.
437 Matt. 12.37. 438 Ps. 19.14.
439 Matt. 13–20. 440 Hag. 2.7.
441 Matt 18.18. 442 Acts 1.41.
443 Isa. 22.22. 444 Acts 1.23–6.
445 Acts 6.5–6. 446 Acts 16.
447 Gal. 2.11. 448 Mark 9.34; Luke 9.46; Matt. 18.1.
449 Possibly an allusion to John 21.14–19.
450 Acts 10. 451 Acts 28.30.
452 Gal. 2.11.
453 'His arm ... active repentance' from facing p. 281 marked for insertion here to replace the deletion.
454 Collect for fifteenth Sunday after Trinity.
455 I can find nothing in Prov. to match this. There is an allusion to Ps 73.3.
456 Ps. 37.35–6. 457 I Cor. 2.9; Isa. 64.4.
458 Heb. 12.7. 459 I Pet. 4.19.
460 Matt. 25.14–30. 461 Matt. 6.20.
462 In a later hand. 463 An allusion to Gen. 25.31–4.
464 Jas. 5.12.
465 'For tho' ... bear, Yet etc' from facing p. 220a intended to be inserted here.
466 'is it certain ... truths of religion' from facing p. 220a in Saurin's hand but with a different pen and ink and clearly added later to the first part of the paragraph.
467 'and which ... their worth' in a different ink to the first part of the insertion.
468 Ps. 66.16. 469 Mal. 3.16.
470 Ps. 101.5.7. 471 Prov. 12.19.
472 Ps. 15.1.3. 473 Ps. 34.13.
474 'And it is ... hurtful & pernicious' from facing p. 229 marked for insertion here.
475 Prov. 10.19.
476 'all talkitivness ... all neglect etc' from facing p. 237 markd to be inserted here.
477 Prov. 10.19. 478 Eph. 4.29.
479 Matt. 6.21. 480 Allusion to Eph. 5.4.
481 I Pet. 1.15. 482 Matt. 12.37.
483 Matt. 12.34; Luke 6.45. 484 Ps. 19.14.

APPENDIX I

Catalogue of the surviving sermons

Sermons have been numbered consecutively. Copies made during Saurin's lifetime by him have been allocated numbers in the sequence. Copies made after his death by others and other items not by Saurin have not been assigned numbers but are printed in italics.

	pages	Times preached by Saurin[1]	No. in this edition
VOL 1			
1. II Cor. 5.7	1–29	18	
2. Matt. 5.16	30–57	15	
3. Eccles. 8.11	58–84	14	
4. Gen. 42.21	85–121	15	
5. Jas. 4.3	122–44	13	
6. Matt. 28.19	145–79	3	I
7. Exod. 34.6	180–215	13	
8. Acts 24.26	216–53	10	
9. Isa. 55.7	254–98	11	
10. II Tim. 3.5	299–338	10	II
VOL 2			
11. Prov. 16.5	1–39	12	III
12. Hos. 4.6	40–91	16	IV
13. Prov. 14.29	92–123	10	V
14. Ps. 119.60	124–56	9	
15. Acts 17.23	157–89	15	VI
Copy of no. 15 made post 1781	*190–220*		
16. Acts 17.26	221–50	9	VII
17. I Cor. 11.29	251–89	9	VIII
18. Rev. 3.16	290–321	7	
19. Matt. 5.20	322–39	11	
20. Matt. 5.48	340–53	unknown	
VOL 3			
21. Luke 22.19	1–36	8	
22. II Tim. 2.8	37–69	7	IX
23. Col. 3.13	70–106	10	X
24. John 16.7	107–42	13	

1 This includes only the number of times preached by James Saurin. No account is taken of the activities of later preachers.

25. Matt. 26.41	143–87	10	
26. Ps. 119.148	188–228	13	
27. II Cor. 5.10	229–67	13	XI
28. John 1.14	268–98	6	XII
29. Ps. 30. 11–12	299–334	1	XIII
30. Copy of no. 17	335–61		
Short commentaries on Colossians, Thessalonians, 1, 2 Timothy, Titus, Philemon, Hebrews, 1, 2 Peter, 1, 2 John, Jude, Revelations, in a later hand than Saurin.	*362–84*		
VOL 4			
31. Slightly edited copy of 32	3–35		
32. Phil. 4.11	36–72	unknown	
33. Copy of no. 34	73–94		
34. Luke 18.24–5	95–130	unknown	
35. Matt. 6.34	131–169	12	
36. Copy of no. 35	170–203		
37. Luke 16.31	204–236	12	
38. Copy of no. 37	237–77		
39. Copy of no. 40	278–305		
40. Exod. 20.5	306–35	12	XIV
41. Ps. 19.12	336–59	14	
42. Copy of no. 41	360–96		
VOL 5			
43. Matt. 20.15	1–35	15	
44. Copy of no. 28	36–71		
45. Heb. 6.1	72–97	11	
46. Eph. 5.16.	98–130	12	XV
47. Job 28.28	131–66	16	XVI
48. I Cor. 15.56	167–200	6	XVII
49. Acts 5.3–5	201–31	12	
50. I Thess. 4.6	232–66	8	XVIII
51. Prov. 11.18	267–87	unknown	
52. Acts 10.1–4	288–325	9	
53. Copy of no. 52	327–48		
VOL 6			
54. I Thess. 5.17	1–33	7	XIX
55. Matt. 22. 11–13	34–61	9	
56. Heb. 3.7–8	62–87	11	
57. Prov. 14.12	88–110	11	XX
58. Matt. 5.5	111–32	10	
59. Matt. 17.1–2	133–59	10	
60. Matt. 22.37	160–84	13	
61. Luke 2.32	185–216	4	
62. Eph. 5.4	218–59	9	XXI
63. Matt. 16.18–19	260–83	8	XXII
64. Unknown	284–314	unknown	XXIII

VOL 7

65 John 7.17	1–41	10	
66. Copy of no. 65	42–71		
67. Exod. 20.8	72–116	3	
68. Copy of no. 67	117–46		
69. I Thess. 5.16	147–73	15	
70. Copy of no. 69	174–208		
71. Col. 4.6	209–46	5	XXIV
72. Copy of no. 71	247–85		
73. II Pet. 3.11	286–310	10	
[post 1820 copy of no. 73]	*312–53*		
74. Ps. 103.1–2	354–80	9	
75. Copy of no 74	381–410		

APPENDIX 2

James Saurin's preaching

The date and place of preaching is noted at the beginning of each sermon. Where no place of preaching is given in this list it is Belfast. In cases of multiple copies of sermons the version with the most complete list of preaching dates and places has been used. Dates before 1752 are given old style as recorded by Saurin.

Date	*Sermon no.*	*Place*
1742/3		
20 Mar.	3	Irishtown, Dublin
1743		
24 July	32	Donnybrook
31 July	32	Irishtown, Dublin
14 Aug.	32	St Michael's, Dublin
28 Aug.	3	St Michael's Dublin
11 Sept.	32	St Michan's, Dublin
1744		
19 Aug.	1	Donnybrook
2 Sept.	1	Christ Church, Dublin
11 Nov.	3	St Michan's, Dublin
16 Dec.	2	St Peter's, Dublin
30 Dec.	1	St Michael's, Dublin
1744/5		
4 Jan.	32	St John's, Dublin
27 Jan.	2	Crumlin
1745		
6 Oct.	1	St Ann's, Dublin
1746		
13 Apr.	4	St Luke's, Dublin
4 May	4	Donnybrook
10 Aug.	36	Donnybrook
24 Aug.	36	St Ann's, Dublin
7 Dec.	1	St Peter's, Dublin
1746/7		
18 Jan.	36	
22 Feb.	1	St Luke's, Dublin
22 Mar.	34	St Ann's, Dublin
1747		
29 Mar.	2	St Michan's, Dublin
26 Apr.	34	St Peter's, Dublin
3 May	4	St Ann's, Dublin
10 May	4	Christ Church, Dublin
28 June	5	
12 July	2	
19 July	3	
22 July	6	[confirmation]
2 Aug.	4	
11 Oct.	37	
25 Oct.	40	
8 Nov.	42	
22 Nov.	7	
29 Nov.	66	
6 Dec.	8	
1747/8		
19 Feb.	42	St Ann's, Dublin
28 Feb.	37	St Michael's, Dublin
1748		
3 Apr.	9	[Sunday before Easter]
10 Apr.	22	[Easter]
17 Apr.	10	
24 Apr.	23	
15 May	11	
5 June	25	
12 June	34	
19 June	12	
3 July	36	
10 July	2	
17 July	26	
31 July	27	
7 Aug.	1	
14 Aug.	66	

21 Aug.	4	
11 Sept.	32	
11 Dec.	43	
18 Dec.	3	
25 Dec.	28	
1748/9		
8 Jan.	45	
15 Jan.	46	
29 Jan.	47	
5 Mar.	26	St Michael's Dublin
1749		
26 Mar.	48	[Easter]
2 Apr.	5	
23 Apr.	49	
25 Apr.	29	['upon the peace']
7 May	50	
29 May	24	[Whitsunday]
4 June	13	
11 June	37	
18 June	52	
25 June	7	
2 July	14	
9 July	66	
16 July	15	
23 July	10	
30 July	16	
6 Aug.	40	
13 Aug.	69	
20 Aug.	23	
27 Aug.	72	
3 Sept.	11	
17 Dec.	12	
24 Dec.	17	
31 Dec.	8	
1749/50		
7 Jan.	34	
26 Feb.	27	St John's Dublin
28 Feb.	15	St Luke's, Dublin
1750		
25 Mar.	10	St Anne's Dublin
1 Apr.	42	
22 Apr.	36	
13 May	18	
20 May	25	
10 June	19	
3 June	24	[Whitsunday]
15 July	1	
29 July	54	
5 Aug.	27	
12 Aug.	3	
26 Aug.	2	'New Church'[1]
2 Sept.	47	
9 Sept.	13	
16 Sept.	55	
23 Sept.	26	
30 Sept.	4	
7 Oct.	49	
21 Oct.	49	St Andrew's, Dublin
28 Oct.	47	St Ann's, Dublin
25 Nov.	47	St Michael's, Dublin
16 Dec.	15	St Werburgh's, Dublin
23 Dec.	9	
25 Dec.	28	
30 Dec.	43	
1750/1		
6 Jan.	68	
13 Jan.	56	
27 Jan.	32	
10 Feb.	37	
16 Mar.	15	St Ann's, Dublin
1751		
7 Apr.	22	[Easter]
14 Apr.	57	
21 Apr.	15	
28 Apr.	16	
19 May	58	
1 June	66	
9 June	69	
23 June	15	'New Church'
30 June	59	
7 July	45	
28 July	5	
18 Aug.	60	
25 Aug.	25	
15 Sept.	73	
22 Sept.	52	
29 Sept.	2	
13 Oct.	14	
27 Oct.	7	

1 Presumably Anahilt, Co. Down, where he preached on 11 Aug. 1754. The church had been rebuilt in 1741; E.D. Atkinson, *Dromore: an Ulster diocese* (Dundalk, 1925), p. 181.

3 Nov.	11	
8 Dec.	50	
15 Dec.	12	
22 Dec.	17	
1752		
12 Jan.	23	
26 Jan.	43	St Andrew's, Dublin
22 Mar.	9	[Sunday before Easter]
29 Mar.	48	[Easter]
5 Apr.	10	[Sunday after Easter]
19 Apr.	19	
26 Apr.	8	
19 July	6	[confirmation]
26 July	47	New Church, Co. Down
8 Oct.	57	
22 Oct.	46	
29 Oct.	36	
26 Nov.	34	
3 Dec.	18	
10 Dec.	56	
24 Dec.	55	[Sunday before Xmas]
25 Dec.	61	
31 Dec.	1	
1753		
7 Jan.	13	
11 Mar.	43	
18 Mar.	60	
1 Apr.	7	
8 Apr.	47	
29 Apr.	54	
6 May	27	
13 May	26	
19 May	58	
27 May	32	
3 June	59	
10 June	24	[Whitsunday]
1 July	4	
8 July	37	
15 July	73	
22 July	62	
29 July	68	
12 Aug.	40	
9 Sept.	69	
30 Sept.	45	
7 Oct.	11	
18 Nov.	62	St Ann's, Dublin
25 Nov.	11	St Luke's, Dublin
2 Dec.	49	St Peter's, Dublin
23 Dec.	17	
25 Dec.	28	
1754		
6 Jan.	25	
13 Jan.	12	
17 Feb.	69	St Ann's, Dublin
24 Feb.	69	Donnybrook
17 Mar.	40	St Andrew's, Dublin
30 Mar.	62	St Peter's, Dublin
7 Apr.	9	[Sunday before Easter]
14 Apr.	22	[Easter]
21 Apr.	5	
5 May	56	
12 May	66	
19 May	49	
9 June	72	
14 July	15	
18 July	16	
4 Aug.	2	
11 Aug.	69	Anahilt, Co. Down
27 Aug.	72	
1 Sept.	10	
29 Sept.	36	
6 Oct.	57	
13 Oct.	50	
20 Oct.	14	
27 Oct.	63	
4 Nov.	3	
10 Nov.	23	
17 Nov.	19	
24 Nov.	42	
1 Dec.	52	
15 Dec.	47	
22 Dec.	21	
1755		
12 Jan.	34	
26 Jan.	1	
2 Feb.	27	
9 Feb.	26	
16 Feb.	7	
2 Mar.	60	
16 Mar.	54	
23 Mar.	55	[Sunday before Easter]
30 Mar.	48	[Easter]

6 Apr.	43	
20 Apr.	12	
18 May	24	St Andrew's, Dublin [Whitsunday]
1 June	42	St Peter's, Dublin
6 July	59	
26 Oct.	42	Abbey Church, Bath
7 Dec.	8	St Anne's, Dublin
25 Dec.	61	
28 Dec.	46	
1756		
18 Jan.	42	St Andrew's, Dublin
23 Jan.	5	
1 Feb.	42	St Michan's, Dublin
23 Feb.	8	
11 Apr.	25	
16 Apr.	21	[Good Friday]
25 Apr.	58	
2 May	69	
9 May	9	
23 May	43	St Ann's, Dublin
14 June	24	St Mary's chapel, Dublin [Whitsunday]
27 June	12	St Ann's, Dublin
4 July	12	St Michael's, Dublin
18 July	43	St Peter's, Dublin
25 July	4	
8 Aug.	11	
22 Aug.	32	
29 Aug.	62	
12 Sept.	63	
19 Sept.	57	
3 Oct.	47	
10 Oct.	19	
17 Oct.	3	
31 Oct.	49	
14 Nov.	37	
5 Dec.	73	
12 Dec.	13	
19 Dec.	17	
26 Dec.	66	
1757		
3 Jan.	7	
16 Jan.	42	
30 Jan.	56	
13 Feb.	18	
20 Feb.	68	
27 Feb.	40	

6 Mar.	45	
13 Mar.	10	
27 Mar.	52	
10 Apr.	22	[Easter]
17 Apr.	60	
24 Apr.	23	
8 May	15	
15 May	16	
29 May	24	[Whitsunday]
5 June	14	
26 June	36	
17 July	26	
31 July	59	
14 Aug.	50	
21 Aug.	27	
11 Sept.	54	
18 Sept.	34	
25 Sept.	1	
2 Oct.	8	
16 Oct.	43	
30 Oct.	12	
6 Nov.	58	
27 Nov.	57	
5 Dec.	62	
1758		
15 Jan.	46	
12 Feb.	69	
19 Feb.	25	
26 Feb.	19	
12 Mar.	11	
19 Mar.	21	[Sunday before Easter]
23 Apr.	73	
7 May	47	
21 May	49	
28 May	3	
2 July	37	
9 July	32	
16 July	4	
23 July	5	
30 July	63	
13 Aug.	42	
27 Aug.	60	
17 Sept.	56	
24 Sept.	66	
5 Nov.	75	
12 Nov.	23	
26 Nov.	12	
3 Dec.	14	

17 Dec.	9	
24 Dec.	17	
25 Dec.	61	
1759		
7 Jan.	52	
14 Jan.	40	
21 Jan.	18	
28 Jan.	59	
4 Feb.	72	
11 Feb.	58	
25 Feb.	26	
4 Mar.	15	
11 Mar.	57	
18 Mar.	68	
25 Mar.	45	
1 Apr.	16	
15 Apr.	48	[Easter]
6 May	1	
13 May	43	
20 May	36	
3 June	24	[Whitsunday]
9 June	72	
8 July	69	
22 July	27	
29 July	46	
26 Aug.	60	
16 Sept.	50	
23 Sept.	54	
30 Sept.	10	
7 Oct.	42	
21 Oct.	7	
23 Dec.	21	
25 Dec.	28	
1760		
13 Jan.	63	
20 Jan.	34	
27 Jan.	47	
17 Feb.	73	
2 Mar.	75	
9 Mar.	8	
16 Mar.	19	
4 May	3	
10 May	9	
15 June	25	
29 June	66	
27 July	5	
3 Aug.	46	
10 Aug.	56	
24 Aug.	37	
31 Aug.	4	
7 Sept.	45	
14 Sept.	49	
21 Sept.	11	
2 Nov.	12	
30 Nov.	40	
14 Dec.	27	
21 Dec.	17	
1761		
4 Jan.	62	
11 Jan.	15	
18 Jan.	57	
25 Jan.	16	
8 Feb.	43	
11 Feb.	58	
1 Mar.	26	
8 Mar.	52	
22 Mar.	22	[Easter]
5 Apr.	75	
19 Apr.	68	
26 Apr.	68	'New Church'
5 July	56	
12 July	2	
19 July	47	
2 Aug.	1	
9 Aug.	42	
16 Aug.	60	
23 Aug.	72	
30 Aug.	36	
6 Sept.	13	
13 Sept.	59	
20 Sept.	7	
17 Oct.	4	
9 Dec.	27	
13 Dec.	23	
20 Dec.	55	
25 Dec.	61	
27 Dec.	10	
1762		
31 Jan.	15	Dublin Castle
4 Apr.	21	[Sunday before Easter]
2 May	46	
9 May	75	
23 May	63	
30 May	24	[Whitsunday]
13 June	25	

18 July	45	
1 Aug.	57	
8 Aug.	73	
15 Aug.	62	
29 Aug.	37	
5 Sept.	40	
12 Sept.	5	
26 Sept.	69	
3 Oct.	43	
10 Oct.	60	
24 Oct.	49	
31 Oct.	32	
7 Nov.	50	
14 Nov.	56	
25 Dec.	28	
26 Dec.	66	
1763		
9 Jan.	18	
16 Jan.	12	
23 Jan.	58	
20 Feb.	69	St Andrew's, Dublin
27 Feb.	66	St Peter's, Dublin
6 Mar.	2	
13 Mar.	19	
20 Mar.	3	
27 Mar.	17	[Sunday before Easter]
3 Apr.	48	[Easter]
10 Apr.	26	
24 Apr.	11	
1 May	47	
29 May	13	
10 July	46	
17 July	1	
14 Aug.	9	
21 Aug.	68	
18 Sept.	59	
25 Sept.	36	
13 Nov.	75	
11 Dec.	7	
18 Dec.	55	
1764		
8 Jan.	42	
22 Jan.	60	
29 Jan.	5	
5 Feb.	23	
19 Feb.	52	
26 Feb.	15	
4 Mar.	16	
11 Mar.	72	
18 Mar.	34	
25 Mar.	27	
8 Apr.	9	
22 Apr.	22	[Easter]
6 May	69	
3 June	37	
10 June	24	[Whitsunday]
1 July	45	
22 July	43	
29 July	73	
26 Aug.	57	
2 Sept.	63	
16 Sept.	14	
23 Sept.	26	
30 Sept.	32	
14 Oct.	40	
21 Oct.	50	
28 Oct.	66	
4 Nov.	75	
11 Nov.	46	
16 Dec.	2	
1765		
6 Jan.	19	
27 Jan.	56	
3 Feb.	12	
10 Feb.	36	
25 Feb.	49	
3 Mar.	13	
17 Mar.	4	
24 Mar.	47	
31 Mar.	21	[Sunday before Easter]
21 Apr.	10	
28 Apr.	75	Connor, Co. Antrim
1 May	62	
19 May	69	St Audoen's, Dublin
26 May	24	Chapelizod, Dublin [Whitsunday]
2 June	75	St Peter's, Dublin
16 June	58	
23 June	8	
30 June	7	
7 July	11	
21 July	37	'New Church', Co. Down
4 Aug.	68	

22 Dec.	55	
29 Dec.	25	
1766		
5 Jan.	3	
19 Jan.	60	
9 Feb.	27	
16 Feb.	5	
23 Feb.	14	
16 Mar.	1	
20 Apr.	75	Abbey church, Bath
25 May	24	Bath Chapel in the Square, Bath
24 Aug.	15	Abbey Church, Bath
28 Sept.	43	Abbey Church, Bath
26 Oct.	15	St Peter's, Dublin
2 Nov.	15	St Audoen's, Dublin
23 Nov.	2	
14 Dec.	26	
1767		
8 Mar.	69	
15 Mar.	56	
22 Mar.	12	
12 Apr.	66	
17 Apr.	17	[Good Friday]
26 Apr.	45	
10 May	32	
17 May	59	
24 May	60	Connor, Co. Antrim
21 June	52	
19 July	75	
26 July	40	
2 Aug.	47	
9 Aug.	72	
15 Aug.	6	[confirmation]
23 Aug.	42	
30 Aug.	49	
27 Sept.	73	
11 Oct.	57	
18 Oct.	13	
25 Oct.	18	
15 Nov.	68	
22 Nov.	63	
29 Nov.	16	
20 Dec.	55	
25 Dec.	28	
1768		
3 Jan.	7	
10 Jan.	9	
17 Jan.	4	
24 Jan.	46	
7 Feb.	43	St Audoen's, Dublin
14 Feb.	66	St Audoen's, Dublin
18 Feb.	72	St Audoen's, Dublin
13 Mar.	69	St Peter's, Dublin
20 Mar.	47	St Audoen's, Dublin
3 Apr.	48	[Easter]
10 Apr.	10	[Sunday after Easter]
24 Apr.	37	
1 May	43	
8 May	8	
22 May	24	[Whitsunday]
19 June	5	
31 July	23	
21 Aug.	12	
4 Sept.	60	
11 Sept.	50	
18 Sept.	1	
2 Oct.	14	
16 Oct.	2	
30 Oct.	26	
6 Nov.	27	
20 Nov.	25	
4 Dec.	36	
11 Dec.	3	
18 Dec.	21	
1769		
15 Jan.	56	
12 Feb.	45	
19 Feb.	58	
2 Apr.	73	
16 Apr.	54	
23 Apr.	59	
2 May	34	
4 June	11	
11 June	75	
2 July	40	
9 July	52	
16 July	13	
30 July	46	
13 Aug.	68	
27 Aug.	4	
3 Sept.	32	
10 Sept.	49	
24 Sept.	47	
1 Oct.	62	
8 Oct.	57	
15 Oct.	66	

22 Oct.	19	
29 Oct.	2	
12 Nov.	42	
19 Nov.	1	
17 Dec.	7	
24 Dec.	17	
1770		
18 Mar.	36	St Audoen's, Dublin
22 Apr.	16	
29 Apr.	5	
13 May	18	
6 May	63	
27 May	14	
3 June	24	[Whitsunday]
10 June	70	
22 July	8	
5 Aug.	38	
12 Aug.	27	
26 Aug.	23	
9 Sept.	43	
30 Sept.	26	
7 Oct.	3	
14 Oct.	60	
23 Dec.	55	
30 Dec.	19	

1771		
13 Jan.	12	
20 Jan.	73	
27 Jan.	66	
10 Feb.	58	
7 Apr.	22	[Sunday after Easter]
28 Apr.	45	
6 June	36	
23 June	42	
30 June	7	
7 July	72	
1 Dec.	11	
22 Dec.	21	
1772		
5 Jan.	46	
19 Jan.	5	
2 Feb.	2	
9 Feb.	19	
1 Mar.	1	
22 Mar.	12	
29 Mar.	54	
5 Apr.	40	
12 Apr.	59	
17 May.	13	

INDEX OF SCRIPTURAL QUOTATIONS AND ALLUSIONS

The pages given are those on which the text is cited. The biblical reference is given in the relevant note.
* indicates an allusion rather than a quotation.
†indicates a text that was the basis of a sermon by Saurin.